# THE #METOO EFFECT

GENDER AND CULTURE

GENDER AND CULTURE

A SERIES OF COLUMBIA UNIVERSITY PRESS

Nancy K. Miller and Victoria Rosner, Series Editors
Carolyn G. Heilbrun (1926–2003) and Nancy K. Miller, Founding Editors

SELECTED NEW BOOKS

My Brilliant Friends: Our Lives in Feminism
Nancy K. Miller

Tainted Witness: Why We Doubt What Women Say About Their Lives
Leigh Gilmore

"How Come Boys Get to Keep Their Noses?": Women and Jewish American Identity
in Contemporary Graphic Memoirs
Tahneer Oksman

Extreme Domesticity: A View from the Margins
Susan Fraiman

Nomadic Theory: The Portable Rosi Braidotti
Rosi Braidotti

Graphic Women: Life Narrative and Contemporary Comics
Hillary L. Chute

SELECTED CLASSICS

Between Men: English Literature and Male Homosocial Desire (1985, 2015)
Eve Kosofsky Sedgwick

The Poetics of Gender (1986)
Edited by Nancy K. Miller

Gender and the Politics of History (1988, 2018)
Joan Wallach Scott

Hamlet's Mother and Other Women (1990)
Carolyn G. Heilbrun

The Apparitional Lesbian: Female Homosexuality and Modern Culture (1995)
Terry Castle

Second Skins: The Body Narratives of Transsexuality (1998)
Jay Prosser

For a complete list of books in the series, please see the
Columbia University Press website.

# THE #METOO EFFECT

## WHAT HAPPENS WHEN WE BELIEVE WOMEN

LEIGH GILMORE

Columbia University Press

*New York*

Columbia University Press
*Publishers Since 1893*
New York    Chichester, West Sussex
cup.columbia.edu

Library of Congress Cataloging-in-Publication Data
Names: Gilmore, Leigh, 1959– author.
Title: The #MeToo effect : what happens when we believe women / Leigh Gilmore.
Description: New York : Columbia University Press, [2023] | Series: Gender and
culture | Includes bibliographical references and index.
Identifiers: LCCN 2022039941 (print) | LCCN 2022039942 (ebook) |
ISBN 9780231194204 (hardback) | ISBN 9780231550703 (ebook)
Subjects: LCSH: MeToo movement. | Sexual harassment of women. |
Women—Crimes against.
Classification: LCC HQ1237 .G55 2023 (print) | LCC HQ1237 (ebook) |
DDC 305.42—dc23/eng/20220607
LC record available at https://lccn.loc.gov/2022039941
LC ebook record available at https://lccn.loc.gov/2022039942

Cover image and design: David Gilmore

FOR BETH MARSHALL

# CONTENTS

# PREFACE

When President Biden nominated Judge Ketanji Brown Jackson to the U.S. Supreme Court, fulfilling his campaign promise to appoint a Black woman, it should have been cause for celebration. Instead, it devolved into a rerun of the mistreatment of Anita Hill, a Black law professor, and Christine Blasey Ford, a white psychology professor, who had accused previous nominees of sexual misconduct. How does #MeToo enable us to connect two witnesses who testified about sexual harassment (Hill) and assault (Blasey Ford) to a third, herself a nominee to the Court, and the bizarre accusation that she harbored sympathy for child molesters? When #MeToo transformed the iterative phenomenon of one wretched case after another into a demand for accountability, it exposed a pattern of how institutions use formal processes against those who report sexual harassment, draw on a supply of racist and sexist bias to slander them, and turn their allegations against them in lurid and parodic ways. Anita Hill, Christine Blasey Ford, and Ketanji Brown Jackson, although distant in time and circumstance from one another, were denigrated by gendered and racialized smear tactics honed over time. Although the individuals change, every week brings new examples that expose the prevalence of abuse and the inadequate response to systemic sexual violence. So many, in fact, that I stopped trying to include the latest outrage in this preface and to focus instead on what enables its repetition. The pattern persists because the racist and sexist associations required to reproduce it are entangled in processes that are enshrined as positive and fair. For this reason, our first thoughts about justice and protection are often for abusers rather than survivors.

Those who try to report sexual abuse are ensnared in Kafkaesque processes. They are often told there are no procedures for their complaints, or their complaints are recorded only to be shelved. When they follow up, often years later, they are told the statutes of limitations have expired. In contrast, abusers are often familiar to authorities—including police, religious leaders and school administrators—and benefit from the appearance of a fair process that entails no accountability.[1] These same formal processes allow men, especially white men, to defame women, especially women of color, as threatening to the rule of law, confused about sexual abuse, and undeserving of respect. While the similar mistreatment of Anita Hill and Christine Blasey Ford demonstrates that nothing changed between 1991 and 2017 to clarify how a charge of sexual abuse could be communicated, equally important is how Republican senators were able to transfer their attacks from these witnesses to a historic nominee in 2022 by acting as if she were on trial, sexually suspect, and ultimately illegitimate. I begin with a recent Supreme Court nomination not because it uniquely captures the essence of #MeToo, but because it is one among many examples whose appalling familiarity demonstrates why "MeToo" struck a global public as both necessary and long overdue when it appeared in October 2017.

#MeToo erupted on social media a few months after the publication of my book *Tainted Witness: Why We Doubt What Women Say About Their Lives*.[2] In it, I examine how cultural practices of judgment diminish women as knowers and persons worthy of justice. I theorized that women count less than men as truth-tellers because we are trained to believe men, to value their futures and care about what might injure them in ways that simply do not apply to women.[3] In addition to holding men in regard, we learn to doubt women. Doubting women is reaffirmed by the law and reproduced in workplaces, disciplinary processes, and everyday life. This doubt has the force of common sense, and it feels rational and ethical to direct it at women. Because doubt welds sexism to other forms of abuse and bias, like racism, homophobia, and transphobia, those who speak out are often discredited before any evidence is examined. #MeToo raises a new proposition: What happens when we believe women?

I use "women" here and throughout this book as a name people call themselves and also as a category of feminist analysis. Within feminist scholarship, "women" is not a neutral biological descriptor but a concept that carries a range of legal, religious, political, and cultural meanings. It is inconceivable that we would minimize sexual violence as "not that bad," "a case of he said/she said," or an inevitable byproduct of women entering the workforce if we didn't already consider women to be worth less than men. There is no comparable dismissal of entire categories of harm without the related disparagement of the groups harmed. Racist, settler, and gendered regimes rationalize the violence they benefit from by defining its targets as essentially different and less than. For this reason, the use of "women" and "men" is not about nomenclature as much as who counts and who does the counting.[4] Although #MeToo has a global reach, some feel empowered by it while others feel excluded, for some of the same reasons they feel included in or alienated from the category of "women." At Judge Brown Jackson's nomination hearing, Republican senator Marsha Blackburn, a southern white woman, using a transphobic trope, challenged Brown Jackson to define "what a woman is." Blackburn's demand was a potent reminder that words are charged with political meanings and histories of exclusion. Survivors who are young, trans, queer, poor, brown, Black, or Indigenous often find formal processes revictimizing because they direct the powers of state, including carceral power—the power to imprison—at them. This is especially evident when they speak out about sexual violence.

#MeToo offers an alternative. As a response to hostile formal processes, #MeToo uses the power of stories to raise the credibility of all survivors. Although #MeToo is sometimes caricatured as a threat to due process or an example of carceral feminism most likely to harm people of color, the strategy of narrative activism is neither. At least not necessarily. While it seeks to hold abusers and their enablers accountable, and often does so by placing its faith in activism rather than courts, it typically builds a case through testimony—truth-telling, evidence gathering, fact checking, and public disclosure—when that testimony is blocked by the law. It relies on journalists to provide what police and courts often refuse survivors, uses labor actions to demand third-party investigations and other alternatives to forced mediation, and embraces the power of storytelling to create empathy and understanding in diverse audiences. I draw on the humanities—literary criticism, narrative theory, and feminist criticism, specifically—to describe how survivors used narrative rather than strictly legal, administrative, or policy tools to revive a longstanding public conversation about sexual justice.[5] This approach to #MeToo exposes the asymmetry between two threats: one posed by sexual violence, which is decried by survivors and activists, and the other by truth-telling about it, which is characterized by its critics as dangerous and retributive. #MeToo exposes this pattern of false equivalence and demands that we learn how to listen when survivors tell the truth. This book diagnoses why this is so difficult and how narrative activism makes it less so. It shifts the focus from demanding that survivors speak out to the features of narrative and reception that enable us to hear them.

# THE # METOO EFFECT

# INTRODUCTION

---

## The #MeToo Effect

*The best way to fight against misrepresentation is to*
*represent oneself in radical numbers.*
—JUDITH BUTLER, "GENDER, IDENTITY, MEMOIR"

*We sound louder when we are heard together; we are louder.*
—SARA AHMED, *COMPLAINT!*

**M**uch of the #MeToo story is familiar. In October 2017 the hashtag blazed across social media when millions acknowledged personal experiences of sexual violence. Touched off by revelations of sexual abuse in Hollywood, #MeToo blended celebrity scandal with grassroots feminist activism to ignite a conversation about accountability. The rush to cover that breaking story, however, was limited to recent events and overlooked the broader literary and cultural context necessary to make sense of its rapid adoption as well as the backlash against it. As a result, #MeToo was viewed variously as an extralegal movement that threatened to substitute retribution for due process, an overreaction to the risks of sex that women once handled with silence, or an example of carceral feminism that would further fuel the criminal-legal system's propensity to punish men of color. But women have been telling their stories for a long time, and none of those factors alone—not social media, celebrity, or even the sheer prevalence of sexual violence—explains why a global public heard them. By restoring #MeToo to the broader context of life writing and survivor narratives, this book reframes the novelty of #MeToo as a powerful episode of narrative activism within a longstanding intersectional feminist lineage. When previously silenced survivors—including whose who are nonwhite, nonbinary, trans, young, or male—were heard as both "me," singular and authoritative, and "too," part of a testimonial collective of truth-tellers, disparate accounts fused into a shared story. This genre had a new name—#MeToo—but its roots in intersectional feminism explain how far and fast it traveled, how it has been blocked, and how it might continue to provide survivors with the collective credibility necessary to be heard at all.

#MeToo shifted the deeply engrained response to women's accounts of sexual violence from doubting all of them to believing some of them. This rise in credibility upended the false equivalence between women's allegations of abuse ("she said") and men's denial of it ("he said"). He said/she said misrepresents a gendered hierarchy of credibility as a neutral binary. Through it any individual woman's account is seen as less credible than every man's, which effectively suppresses knowledge about patterns of abuse. Yet where it once ended conversations about consent and harm, #MeToo forced a new hearing. What changed? Although the downfall of Hollywood producer Harvey Weinstein seemed to usher in a new era of accountability for powerful men overnight, the elements that converged to transform a handful of high-profile cases into a global demand for justice had been rising for a long time. Narrative activism—which I define as storytelling in the service of social change—propelled #MeToo beyond courts and isolated cases into a global movement, with survivors as authorities on sexual violence. James Phelan defines narrative as "somebody telling somebody else on some occasion and for some purpose(s) that something happened."[1] Precisely at a time when the cultural conversation about sexual justice was unhelpfully fixated on appeals to legal and bureaucratic systems, storytelling by survivors knit together concerns about consent and accountability into an existential demand for sexual justice and the right to be heard. Survivors told everybody that sexual violence happened in order to make it to stop.

This is not the first time stories of sexual violence have motivated audiences to take action. #MeToo is part of an activist feminist lineage that uses autobiographical narrative to inform, move, and persuade diverse audiences about structural inequalities. Just as "the personal is political" summarized a key insight of feminism in the 1970s, #MeToo referenced Black feminist activist Tarana Burke's recent work with survivors.[2] Both phrases are shorthand for feminist praxis rooted in the creation of community. Both distill a shareable insight that translates the community-building side of activism for a broad audience. Sharing stories—whether through consciousness-raising groups, in print, in whisper networks, or online—is a core feminist practice that produces critical language about harm and justice. Where previous generations passed pamphlets, #MeToo launched a global campaign on Twitter. Both used available technologies to speed testimonial accounts through well-traveled networks.

Harriet Jacobs's *Incidents in the Life of a Slave Girl*, a slave narrative published in 1861, offers a provisional starting point for this tradition.[3] Like Jacobs, Me Too founder Tarana Burke chose life writing, a genre that connects the personal and the political. Her memoir *Unbound: My Story of Liberation and the Birth of the Me Too Movement*, locates the origin of the movement in an episode of thwarted storytelling with Heaven, a young girl whose story of sexual abuse Burke resisted hearing because *"She was me."*[4] Burke's focus on girlhood—Heaven's and her own—recalls Jacobs's attention to the disruption of her childhood by a slaveholder's sexual predations. To convince readers that she was degraded by the threat of rape, Jacobs persuades them to put themselves in her place and sympathize. She urges white women readers, in particular, toward a "me too" recognition of the harm white men do. "Me too," the words Burke realized would place survivors in a position of recognition and trust, came to her when she began to process her own sexual trauma.[5] Her distillation of an intersectional feminist stance on survivor identification into a shareable two-word statement of empathy invited participation. Following the global sharing of #MeToo on social media, personal stories like Heaven's and Burke's would soon pour out, prompting reinspection of patterns previously hidden or denied. Placing these accounts front and center enables a new perspective on how the credibility of survivors rose when women's vivid, personal accounts were propelled into the court of public opinion, carrying a tradition of feminist activism with them.

By clarifying the roots of #MeToo, we can understand how survivors have used narrative to reframe themselves as authoritative and credible, to see abusers as accountable, and to identify sexual violence as an urgent problem requiring structural solutions. #MeToo tapped into a lineage that links Jacobs to Burke to become another episode in the longstanding tradition of using personal narrative as a call to action. When social networks like Twitter enabled an outpouring of stories of sexual abuse, ignorance of this narrative tradition caused many to call #MeToo unprecedented, highlighting the overnight change in accountability while omitting the feminist intellectual, aesthetic, and political context necessary for understanding three of its key features: why storytelling is the signature form of #MeToo; how literature and life writing serve as a resource in the long struggle against sexual violence; and why narrative testimony rebalances the cultural conversation away from law, where survivors are structurally unequal to those who abuse them, and toward life writing, where they have greater flexibility in telling their stories and having them heard.

As the group credibility of survivors rose, it created what I call the #MeToo effect: the gelling of millions of diverse accounts into a collective voice that exposed systemic bias. Data on Twitter confirms that people posted #MeToo after seeing six of their contacts do the same.[6] They responded to what they saw with their own eyes: the voluntary assembly of a group to which they belonged.[7] This collective assembly contextualized the October 2017 cases breaking on social media with other examples of multiple accusers coming forward to condemn specific abusers. Allegations by actors Ashley Judd, Rose McGowan, and dozens more led to Weinstein's resignation, criminal trial, conviction, and twenty-three-year sentence.[8] Prior to that, the hashtag #TheEmptyChair referred to anonymous victims of comedian Bill Cosby, whom Andrea

Constand and more than thirty-five other women accused of drugging and raping them.[9] Although social media alone does not account for the global reach of #MeToo, it is difficult to imagine its spread without Twitter's narrative power. Twitter embeds citation as a narrative device: hashtags announce and remind users of a story, mark individual contributions as part of that story, and grow it through participation in a shared narrative. Like #MeToo, Black Lives Matter broke on Twitter. Twitter was crucial to organizing actions in the Arab Spring and the Occupy movement launched with the hashtag #OccupyWallStreet. Twitter doesn't simply aggregate; it consolidates individual tweets into a shared narrative. When this happened with #MeToo, a new narrator emerged: the credible witness, a collective identity for survivors wherever they were located.

Feminist publics have previously emerged on Twitter around the issue of sexual violence, and #MeToo tweets referenced that history through the citation of hashtags. #MeToo connected cases outside social media to the history of protesting them online. Resonating within this frame were Brooke Nevils's allegations of sexual harassment and rape against Matt Lauer coupled with knowledge of his behavior by NBC staff and management, who protected Weinstein.[10] Rachael Denhollander's public allegations about sports doctor Larry Nassar led to over 160 women offering victim impact statements at his sentencing hearing, including some who had reported Nassar to police, to Michigan State athletic department staff, and to USA Gymnastics before their collective witness was allowed a place in court.[11] As it became a frame of reference, #MeToo offered an alternative jurisdiction for publicizing accounts previously smothered by indifferent or hostile authorities, including cases long silenced by statutes of limitation.[12] This extrajudicial space nonetheless followed the rules of evidence and due process denied survivors by police and courts, with journalists taking on the ethical and legal responsibilities of evidence gathering, fact finding, and fact checking, and offering those named as abusers an opportunity to review and rebut their reporting.

Signs of skepticism about #MeToo were present almost immediately. Masha Gessen worried it would become a sex panic in the pages of the *New Yorker* on November 14, 2017, one month after the hashtag went viral. Through the end of the year and into the beginning of 2018, workplaces were conflated with dating culture in op-eds that presented objections to sexual harassment on the job as an overreaction to normal male dating behavior. A backlash took shape as writers like Katie Roiphe and Daphne Merkin sought to shift the burden of accountability back onto women, mocking them for viewing sexual interactions as something that could be more egalitarian, or even just less damaging, insisting that workplaces could not rein in men's behavior because "boys will be boys" everywhere.[13] Iconic actress Catherine Deneuve and ninety-nine prominent French women cosigned an op-ed affirming men's "right to bother," endorsing a free pass for any and all sexual harassment.[14]

Because #MeToo exposed decades of abuse within specific organizations, often by serial harassers, multiple survivors came forward to attest to patterns of abuse and retaliation. Abusers sought to describe these allegations as a witch hunt. They accused survivors of materializing from the shadows to terrorize innocent men with false accusations. The specter of the witch hunt seeks to scandalize the public with the fear of extrajudicial mob violence. It conflates survivors themselves with lawlessness and defends those accused of abuse by raising a seemingly reasonable concern for due process. This feature of the backlash united self-described feminists with antifeminists. Some charged that even the moderate demand for a hearing represented a wild swing of the pendulum, dangerously overcorrecting the tendency toward doubt with a new requirement to "believe all women."[15] This caricature falsely presented survivors as demanding what justice can never offer: which is to be believed a priori. #MeToo offered a different standard: a credible witness is one who *can* be believed, not one who *must* be believed.

The backlash against #MeToo as extrajudicial echoes the ways that formal procedures deny due process to victims. Held outside the law, but also blamed for not pressing a legal claim, due process represents a catch-22 for survivors. Jessica A. Clarke argues in her article "The Rules of #MeToo" that because traditional formal legal procedures fail to redress sexual harassment and assault, ad hoc processes have emerged to fill the gap.[16] When victims seek redress through formal processes, they often discover they have two choices: either see the process through and be treated as the problem or fall silent. Deborah Turkheimer observes that because formal mechanisms for reporting sexual harassment are so inadequate, women are forced into informal channels.[17] In her recent book on the failures of the complaint process in higher education, Sara Ahmed observes that formal reporting exhausts, undermines, and typically defeats those compelled to use it. Disregard for survivors is built into the operations of the university. As Ahmed explains: "We learn *about* institutions from the wear and tear of coming up against them. And, we learn *from* the embodied nature of the work of complaint: we can be worn down as well as worn out by what we go through when we go through a complaints process."[18] And yet survivors go to great lengths to stay within formal processes, pursuing alternatives only after available processes prove more obstructive than responsive. Indeed, so-called informal procedures offer more rather than less due process. As Clarke argues, "Rather than flouting due process values, #MeToo's informal procedures have a number of advantages in addressing sexual misconduct while providing fair process when the accused person is a prominent figure."[19]

Survivors confront a criminal-legal system that is hostile to their experience. Police, courts, and disciplinary processes in workplaces are nonresponsive to sexual violence when they are not demonstrably hostile to survivors. This treatment explains why no survivor groups of which I am aware argue for extra policing or additional punishments. They demand, instead, fair and transparent processes for reporting, accountability within those processes for those who usually enjoy impunity, and independent investigations rather than forced mediation. Some also advocate for restorative justice, including programs for sex offenders within prisons, recommending reduced sentences for those who fulfill the requirements of these programs. They most frequently say they want to prevent further abuse. They often speak about wanting to spare their daughters and other girls what they have suffered. They seek to end the reproduction of violence and the processes that permit it.

Finally, the assertion that extrajudiciality is itself the problem not only fails to address why the same survivors who are barred from legal redress by statutes of limitations might choose public personal testimony as a platform, it grants #MeToo a force it does not possess. Unlike a change in law, the #MeToo movement made no structural or institutional changes overnight. #MeToo did not compel compliance across public and private institutions. Instead, it changed the public narrative. It shifted perspective and sympathies, introduced new voices and stories, and challenged dominant epistemologies about consent. Above all, it confronted a broad audience with a changed reality about the pervasiveness of sexual violence.

When #MeToo disrupted the routine minimization of sexual violence, it revealed two different ways to think about the chronic tolerance of a massive problem. The first is that because sexual violence is everywhere, it must be natural. Horrible, yes, but unremarkable. Although the right of men to engage in sexual violence per se is rarely asserted, a propensity for violence is frequently naturalized as an intrinsic aspect of masculinity. When men act in sexually abusive ways, their harm is often minimized as something intimate partners must tolerate because it cannot be changed. Yet every institution in which work, study, worship, and play take place is also a location of sexual abuse because the reproduction of power allows it. The ideology that the institution is good, the law is fair, and abuse results from the actions of a few bad actors has a commonsense appeal. Common sense relies on the self-reinforcing logic that those in power stay in power for the good of the institution. Abusers retain positions of influence because they are often more aligned with institutional norms than are those who complain. Abuse is supported by processes that punish those who speak out, shield abusers from repercussions, and allow willing enablers and passive bystanders to thrive. Sexual abuse is adjudicated within structures that claim to be neutral regarding gender and race, but which embed this bias within their rules and norms.

A very different way of thinking comes from survivors. Consent comes freighted with power imbalances, as a multitude of #MeToo cases demonstrate. When there is a conflict over a claim of consent, power can be translated into credibility, enabling courts to favor men's claims of consent over women's claims of rape. Reading individual accounts of rape as examples of a collective problem, which is the core of #MeToo, clarifies that women's diminished right to lodge credible complaints in processes that grant men impunity from those complaints is a structural problem. The minimization of sexual violence as "no big deal" and rewriting of coercion as "consent" represents "he said" as a position of privilege: the privilege to name reality, backed up by the force of law. Survivor storytelling counters the normalization of sexual abuse and the myth that sexual violence is merely desire that gets out of hand. It reframes the consequences of excusing sexual violence to focus, instead, on the long-lasting negative effects on education, employment, and health that survivors experience.

Framing #MeToo as a threat to due process or a novelty rather than a resurgence of feminist activism resulted in crucial omissions and distortions even as the movement gained ground. It threatened to leave behind the intersectional lineage represented by Tarana Burke to focus, instead, on a Hollywood-centric story and primarily white actresses. Burke's activist lineage behind the creation of #MeToo was absorbed into another longstanding tradition in which white feminists bring the work of Black feminists to white audiences, with and without acknowledging their indebtedness. This tradition was amplified as #MeToo traveled across legal, literary, political, and national boundaries and shaped what different institutions believed they owed survivors. #MeToo was a story in need of a historical view on how personal testimony propels social change. For that, it had to recognize its roots in Black feminist activism and testimony.

A different framing for #MeToo was offered by feminists who saw it as a rerun of the sex wars of the 1980s in which divisive cultural debates focused on pornography and legal efforts to restrict it. At the Barnard conference in 1982, "Toward a Politics of Sexuality," activists, scholars, and artists gathered to debate feminist sexuality. Historian Lorna Bracewell describes the energies unleashed in the clash between antipornography activists interested in legislative change at a broad level and a sex-positive queer feminist left worried about censorship as "sorocidal ferocity" that would define a generation of participants. The stakes were high. Antiporn feminists lumped together consensual s-m queer practices with pornography made about trafficked women and children as "patriarchal sexuality."[20] In contrast, writers like Dorothy Allison, whose autobiographical novel *Bastard Out of Carolina* dealt with child sexual abuse rooted in her experience, denounced the policing of radical sexuality and the likely use of antipornography ordinances to target queer persons and businesses.[21] For those who saw in #MeToo the resurgence of a censoring spirit, a new sex panic seemed to be underway. As I will show, this framing misses how the intersectional lineage of narrative activism tilts away from legal interventions to focus more on accountability than punishment, on working conditions, and on the impact of sexual trauma on health.

Taken together, these debates about the legitimacy of #MeToo highlight the threefold power of narrative activism: (1) it shifts authority to individuals who critique the structures in which they are routinely discredited and, instead, draw on a range of storytelling techniques to reach broader audiences; (2) it replaces legal action with journalistic testimony and memoir, refuting the courtroom as space in which survivors can expect fair treatment; and (3) it provides a resource for survivors, activists, and advocates as they focus attention on justice and healing. When individuals cite the #MeToo era as the frame of reference in which they want to be heard, they rely on narrative activism to place their personal story in the context in which it makes sense as testimony. Testimony addresses itself to a public. In framing sexual violence as something someone must be accountable for and positioning survivors as someone to be accountable to, it asks, "What do we owe survivors?" As a moral question, it demands that we think beyond the limits of the law and consider which forms of justice are adequate and suitable to this harm.

Burke's approach to this question is intersectional—that is, focused on structural inequalities at the confluence of race, gender, class, and sexuality. This framework connects women's sexual agency to the conditions in which they perform waged and unwaged labor and to their capacity to be heard as truth-tellers. Before the coinage of "intersectionality" by Kimberlé Crenshaw, the Combahee River Collective theorized in 1977 that "systems of oppression are interlocking ... [and] the synthesis of these oppressions creates the conditions of our lives."[22] This Black feminist lesbian group of scholars and activists grounded in anti-capitalist, anti-imperialist critique argued that neither the white women's movement nor the Civil Rights movement addressed the lived realities of Black women.[23] Their legacy would prove salient for #MeToo and the concerns about whether it might be used against men of color. The criminal-legal system has a malignant and active history of enabling white men to punish Black men for alleged crimes against white women.

It has long been the case that in the absence of group credibility, sharing an individual story does not guarantee a fair hearing or prompt a new understanding of sexual violence.[24] In fact, personal stories can generate victim blaming and the reflexive defense of accused men. The insistence that women tell their stories in such conditions obscures what survivors need in order transform trauma into testimony: fair processes for reporting, adequate and timely investigations, and proportional forms of resolution. As #MeToo stories from across the globe attest, such pathways to justice are the exception rather than the rule. Instead, patriarchy stacks the deck against women and in favor of men structurally; that is, the same processes in which women are compelled to pursue redress and the same authorities to whom they must appeal offer men the unearned benefit of the doubt.[25] Thanks to #MeToo, however, the public conversation is no longer restricted to men's denials, women's defenses of men, the exonerating shrug of "he said / she said," and survivors' discounted testimony. There is a new focus on abusers' words and actions. Whether on the *Access Hollywood* tape that captured Donald Trump casually bragging about grabbing women by the pussy, the livestreamed diatribe by Isla Vista incel mass murderer Elliott Rodgers, or Bill Cosby's admission at his civil trial that he drugged and raped women, large public audiences heard what "he said" in his own words rather than his scripted denials. #MeToo changes the visual and audio archive of sexual violence from the disclaimers and denials of accused men to a record of their behavior, often in their own voices. Rereading these stories through the #MeToo effect gives us a new perspective on the familiar cases we thought we understood and amplifies what was not heard loudly enough in much of the reporting of these cases: the coarse textures of what "he said," the silencing of what "she said," and the reverberating #MeToo effect created by what "we said."

The rise of #MeToo coincides with a debate about life writing, specifically, the entrenched judgment that memoir is fixated on trauma and, further, that the meaning of trauma has become diluted through overuse. *New Yorker* writer Parul Sehgal recently explored this criticism in her article, "The Case Against the Trauma Plot."[26] Briefly, Sehgal argued that the trauma plot was a shortcut to unearned feeling, a cheap device that sent audiences into the past to ask, "What happened to her?," rather than orienting them toward future action. Although reasonable in the context of trauma's seeming ubiquity, her criticism echoes the standard dismissal of memoir that emerged in the 1980s as those who had not previously been represented by memoir and life writing began to publish in large numbers. Much of their life experience included trauma. Criticism of memoir (as being narcissistic, trauma-obsessed, and disrespectful about privacy) also resembles criticism directed at survivors. Objections to memoir are rarely restricted to aesthetic criteria; instead, U.S. literary culture consistently applies norms of decorum around speaking about domestic violence, women's bodies, and intergenerational trauma to women's memoir and faults it for being personal and partial.

In the 1970s and 1980s many feminists used autobiographical writing in multiple genres—essays, manifestos, memoirs, and poetry—to articulate the principle that the personal is political. The centrality of personal experience to the expression of political resistance to racism, sexism, and homophobia connects the radical women of color whose writing is collected in the landmark volume *This Bridge Called My Back* across their diverse identities and histories and to the lineage of Jacobs and Burke.[27] Drawing on confessional poetry, political analysis, and narrative, these writers focus on the communion of family, the joys of erotic love, and political passion through multiply situated "I's." The centrality of autobiography in their work reaches back to the testimonial genre of the slave narrative as well as the confessional genre of the spiritual autobiography. Women reworked both genres to tell stories of longing, pain, and resolve and to seize the authority associated with the "I." When marginalized writers take up life writing, it is often to wield the "I" in the formation of collective identity, to insist on feminist solidarity within experiences of discrimination and violence. Personal writing by women can be an act of resistance.[28]

Life writing from and about the perspective of survivors is the signature form of the #MeToo movement, so this is the context in which #MeToo must be framed. Life writing is heterogeneous in style, organization, and voice. It comprises different media and genres—from social media posts, victim impact statements, essays, poetry, and memoir—united by their focus on self-representation. Sometimes the testimonial "I" breaks into genres where it layers autobiographical reference into fiction or infuses bureaucratic depositions with an autobiographical perspective. Life writing typically features the author as narrator and includes the stylization of dialogue, scenes, and characters. Chronology is variously compressed or expanded in order to represent the intensities of experience. The "I" in life writing aims for truthfulness within the constraints of memory. In testimonial forms like the slave narrative, memory is assumed to be reliable for the specific purposes of truth telling.

As a narrative form, an account of a person's experience in their own voice is less constrained than legal testimony. For example, a choice as simple as where and how to begin offers a way to reenter the past with more agency. From retrospective narrative to flashbacks and flashforwards, from direct address to the reader and the use of dialogue, life writing uses literary techniques that enable us to imagine shared *and* unshared experience, to feel moved by characters whose violence—suffered and inflicted—appalls us, and, to abide with scenes and feelings from which we too rapidly turn away. Life writing expands both our archive of testimony and our understanding that judgment is not confined to law. Personal stories connect survivors to audiences and to each other beyond the legal courts of specific nations. The #MeToo effect happens as testimony moves out of official forums of judgment like courts and workplace complaint processes, circulates to new audiences, and establishes an alternative jurisdiction.[29] Life writing offers a resource with which to think about the limits of individual action and the role of communities and legal systems in holding wrongdoers accountable.

As a life writing genre, #MeToo needs an interpretive practice that places individual examples in a context that supplies meaning. I propose "survivor reading" as a feminist critical practice grounded in ethical listening and informed about the transformational power of storytelling by and about survivors. Reading like a survivor enables us to apply the care we feel for literary characters to actual survivors and, reciprocally, to bring the knowledge gained from listening to survivors to how we read. Just as #MeToo demonstrates the centrality of testimony to drive change, survivor reading recognizes the role of the witness. Survivor reading offers listeners a way to say "me too" as a response to representations of sexual violence and agency. It resonates with Tarana Burke's movement through its emphasis on empathy and identification. As such, it can be meaningfully brought to bear on any representation of sexual violence regardless of time, language, or genre: not because it evaluates texts according to a fixed #MeToo standard, but because it offers a way to pay attention to agency and violence. Not everyone has a personal story of sexual violence, but it is exceedingly likely that everyone knows someone who does. We will all be called on to attend to such stories in a range of contexts. Some will lend a sympathetic ear; others will be finders of fact. Survivor reading equips a broad public to engage in narrative activism by witnessing it.

In addition to the nonfictional form of life writing, literary fiction can serve as a resource for understanding survivors. So, too, the range of innovative strategies writers use to forge new forms of knowing cross boundaries of genre, picking up storytelling techniques as they go, shedding readings that proceed as if by police investigation.[30] Reading literary fiction can generate identification and empathy for characters beyond our personal experience—expanding our understanding of human motivation and diversity, casting new light on unsympathetic characters and unreliable narrators, and teaching us to survive. Fiction can unsettle our assumptions about who is worth protecting or easy to sacrifice. We can pay attention anew to characters we have been taught are minor and whose casual and even brutal treatment we have hardly noticed, so focused are we on protagonists with whom our attention is aligned. Representations of sexual violence are part of literary and religious texts from antiquity, yet these texts also model agency, resistance, and resilience. They contain submerged narratives we have been taught not to value, narrators we consider unreliable, and representations of sexual violence we minimize or consider mainly metaphorical. If literature were an empathy machine capable of generating the same effects in everyone, these texts would already have been read differently. Yet reading is responsive to and changes cultural understanding. Reading life writing together with other representations of sexual violence, whether they be fictional, legal, or religious, provides an ongoing benchmark against which to measure whether survivors are being heard or silenced and contributes new knowledge about the impact of sexual violence.

The #MeToo effect enables us to read the current outpouring of cultural productions as part of a broader shift that opens a new perspective on settled views of the past. In this sense, the #MeToo effect carries on the work of previous feminist generations, offering material for what Michèle LeDoeuff calls the "prospective memory of a movement which constantly needs to be taken up again."[31] There is a recursive quality to this work. Trauma seems to lie buried for years until victims find an opening to tell their stories. Sexual violence, even after it is spoken about by victims, can be folded into amnesiac narratives that exonerate abusers. Intersectional feminist critiques of sexual violence along with successes in rape prevention are purposefully left out of public history, officially forgotten, or rewritten as signs of progress secured. Yet, as psychologist and feminist trauma theorist Judith Herman explains, "Remembering and telling the truth about terrible events are prerequisites both for the restoration of the social order and for the healing of individual victims."[32] Therefore I return to a history that predates #MeToo and the feminist lineage Tarana Burke represents to unpack the events that erupted in the 2017 frame of #MeToo and explore lingering cases that received new scrutiny because of it.[33] Although I cannot tell a wholeheartedly positive story about what the #MeToo movement has accomplished and might still do, I refuse to tell a hopeless one. Instead,

I identify how survivors, who often reflect on their experience long after sexual assault, offer the best perspective on trauma, justice, and the future.

As to organization, I trace a line of argument through examples—some of which will be familiar to those who followed #MeToo, others less so—to show a pattern over time of survivor credibility emerging and then being moved to the edges of attention—even as activism continues. Narrative offers a record of persistence. From classical drama and myth to canonical literature and modern texts, survivors are sometimes protagonists, but often minor characters. The theme of doubting women, of hiding sexual violence in plain sight and calling it by false names, of pretending to offer justice to women in the form of a trial, of focusing on the sordid dailiness of the harm men do without delving as deeply into the complex lives of those to whom it is done fill literature, to be sure. But because we are also habituated to ignore the presence of survivors, seeing them differently is a promising option. We can learn to read "like a survivor"; that is, to embrace multiple positions of identification and understanding, whether or not we have experienced sexual violence ourselves in the ways in which specific examples present it. To that end, I offer a map of testimonial connections to amplify the #MeToo effect. From Harriet Jacobs and Tarana Burke to Anita Hill and Christine Blasey Ford; from the Women's March and Black Lives Matter to Chanel Miller, Vanessa Springora, and those whose testimony—legal and literary—forced changes in law; and from fictional figures like Philomela, Antigone, and Shakespeare's Lavinia to an emerging archive of #MeToo storytelling in multiple genres and media, the #MeToo effect draws in a range of reference beyond its most recent episode. Although my analysis centers life writing, #MeToo storytelling traverses genre. I do not offer a full taxonomy of how survivors tell #MeToo stories, where, and to what audiences, but I note how key figures and formations recur. Survivors can be trapped in stories, as well as in legal processes or cultural silences, where they are misread and dismissed. Narrative activism offers the opportunity to change the stories we tell and survivor reading equips us to hear them.

Part 1 makes the case that survivor testimony is the signature form of the #MeToo movement and defines it as an episode of narrative activism within an intersectional feminist lineage. It examines a series of recent cases clustered around the #MeToo breakthrough in 2017 in the context that I argue was absent in the commentary on that eruption. Chapter 1 contextualizes the competing temporal framings offered for #MeToo within this lineage and charts the shift from "he said / she said" to "we said." It focuses on how Anita Hill's testimony staged a public spectacle of doubting credible women while also sweeping a wave of women into elected office. This bifurcated response illustrates the mobility of "he said / she said" across multiple locations in which women's testimony is heard and the backlash feminist social processes face.

Chapter 2 examines how events in the year preceding #MeToo set the stage for it. It charts how the growing visibility of survivor-centered experience and knowledge moved the credible witness into public view. It reads Chanel Miller's testimony at the rape trial of Brock Turner as the template for contemporary #MeToo narrative activism and evidence of the power of autobiographical narrative to challenge law from outside the courtroom. It reframes Trump's *Access Hollywood* tape and the Women's March within the context created by Chanel Miller's testimony and Brock Turner's defense of the right to rape.

Chapter 3 theorizes #MeToo as a breakthrough rather than a novelty. The conditions of its emergence can be located as four elements converged: temporality, saturation, visibility, and participation. The connections between #MeToo and other recent social movements, most notably Black Lives Matter, demonstrate how elements combine to catalyze witness and action. It analyzes the #MeToo tweet, and the tropes, events, and people associated with silence breaking.

Chapter 4 identifies #MeToo as an event that belongs to a complex history beginning with Harriet Jacobs's use of autobiographical narrative to critique sexual violence and slavery and connecting the Combahee River Collective's statement on interlocking systems of oppression to Burke's message of empathy and identification. I consider how anti-rape activism from the nineteenth century to the 1970s, the free love movement in the nineteenth century, and the sex wars in the 1980s are interwoven with but distinguishable from Burke's lineage, and I note the use of literary criticism in 1970s antirape activism to move survivors to the fore.

Chapter 5 examines Christine Blasey Ford's allegations that Brett Kavanaugh sexually assaulted her as a stress test for #MeToo. Her allegations recalled Anita Hill's testimony that Clarence Thomas sexually harassed her and raised expectations that Blasey Ford's credibility would be informed by the #MeToo context. Hill's testimony and treatment haunted the hearing, which proceeded as a trial, a setting in which survivors are structurally disadvantaged. Through the partisan questioning of Blasey Ford, the Senate Judiciary Committee conducted two hearings: one in which she could be credible, and another in which she must be doubted. The hearing offered the appearance of being heard in the presence of being silenced.

Part 2 provides a broader narrative context for the cases in part 1 and identifies narrative justice as the goal of survivor testimony. This is not the only goal of feminist movements to end sexual violence; rather, it emerges as a counterdiscourse to the legal framing of testimony and underscores the insufficiency of carceral solutions. Chapter 6 identifies narrative justice—the right to be heard—as a demand that arises in survivor life writing. It draws on the concept of epistemic violence to ask how narrative justice counters the harm done to a person denied the status of knower. I propose survivor reading as a practice for grappling with the complexity and nuance of survivor storytelling. Survivor reading reframes past sexual violence within the #MeToo effect to imagine victims as credible and abusers as accountable in relation to the forces—in law and culture—that resist this reframing.

Chapter 7 identifies narrative activism through an emerging archive of #MeToo storytelling. #MeToo storytelling and narrative activism are generically diverse and growing. My analysis centers on life writing, but narrative exists in multiple media, and many conventions of #MeToo storytelling traverse genre. I describe this as testimony in motion and evidence of the epistemic power of #MeToo to frame collective witness.

Chapter 8 returns to the subject of consent, which is never far from the nexus of desire, agency, and autonomy. #MeToo offers survivors a new position here: the "I" whose silence breaking navigates the "gray areas of consent," bringing testimonial agency to experiences of coercion and abuse. Consent, I argue, shifted some of its meanings after #MeToo, but it remains an artifact of systemic bias refashioned with variable success as a tool through which to assert sexual autonomy. In examples that originate in the #MeToo buildup and find their largest public audience after its breakthrough, consent emerges in high-stakes battles over accountability in formal structures. The chapter concludes by reading Vanessa Springora's memoir as an example of how narrative activism led to the establishment of age of consent laws in France.

---

The aim of this book is to show how the #MeToo effect accomplished something important but not unprecedented when it enabled millions of individual stories to coalesce into a collective witness. The #MeToo effect represents a breakthrough in norms of silencing. In the fracturing of doubt and discrediting, survivors reach toward new ways of being in relation to each other. As an intersectional feminist practice within a history of narrative activism, it not only exposed institutional bias, it revealed and fostered networks of connection. For survivors, telling about abuse risks retraumatization, especially in processes that reinforce the structures in which abuse occurred or promise little in the way of resolution or justice. The #MeToo effect enabled survivors to reimagine the scene of violation as one of solidarity, healing, and justice, where previously muffled voices could be heard together. I conclude by considering the debt we owe those whom we doubt and offer concrete solutions based on storytelling by survivors.

# I

# NARRATIVE ACTIVISM AND SURVIVOR TESTIMONY

# 1

## THE #METOO EFFECT

From He Said/She Said to Collective Witness

*You took away my worth, my privacy, my energy, my time,*
*my safety, my intimacy, my confidence, my own voice,*
*until today.*

—CHANEL MILLER, *KNOW MY NAME*

When #MeToo corrected the false view of sexual violence as rare with a more accurate understanding of its prevalence, it directly challenged the claim that women often and even characteristically lie about assault. That view is both entrenched and false, the classic pairing of attributes central to stereotype. "He said / she said" operates as a cultural norm, a shared belief in what fairness looks like. It is woven into legal guidelines that influence how police question witnesses and suspects, whether prosecutors bring charges, and, in the rarity that the case goes to court, how juries decide. With deep roots in racism and misogyny, legal and religious traditions discount testimony about sexual violence in order to make those who are the targets of it less credible than those who abuse them. This occurs not only in the case of abuse, but as a mechanism to reproduce patriarchy in general. When the #MeToo effect displaced "he said / she said," it exposed an interlocking set of assumptions and law supporting male impunity and inaugurated a paradigm shift toward accountability.

As recently as 1972, every element of a woman's testimony about rape required corroboration because, as New York jurist Morris Plescowe opined in opposition to repealing the requirement, "ladies lie." The legal origins of "he said / she said" can be traced to English law and the carving out of a new testimonial standard for a woman's allegation of rape: "Victims of any other type of crime—muggings, robberies, physical assaults—could provide the sole testimony at trial. Rape victims were uniquely excluded from the criminal justice system."[1] The corroboration requirement ended in the 1970s following an outcry of feminist activism, but the exclusion of survivors from due process persists in the form of doubt. Doubt hounds women, especially when they speak about sexual abuse, for three reasons: because they are women, because what they say conflicts with paternalistic notions about harm and care, and because they possess less symbolic and material capital than men as witnesses in courts of law and the court of public opinion.[2] Once doubt is raised, it sticks, tainting women as witnesses to their own experience. In contrast, we are trained to believe men, to value their prospects and reputation.[3]

"Ladies lie" and "he said / she said" exemplify a range of legal tactics that silence women. When such methods cross from the law into the realm of common sense, they represent a form of judgment readily directed at any survivor. A series of examples illustrates how this judgment suppressed the #MeToo effect in public conversations about sexual harassment. From Anita Hill and the women who complained about Senator Robert Packwood (R.-Ore.), to faculty members and graduate students in higher education, to a young rape victim pressured to recant her true testimony, the refusal to hear what "she said" reveals the connective tissue of doubt muffling women's speech in testimonial contexts. Yet as a dominant method for tilting the credibility balance away from women, "he said / she said" has an astonishing grip on the cultural imagination as a fair standard.

Twenty years after the repeal of the law that made women's testimony about rape less credible than men's denial of it, Anita Hill faced the same standard in her testimony that Clarence Thomas, a nominee to the Supreme Court in 1991, sexually harassed her when she worked for him at the Equal Employment Opportunity Commission. *TIME* magazine presented Hill's testimony as "he said / she said" in a cover story that featured photographs of Hill and Thomas in split screen.[4] On the left, a tense Thomas, purses his lips as if about to spit out his searing indictment that his nomination hearing was a "high tech lynching for uppity blacks"; on the right, Hill, composed and wary, glances over her right shoulder. Like the juxtaposed images on the cover, the story attempts to equalize Hill and Thomas as reluctant witnesses despite describing them as a study in contrasts. She is "cool and unflappable," answers every question, and is cooperative rather than defensive. He swings from anguish to rage and describes himself as "shocked, surprised, hurt and enormously saddened." Despite the binary framing of "two credible, articulate witnesses" with "irreconcilable views of what happened nearly a decade ago," there was never any evidence that Hill was lying and, instead, ample accounts supporting her descriptions of Thomas's behavior.[5] Framing their positions as "both sides" minimized Hill's testimony and isolated her from other women who were prepared to testify about Thomas's sexual harassment, suppressing the formation of the #MeToo effect.

When Hill testified that Thomas talked about pornography in the office and pressured women for dates, Angela Wright, who worked for and dated Thomas, was watching the hearings on television. She recognized her former boss: "I didn't know her. . . . But I knew that Clarence Thomas was capable [of what he stood accused of] because he had made similar remarks to me and in my presence about my body and other women's bodies, and he did—he was very egotistical, and he did pressure me to date him, and he did drop by the house when unannounced."[6] Sukari Hardnett, who worked in a similar position at EEOC as Hill, also recognized Thomas's behavior as she watched the televised testimony. Hardnett provided an affidavit saying she had witnessed the sexualized atmosphere Hill described: "What I wanted to do was corroborate the fact that Anita Hill, like so many other young females at the commission, would be an audition by Clarence for whatever purpose. He would call them into his office. In particular with me, Clarence expected me to be available to him every morning and for lunch, and I would run down to a friend of mine's office and hide just to avoid being in the situation with Clarence where I would have uncomfortable conversations."[7] Although Wright was subpoenaed by the Senate Judiciary Committee and waited in her attorney's office in Washington during the hearing, Senator Alan Simpson, Republican from Wyoming, falsely stated that Wright "got cold feet." She was never called.

Outrage over Hill's mistreatment and Thomas's confirmation swept a record number of women into elected office in 1992. In an early test of the hoped-for sea change in attitudes toward sexual harassment, Congress opened an ethics inquiry into allegations against Senator Packwood. There were many. Packwood denied each allegation as an example of "she said." In a recognizable pattern of multiple allegations against a single abuser, the Ethics Committee accumulated testimony from multiple women, each of whom echoed the testimony of Julie Williamson, a young staff assistant in Packwood's office. Williamson described an incident in which she was on the phone when Packwood came up behind her and kissed her neck: "I was startled by that, finished the phone conversation, hung up the phone and turned and said to him, 'Don't you ever do that again.'" After Williamson verbally rebuffed him, she battled through a sexual assault: "Finally, he grabbed her; when she tried to kick him in the shins, he stood on her feet. He grabbed her ponytail with his left hand, pulled her head back forcefully, and gave her a big wet kiss, with his tongue in her mouth. She did not smell or taste any alcohol. With his right hand, he reached up under her skirt and grabbed the edge of her panty girdle and tried to pull it down. She struggled, got away from him, and ran into the front office. He stalked out past her, paused at the threshold to the hallway, and told her, 'If not today, someday,' and left." Williamson immediately told a friend, who corroborated her testimony to the Ethics Committee.[8]

Williamson showed precisely the kind of "gumption" that Senator Dennis DeConcini (R.-Ariz.) implied during the Clarence Thomas hearing that Anita Hill, and by extension any woman who did not successfully stop sexual harassment, failed to exhibit: "If you're sexually harassed you ought to get mad about it, and you ought to do something about it and you ought to complain, instead of hanging around a long time and then all of a sudden calling up anonymously and say 'Oh, I want to complain.' I mean, where is the gumption?"[9] DeConcini's folksy locution conjures a scene in which a firm "no" from a principled woman halts a handsy boss in his tracks. In contrast to this invented scenario, both Hill and Williamson verbally resisted. If the standard is that a woman should say "no" and report the incident contemporaneously, Williamson met it. Yet the Ethics Committee did not respond to any of the women who gave sworn statements about Packwood for two years. When California Democrat Barbara Boxer called for public hearings, Republicans in the Senate blocked her request.

Neither the testimony of Julie Williamson nor that any of the other women who provided evidence of a longstanding pattern of sexual abuse shifted opinion against Packwood. What finally did was what "he said" in the form of a voluminous diary he kept during his career in the Senate. It included entries like this: "I have one question—if she didn't want me to feather her nest, why did she come into the Xerox room? Sure, she used that old excuse that she had to make copies of the Brady Bill, but if you believe that, I have a room full of radical feminists you can boff. She knew I was copying stuff in there. I had my jacket off and my sleeves rolled up, revealing the well-defined musculature of my sinewy arms which are always bulging with desire. I know what she wanted. This didn't require a lot of thought."[10] Three years after public allegations about Packwood surfaced in the wake of Anita Hill's testimony, and after twenty women had given evidence of sexual assault and rape, the diary prompted the Senate Ethics Committee to vote unanimously to expel Packwood. He promptly resigned.[11]

No new processes for hearing allegations about sexual harassment were developed following Anita Hill's testimony. All the women reporting on Packwood between 1992 and 1995 faced the same lack of access to a timely and transparent process. In 2018, when Christine Blasey Ford wanted to inform the Senate Judiciary Committee that Brett Kavanaugh had tried to rape her when they were teenagers, the process was as unclear and inadequate as it had been in 1991 for Hill. In a male-dominated and influence-saturated context like politics, abuse of power is hardly news, but rules for reporting that insulate sexual abusers from consequences make it hard for survivors to engage the process. Congress, for example, has no human resources department; instead, it polices itself through ethics committees. These committees have no instructions about the timeliness or scope of their investigations, although they do impose statutes of limitations on victims and require mediation, which expose survivors to ongoing contact, including threats of retaliation and potential retraumatization. Hearings are held in secret and are subordinate to the work schedules of committee members. Time and money are disproportionately on the side of elected politicians. Taxpayers pay for the legal representation for accused members of Congress, while accusers are responsible for financing their own counsel. When investigations conclude in settlements, those, too, are paid by taxpayers.

Nor are these conditions confined to government. In a case that preceded the Hill-Thomas hearings and continued for four decades, Harvard enabled Latin American scholar and senior administrator Jorge Domínguez to abuse women faculty members.[12] In 1983 Terry Karl, a junior tenure-track faculty member in the Government Department, filed a complaint alleging that Domínguez had sexually harassed her on multiple occasions over two years. Following an investigation, Henry Rosovsky, dean of Harvard's Faculty of Arts and Sciences, determined the complaint had merit. Yet despite a finding of "serious sexual harassment and abuse of authority," Domínguez stayed and Terry Karl left. She reported that he continued to harass her after her departure from Harvard. Two other faculty members in the Government Department were also investigated and found to have committed sexual assault during the time Professor Domínguez harassed Professor Karl. In the years after this finding, Domínguez rebuilt his stature at Harvard, gaining high-level administrative postings where he continued to exert power over students and faculty. In 2018, when news of decades of his ongoing sexual misconduct was made public, he resigned, characterizing the decision as "retirement."

The Harvard report occasioned by Domínguez corroborates one on sexual harassment in STEM published in 2018.[13] That report identifies higher education, academic medicine, and the sciences as notorious havens for predatory behavior. In them, serial sexual harassers use their positions of authority as cover for wrongdoing, leverage the prestige and credibility of the institution to shield themselves from repercussions, and shape institutional cultures through their influence over those they target and those whose silence they reward. Such gatekeepers wield outsize power over opportunity and advancement. Both reports acknowledge the consequences of not removing sexual harassers who are positioned to retaliate against those who challenge them. They express concern about the harm of sexual misconduct to those victimized. Finally, they tout the role of leadership in establishing norms around not tolerating sexual harassment and emphasize the importance of transparent reporting processes. Yet in 2020 a story in the *Harvard Crimson*, the student newspaper, detailed how three professors in the Anthropology Department had received multiple complaints of sexual harassment during the same decades of sexual misconduct engaged in by professors in the Government Department.[14] Harvard had problems with ongoing sexual harassment reaching back decades. Those accused continued to hold positions of power in their academic fields and the institution. As complaints by graduate students in anthropology about incidents of sexual harassment by a senior faculty member as recently as 2017 show, impunity is an institutional norm.[15]

Outside politics and academia, suspicion against victims is entrenched. In 2008 eighteen-year-old Marie Adler was bound, gagged, and raped at knifepoint by a masked intruder who broke into her apartment while she was sleeping.[16] Adler reported the crime immediately to Lynnwood, Washington police. Despite offering consistent testimony about a traumatizing and violent rape, and in the absence of any disqualifying evidence, Adler was deemed "unbelievable." The investigators accused her of making up a tale of the masked intruder and insisted she had been dreaming. Confirming that everyone is trained to doubt women, two previous foster mothers told the police they, too, doubted Adler. The detectives pressured her to recant, which she did. When they charged her with making a false report, she lost her housing, her job, and her friendships.

After the investigation was closed, the man who attacked Adler continued to rape women in Washington, Oregon, and Colorado. The case only began to crack two years later when Detective Stacey Galbraith was assigned to investigate a rape in Colorado. Galbraith told her husband, also a detective, about the case. He noted a similarity to a rape in a nearby town a few months earlier. Galbraith contacted Edna Hendershot, the detective investigating that case, and their joint effort culminated in the arrest of serial rapist Marc O'Leary, who was tried in Colorado, pled guilty to twenty-eight counts of rape and associated felonies, and was sentenced to 327 and a half years. Had police believed Marie Adler, they might have spared her the traumatization she experienced at their hands and prevented multiple rapes.

Journalists T. Christian Miller and Kevin Armstrong, reporting on this miscarriage of justice, observe that police typically approach a reported rape as a case of regretted consensual sex. "In that way," they write, "rape cases were unlike most other crimes. The credibility of the victim was often on trial as much as the guilt of the accused." Detective Galbraith's approach to investigating sex crimes was markedly different: listen and verify. "A lot of times people say, 'Believe your victim, believe your victim,'" Galbraith said. "But I don't think that that's the right standpoint. I think it's listen to your victim. And then corroborate or refute based on how things go." Galbraith's "listen and verify" may not be substantively different from "believe your victim" as a starting point, but it is worlds apart from "doubt your victim." Edna Hendershot's standard was even higher: "she needed what she called 'definitive' evidence before dismissing a sexual assault allegation."[17] As an ethical stance, "listen" does not require one to embrace survivor testimony uncritically or discard due process for accuser and accused.[18] Instead, it acknowledges that victims deserve to be heard. "Listen and verify" prepares hearers to believe; it does not guarantee that every element of every case will be equally believable. Traumatized people speak in conditions of doubt and bias. Trauma survivors typically struggle to order their accounts, especially under stress. In the processing of traumatic experience, some details are subordinated to the searing memory of others. All this has been well documented in clinical studies of trauma

and, as Galbraith and Hendershot's approach to interviewing demonstrates, incorporated by some members of the criminal-legal system.

I have shown how the "he said / she said" trope enables institutions
to perpetuate cultures of unequal power in which abuse thrives by dismissing women's claims across multiple locations and suppressing the
cumulative knowledge that is gained by listening to their collective testimony. "He said / she said" seeds the testimonial space with hostility
dressed up as due process. Its rebarbative stance toward women often
mobilizes a rescue response on behalf of accused men. It promotes the
false notion that processes profoundly biased against women are fair and
neutral to them. "He said / she said" is not the only example of how law
silences survivors, but it exemplifies how legal notions migrate outside
courts and take root in cultural practices of judgment. In 2016 a growing public awareness of survivor experience created the conditions for
joining disparate #MeToo accounts into a collective witness. As a result,
individual cases about sexual violence began to coalesce in the public
sphere as examples of the same problem.

# 2

## BUILDUP

Survivors in Public, Trump, and the Women's March

*I feel like once you see violence and you see how it lives in our day-to-day lives, you can't unsee it. I knew that until I could point it out to other people, I wouldn't be able to feel sane.*

—CHANEL MILLER, "MAKING ART OUT OF GRIEF: A CONVERSATION"

By 2016 a host of different elements propelling the #MeToo effect were converging. Forms as disparate as protest, memoirs, political campaigns, lawsuits, and musical performance beckoned audiences to engage with a survivor-centered understanding of sexual violence. In February 2016 public audience of 34.4 million people watched Lady Gaga perform " 'Til It Happens to You" at the Oscars, a song from the documentary film about campus sexual violence, *The Hunting Ground*. Lady Gaga used her celebrity and public stance as a survivor to raise awareness of sexual violence through her song and performance, during which she was joined onstage for the final verse and chorus by other survivors.[1] In August Taylor Swift testified that radio DJ David Mueller had reached under her skirt and groped her at a meet and greet in 2013. Mueller sued Swift for defamation because when she spoke out about the assault, he lost his job. He sought $3 million in damages. She countersued him for $1 and won. During Swift's testimony, which both entertainment media and mainstream journalism covered, Mueller's attorney attempted to shift blame away from his client. Asked if she was "critical of" her bodyguard for not preventing the assault, Swift testified, "I'm critical of your client sticking his hand under my skirt and grabbing my ass." Asked if she were to blame, Swift testified, "I am not going to allow your client to make me feel like it is anyway my fault because it isn't."[2] In both examples, the power of celebrity enabled personal stories of sexual assault to reach broad public audiences.[3] While these examples are distinct in form, they became associated by large audiences as part of the same phenomenon occurring within a short time frame: an openness to the complexities and reality of survivor experience. A collective witness was emerging.

## KNOW MY NAME

In addition to celebrities using their star power to bring attention to survivors through the fusion of popular culture, social media, and journalism, a campus rape case in California vaulted from a local news story to an international audience when the survivor shared her victim impact statement on *Buzzfeed* in June 2016. Like Lady Gaga's performance and Taylor Swift's testimony, Chanel Miller's use of personal voice and vivid storytelling invited audiences to engage with survivor-centered testimony. Miller's 2016 statement and her memoir, *Know My Name*, published in 2019 bookend the #MeToo effect of 2017 and illustrate the importance of narrative activism to its emergence and impact.[4] Until she made her identity public, Chanel Miller was known as "Emily Doe," the author of the searing statement addressed directly to Brock Turner, who was convicted on three counts of felony sexual assault for raping her behind a dumpster outside a Stanford fraternity house in 2015.[5] She was unconscious during the assault. Miller's statement begins: "You don't know me, but you've been inside me, and that's why we're here today."[6] The statement was frank and eloquent. As a testament to its power, it was read eighteen million times online and in its entirety on *CNN*. Vice President Joe Biden published an open letter in response to it, and Representative Jackie Speier (D.-Calif.) read Miller's statement into the *Congressional Record*. It set the stage for how first-person narratives would launch #MeToo beyond legal courts and offer broad publics a firsthand account of the harm of sexual violence. It also shifted Miller's public identity from victim to author, from subject of a crime to the authority of its meaning, a position she would amplify in her memoir.

Miller uses life writing to supply the context, perspective, and meaning that was stripped by the rape and at trial. *Know My Name* is divided into three parts and arranged chronologically: the attack, the trial, and the aftermath, both personal and legal. The first part provides a meticulous account of the day of the assault and begins with Miller, who was living with her parents in Palo Alto after graduating from UC Santa Barbara, looking forward to a weekend visit from her sister Tiffany, a junior at Cal-Poly. She agrees to join her sister and friends at a frat party at Stanford later that evening. The plan evolves casually over the afternoon as four friends coordinate to meet on campus and urge Miller to join them. Miller regards frat parties with the ironic remove of a college graduate: "*Should I go, would it be funny if I went.*"[7] They drink champagne the friends bring and some whiskey they find at home. Miller's mother drives them to campus, seven minutes down Foothill Expressway, and they walk to the Kappa Alpha frat. These quotidian details underscore the mismatch between how a person who will become the target of a sexual assault and how a potential assailant prepare. Rape trials focus on minute details about what a victim did before she was assaulted, seizing on what she wore, if she drank, or whether she danced, in order to roll back the timeline on her consent and reframe her prior actions within a temporality imposed by the sexual assault. There is no comparable attention to the minute-by-minute preparation of rapists in rape trials.

At the frat party, Miller recalls, Turner aggressively danced up to her. She rebuffed him, as did her sister, whom Turner also tried to kiss as he worked the room. The whiskey goes to Miller's head: she's unused to college-party-level drinking, and she is about to black out. She will later testify that she remembers leaving the fraternity without her sister and using her cellphone to call her boyfriend. He was so concerned about how she sounded that he called her sister to check on her. Between leaving the party and waking up at the hospital for a rape examination, Miller's memories are blanked by unconsciousness. She is examined for evidence of sexual assault and questioned by police, but she will not learn details of the assault, including Turner's identity, until she reads about them online. She will discover that Turner stalked her after she left the party, maneuvered her behind a dumpster, and sexually assaulted her. They were discovered by two Swedish graduate students biking by who saw Turner humping a figure lying motionless on the ground. Turner had torn off some of Miller's clothing, she was half-naked, and he was digitally penetrating her. They yelled and he ran. One of them caught and held him until police arrived.

In news reports, Turner was described as a star Stanford swimmer and Miller as "drunk" and "unconscious." Descriptors for Miller were restricted to the time of her assault, while Turner was painted as an upstanding college student with a promising future. Imagine if Turner, like Miller, were described as he was found that night: semi-erect, glassy eyed, hunched over a woman he was in the process of raping behind a dumpster. Imagine, too, if Miller, like Turner, were humanized through her accomplishments as a recent college graduate, visual artist, and creative writer. The failure to identify Chanel Miller as a person with a life outside the assault strongly contrasted with the refusal to identify Turner within that context. While rape shield laws prevented Miller's name from being released, rape culture exploited the absence of information. When media repeat information provided by Turner's defense team intended to represent him as an All-American boy, the problem is not with rape shield laws. Rather, it lies with norms of representation and the refusal to grapple with the agency of rapists who are white, privileged college students attending elite institutions.

In her description of the rape examination, Miller offers perspective on the bond among survivors that resonates with Tarana Burke's "me too." Miller writes, "I always wondered why survivors understood each other so well. Why, even if the details of our attacks vary, survivors can lock eyes and get it without having to explain. Perhaps it is not the particulars of the assault itself that we have in common, but the moment after; the first time you are left alone. Something slipping out of you. Where did I go."[8] Her analysis of trauma and her experience within the criminal legal system will also amplify Burke's intersectional feminist lens as the second part of the memoir turns to the trial. Miller confronts how gender, race, and privilege combine to elevate violent white men into figures of sympathy while demonizing women of color, like Chinese American Miller, who dare to speak out. She describes how powerful institutions like Stanford University and Judge Aaron Persky's courtroom shielded Turner and revictimized her.

The second part of the memoir addresses the trial. Miller has a strong case. Turner is caught while attacking her. When confronted, he runs. She is unconscious when she is taken to the hospital. The circumstances—a victim who cannot consent, eyewitnesses to the attack—suggest Miller is a "perfect victim" to receive justice. However, when Turner's team learns that she has no memory of the attack, they rewrite rape as a consensual romantic encounter. Her unconsciousness enables them to place the assault within a gray area, a space in which her consent might seem plausible. They insist drinking dissolves his responsibility but creates hers. Like Brett Kavanaugh, Turner will blame alcohol, he will say "everyone" was drinking, but he will not admit to sexual assault.[9] Turner will say, instead, he asked "to finger her" and that Miller said "yes."

## THE RAPE DEFENSE

Turner's trial offers an opportunity to examine the strategies his legal team successfully employed to reinterpret a violent act against an unconscious victim—a crime that was amply confirmed by physical evidence and witnesses—into a drunken night that was more regrettable than criminal. The strategies Turner's lawyers used are part of a rape defense that makes routine use of the following tactics:[10]

#1: Blame the victim. Turn everything in her life into evidence of her loose morals. Cast doubt on her actions during the time frame of the assault. Focus especially on what she wore and what she drank, as if the natural consequence of getting drunk is not an awful hangover but a sexual attack. Do this to shift responsibility from her attacker to her.

#2: Elicit sympathy for the accused rapist. Emphasize his many accomplishments and bright future (including his career as a promising athlete). When you use the word *ruin*, make sure it refers to the risk to his future and reputation and not to his victim's. Make sure his mug shot is not the primary visual image. Instead, make him appear as clean-cut and respectable as possible.[11] No one should think, "This is the face of rape."

#3: Promote doubt. Instead of focusing on the facts in the case, capitalize on cultural stereotypes about women's unreliability. Substitute a general narrative about rape for one that conforms to the facts of the case. Distort evidence to equalize the victim and perpetrator. Create a parallel story in which there is no real crime, but only a difference of interpretation. Suggest that alcohol rather than the client is responsible for rape.

These strategies create reasonable doubt, the burden of proof the prosecution must meet in criminal cases. And they work. The law allows them, and jurors are susceptible to them because women are often held responsible for the sexual violence men inflict. Just how easy it was to generate sympathy for Turner confirms Rebecca Wanzo's argument that some stories of suffering remain invisible while others are central to the dominant meaning of events.[12] Through her analysis of how sentiment attaches to Black women's suffering, Wanzo illuminates a history of sympathy for white men that associates their violence with their innocence. Like figures in this history, Turner presented himself and Miller as equally victimized (by alcohol) and equally innocent.

Chanel Miller's unconsciousness is a common part of rape. Cressida J. Heyes notes it as a "long-standing feature of sexual assault, whether the victim is asleep, drunk, drugged, anaesthetized, asphyxiated, suffering from a head injury, or in a coma."[13] Joanna Bourke, too, identifies the interest in Victorian England about the role of "stupefying draughts" in sexual coercion.[14] While temperance movements in the late 1800s and early 1900s decried the economic irresponsibility and sexual violence of drunkard husbands, they also alluded to the dangers alcohol posed to women's virtue, sliding responsibility onto women to prevent men's sexual violence. The history of rape and responsibility is a shell game meant to hide men's responsibility. Sometimes women are blamed, but blame is also displaced onto substances like alcohol, which cannot themselves be held accountable. Substances represent mitigation, or factors that reduce responsibility, and they influence sentencing. Comedian Bill Cosby, for example, evaded responsibility for decades during which he drugged and sexually assaulted sixty women. He was finally sentenced in 2018 to between three and ten years in prison for assaulting Andrea Constand in 2004. In his deposition at her civil suit, Cosby testified that he had drugged her without her knowledge and sexually assaulted her while she was unconscious: "I don't hear her say anything. And I don't feel her say anything. And so I continue and I go into the area that is somewhere between permission and rejection. I am not stopped."[15] An unconscious person cannot say no. She cannot speak at all. Yet his defense that this is "consensual" is that Constand did not stop him from raping her.

Turner was convicted on three counts of felony sexual assault. The maximum sentence was fourteen years. Judge Aaron Persky opined from the bench about the harm Turner's conviction meant for his future and worried about the pain Turner might suffer during incarceration. He sentenced Turner to six months and he served three.[16] Turner's father submitted a presentencing statement that lingered over how his son reacted to the trial. He does not reflect on the crime his son was convicted of, suggest his son is remorseful, or mention the victim. Instead, he writes: "He will never be his happy go lucky self with that easy going personality and wide grin."[17] He complains that his son no longer enjoys a grilled ribeye steak. Rebecca Wanzo's analysis of racialized sympathy explains how such homey details persuaded Judge Persky: "Signs of the sentimental are repeated representations of the sweet, innocent, or cute; provoked tears in response to a melodramatic or tortuous turn in a story; repetitive and nostalgic renderings of either a sorrowful event or happy times so that the audience is reminded of how painful or joyous a recent occurrence is."[18] Wringing sympathy from the portrayal of a previously carefree white teen who is now moping at a backyard barbecue neatly illustrates the melodrama of the rape defense. Persky's sentence meant Turner received a summer's worth of punishment for what his father called "20 minutes of action."[19]

Two more events at the center of public attention shaped the #MeToo buildup: the leaking of Donald Trump's *Access Hollywood* tape and the Women's March in 2016. These events featured two transformative elements that shifted "he said / she said" to collective witness: a global audience heard what "he said" in Trump's own words rather than his denial of those words, and a massive public turned out voluntarily to support women in marches held in small towns and metropolises alike.

## TRUMP'S *ACCESS HOLLYWOOD* TAPE

Typically, and unhelpfully, we hear what "he said" from her rather than in his own voice. Like Julie Williamson and Anita Hill, although women testify accurately about what men said and did to them, their speech carries a credibility discount.[20] Men who face allegations, like Robert Packwood, Clarence Thomas, Harvey Weinstein, and Brett Kavanaugh, often deny them. But when we have their words in diaries or on tape, as with Donald Trump's *Access Hollywood* segment, we hear what "he said" from him. As with the power of survivor testimony and collective witness to shift credibility to women, putting abusers' words back in their own mouths restores reality to scenes of violence euphemized by "he said / she said." In October 2016, late in the presidential contest between Hillary Clinton and Trump, a recording from a segment of the nightly entertainment television program in 2005 surfaced. Over a hot mic for five minutes and twelve seconds, Trump offered an unselfconscious admission of sexual assault as his standard operating procedure: "I just start kissing them. It's like a magnet. Just kiss. I don't even wait. And when you're a star, they let you do it. You can do anything. . . . Grab 'em by the pussy. You can do anything." Like the prior exposure of Trump's racism and xenophobia, many political commentators predicted his misogyny would end his political rise. Instead, he became the face and voice of predatory impunity.[21]

Primed to put distance between themselves and the recognition of abuse, listeners routinely refuse to develop a realistic picture of it. Yet, as Arielle Azoulay argues in an analysis of photographic evidence of widespread rape in Berlin at the end of World War II, "Visual documents of rape are not missing; this is just another cliché rooted in the imperial fusion of the perpetrators' points of view with neutral facts. Visual documents of violence perpetrated in the open are not missing; they should be located within available images falsely declared not to be images of rape, even though they were taken in the same place, and at the same time, as the rapes."[22] How do we restore unheard and unsought sexual harassment to the everyday spaces in which it routinely occurs? One way to develop a visual and aural archive is to insist on the documentary status of speech like Trump's.

The video shows a bus pulling slowly onto a lot in standard entertainment mise-en-scène, but with the addition of the audiotape, the voices reveal a scene of workplace sexual harassment. Billy Bush, a host of *Access Hollywood*, and Trump, a guest on a segment about soap operas, can be heard talking, along with more than one unnamed man. All the voices are male, and the video shows only men exiting the bus. In this conversation, middle-aged men are ranking a woman's looks, and Trump boasts about hitting on her. He brags, "I did try and fuck her. She was married . . . and I moved on her very heavily. . . . I moved on her like a bitch. But I couldn't get there." Trump is talking about Nancy O'Dell, who, at the time of the 2005 conversation, coanchored *Access Hollywood* with Bush.[23] The conversation exemplifies both how unsexy harassment is and how far it lies from reciprocity. Trump's "moves" are, by his description, unsought and unreciprocated. His phrasing is so odd it inspired a thread on Reddit entitled, "what does 'moved on her like a bitch' even mean?"[24]

Bush interrupts Trump as cohost Arianne Zucker walks out to meet the bus and redirects Trump's misogynistic reverie to his colleague. Bush awards Trump with Zucker, perhaps as a consolation prize for failing with his colleague Nancy O'Dell, crowing, "The Donald has scored!"

Trump, in appraisal of this prospect, calls Zucker, simply, "a pussy." In this moment, Bush does not offer her name, perhaps to remind Trump of the person they are meeting, nor does he redirect him down a path of professional courtesy. Here, men simply view women as things: this one is yours. Trump understands this symbolic exchange and prepares to claim his prize: "I just start kissing them . . . I don't even wait. And when you're a star, they let you do it. . . . Grab 'em by the pussy. You can do anything." Trump draws Bush into his fantasy of impunity, shares details of sexually assaulting his former coworker, threatens to harass his current coworker, and assures him that "*they* let you do it." "They" includes the women he assaults, but also a broader audience that is tolerant of sexual abuse. Trump libidinizes the men on the bus to his power, to his history of doing whatever he wants. Through their identification with him, Trump enables them to see women as he does, as pussy to grab, and him as a figure to admire. He makes them complicit in hearing an account of a sexual assault in the past about which they are invited to laugh, and in enacting workplace sexual harassment in the present. No one challenges him, and thus, in a performative of rape culture, his power is what he says it is. "They let you do it" because "You let me do it."

Although "grab 'em by the pussy" drew most of the attention, it is worth noticing the rest of the tape because it underscores what workplace harassment sounds like. The bus ride is a staged element of the show's greeting. When Bush and Trump comment on Zucker's body, all three of them are at work. Harassment saturates workplaces. It assigns a position to everyone involved: actual targets, potential targets, reluctant bystanders, eager bystanders ready to become harassers, and harassers themselves. There are more positions than the pairing of perpetrator/victim. There are, instead, to use Michael Rothberg's term, a broad network of "implicated subjects," including those who would never imagine themselves in the position of victim or perpetrator but who are nonetheless "beneficiaries" of this power imbalance.[25] Not only listening to the tape but also seeing the unctuous seamlessness of the transition from the bus conversation to the face-to-face with Zucker gives anyone who watches the segment the queasy experience of being a bystander to casually performed verbal harassment.[26]

## THE WOMEN'S MARCH

It is fitting that #MeToo erupted in the time of Trump, whose misogyny was the centerpiece of his attacks on Hillary Clinton and a key part of his appeal to white men. The Women's March was a direct rebuke to Trump and set the stage for #MeToo, underscoring how political context makes personal disclosure legible as collective witness. The Women's March previewed how the elements in the #MeToo movement would come together. Like #MeToo, the march featured a social media origin story and a summons to gather.[27] Like previous feminist marches, it called women to assemble in public and make a claim on political representation. Estimates place participation at five million worldwide, including the largest single-day protest in Washington, D.C., with a crowd of over 470,000.[28] As a global statement of protest against Trump, the Women's March crystallized an activist response to his misogyny, racism, and xenophobia. In its display of mass embodied assembly, it echoed Black Lives Matter protests from Ferguson to Baltimore and Palestine. It also allowed for a plurality of feminisms to affiliate with an anti-Trump stance, to gesture toward feminist pasts and visions of feminist futures that were not necessarily shared. The march, like #MeToo, brought renewed and broad visibility to a history of protesting an old problem. It did not so much break with history as reveal, again, the conditions of suppressing a feminist past and the necessity to argue again for the legitimacy of its aims.

Protestors brought visibility to generations of feminist activism in the signs they carried. The signage, "I Can't Believe I Still Have to Protest the Shit," represents an amalgam of "enough already"—signaling histories of protest—and "the time for change is now"—indicating a future horizon—fused in the temporality of protest. Many of the posters and graphics associated with the Women's March used images that refer to female anatomy. Signs with fallopian tubes and ovaries transformed into arms with hands balled into fists echoed the visual iconography of abortion protest, the focus of previous women's marches, like the March for Women's Lives in 1989 to protest attacks on reproductive freedom, the Rally for Women's Lives in 1995 to stop violence against women, and the

World March of Women in 2000, focused on ending poverty and violence. By contrast, some #MeToo iconography resisted gendered anatomical reference, preferring instead the figuration of justice, testimony, and protest represented by raised hands.[29] Although the iconic pussy hat provided a rejoinder to Trump, the expanded realm of imagery gave a clue that visibility was widening beyond abortion rights and reaching out to a broad public, tapping into support that would convert bystanders to witnesses. The graphic power of the hand as symbolic of protest also made a direct connection between #MeToo and Hands Up Don't Shoot—an embodied and performed protest following the killing of Michael Brown in Ferguson, Missouri, who witnesses say had his hands raised when he was shot by white police officer Darren Wilson—and a renewed use of the raised fist of the black power movement invoked as protest.[30]

Moving from the visual to the verbal register to understand how witnesses became newly visible to each other, we can think of #MeToo as a speech act that combines protest and testimony through a claim to solidarity.[31] The signs carried in the Women's March were speech acts that identified the assembled throng as *feminist*. They beckoned women to take over the streets through signs that gestured toward previous marches: the phrase "Women of the World Unite" used in the International Women's Day march in 1975 references the clarion call, "Workers of the World Unite," underscoring the political dimension of the protest and a demand for change. Marchers in 2017 carried signs that linked bodily autonomy to speech acts, including linking "my body, my choice" and "keep your laws off my body," which were also chanted, as well as "Whose streets? Our streets!" Protest is both an embodied action in the present and a citational form. It references multiple pasts and creates links across contemporaneous movements. In so doing, it allies with other breakthroughs conjured in a moment of outrage in the conjunction of speech acts and bodily assembly.

The heightened visibility of feminist protest brought new attention to women's anger as the signature emotion fueling and linking global street protest, international and national conventions, and social media activism. Tracing the gendered lesson that anger is "unladylike," Lacy M.

Johnson writes: "Girls are taught that to show anger, to yell, or to fight back ... is unattractive and undesirable; and if we are undesirable, we have no worth."[32] In the Women's March and #MeToo, as with inflection points like the Beijing conference and the movement for racial justice inaugurated through Black Lives Matter, lifetimes of grief and trauma were given public voice, fueled by rage. Many feminists writing about the Women's March and #MeToo identified a history of anger as righteous and empowering. Brittney Cooper, who calls "eloquent rage" her Black feminist superpower, traces how anger manifests in Black women's actions as "a kind of refusal."[33] Soraya Chemaly explains that anger is the emotion women are denied precisely because it is empowering.[34] Rebecca Traister traces how women's anger reemerged from a "feminist deep freeze" to erupt into potent articulation.[35] Because anger fuels feminist action, it has been crafted into a tool to suppress and shame.[36]

Black queer feminist writer and activist Audre Lorde anatomized the "uses of anger" in a powerful essay in 1981 on combatting racism and misogyny that resonates with the embrace of anger by many who marched.[37] Lorde put anger in historical and political context, distinguishing between the anger of racists and her own angry response to racism. The anger of men, she observes, is a component of sexual violence that often underwrites the assertion of impunity. Wanting to dominate, to injure, to "move on her like a bitch," as Trump threatened, names the sexual objective in sexual violence. Such contaminating and toxic anger comes from a position of entitlement, toward which abusers have a libidinal attachment. Following in Lorde's lineage, Cooper, Chemaly, and Traister make it clear that there was always more than anger motivating those who participated in the Women's March and #MeToo: there was empathy and community building, as well as holding allies accountable within the diverse category of women.[38] Just as the #MeToo effect would beckon survivors of all genders to understand their experience as part of an ongoing, if persistently interrupted, project to transform silence through storytelling, the march demonstrated the global reach of a call to mobilize.

# 3

# BREAKTHROUGH

---

### #MeToo Silence Breakers

*I could not keep silent.*

—ANITA HILL, CLARENCE THOMAS SUPREME COURT NOMINATION HEARINGS

*I can't believe I still have to protest this shit.*

—SIGN AT THE WOMEN'S MARCH, JANUARY 2017

When #MeToo decoupled "he said" from "she said," women's credibility rose to something nearer the baseline accorded to men, overcoming what Deborah Turkheimer calls women's "credibility discount."[1] Most journalists and media outlets routinely and understandably called this shift unprecedented. Although accountability was new, sexual violence and antirape activism were not. When millions of voices in the present found a sudden hearing in October 2017, the history represented by Tarana Burke stretching back through generations of survivors and lineages of activism around the globe flooded in. The irruption of that history defines #MeToo as a breakthrough: the moment the past ruptures its framing as marginal, nonexistent, or settled to become breaking news. In a breakthrough, the past is suddenly everywhere it was previously barred: it becomes urgent, vital, present. This chapter identifies four key terms—temporality, satu-ration, visibility, and participation—to clarify how the lineage of narra-tive activism was activated in the #MeToo breakthrough.

Breakthroughs are characterized by uncanny temporal effects. They can feel overdue, inevitable, and utterly unexpected all at once as differ-ent aspects of individual and collective histories are connected and exposed to previously unconcerned, even hostile, publics.[2] The term *unprecedented* refers to what a breakthrough feels like rather than to the actual histories that propel one. When the novelty of men facing reper-cussions became the story, it muted a narrative of the feminist legacies on which #MeToo built; namely, a history of ongoing resistance to sex-ual violence in various forms of protest, organizing, and community support. Nonetheless, the majority of media reports confidently asserted that "we" had never seen anything like this. How feminist resistance is forgotten even while it is actively occurring shows how hard it is to gain and maintain the conditions of being heard.

Multiple historical contexts vied for inclusion in the #MeToo break-ing story, but the absence of shared knowledge about histories of femi-nist resistance and organizing meant that reporting defaulted to a Holly-wood focus, even as activists leveraged #MeToo as a rallying cry in multiple locations. The shock of holding Harvey Weinstein and other powerful men accountable inspired many commentators to substitute that momentous event for an engagement with the lineage of feminist activism that enabled it. It was as if only the effects of feminism or the symptoms of patriarchal impunity could be noticed rather than the con-ditions and structures that produce them. Burke's "me too" places intersectionality squarely at the center of this breakthrough.

Four elements converged in the #MeToo breakthrough: *temporality,* which includes an unsettling of official narratives and their timelines as well as the traumatic return of the past, *saturation, visibility,* and *par-ticipation.*[3] *Saturation* describes the intersection of a pervasive phenom-enon with a new name and context for understanding it. Like replacing "boys will be boys" with "rape culture," the #MeToo effect demonstrated that sexual violence is a structural problem rather than an individual one. It shifted the framing of prevalence from the status quo to the felt sense of "too much for too long." Without this change, sexual violence is a problem for someone else despite its intrusive ubiquity. In a recent U.S. poll, 81 percent of women and 43 percent of men said they have experienced sexual harassment or sexual assault during their lifetimes.[4] Most reported multiple experiences of sexual harm in multiple locations (most reported four to five locations), two-thirds of women experienced workplace sexual harassment, and more than half of women and just under half of men experienced some form of sexual harassment or assault by the age of seventeen. Few filed reports. Data from the Centers for Disease Control indicates that sexual violence, defined as nonconsensual sexual activity, is so routine that one in five women will experience attempted or completed rape in their lifetime. One in three experience rape when they are children between the ages of eleven and seventeen, and one in eight are under ten years old.[5] Young victims face particular hurdles in speaking out. The average age at which a child victim of sexual abuse tells someone is fifty-two.[6] For some trans women, including trans women of color who are subjected disproportionately to lethal violence, their lives are cut short before they can speak. One in sixteen women between the ages of eighteen and forty-four answered "rape" to a question asking them about their "first sexual experience." Laura Hawks, the study's lead author, predicted that if girls under seventeen and women over forty-five were part of the sample, "the absolute number would be higher." "Honestly," she said, "that's the tip of the iceberg."[7] The World Health Organization in 2021 described sexual violence as "devastatingly pervasive," with one woman in three harmed, and young women especially targeted.[8] Although studies like this as well as awareness campaigns strip sexual violence of its typical excuses, publics must not simply see it but see differently.

In addition to the evidence of frequency these studies supply, #MeToo enabled survivors to see themselves in relation to one another: not as anonymous statistics but as part of a collective with shared experience that included, often for the first time, credibility and solidarity. When survivors see themselves in relation to one another and to a collective identity grounded in speaking out, a general public can be compelled to set aside its tolerance of saturation.[9] The Women's March, women's public anger, Chanel Miller's statement, and the #MeToo hashtag are all examples of *visibility* as a shifted stance on saturation. Instead of triggering apathy or voyeurism, visibility prompts an ethical response in which witnesses demand change. In breakthroughs, saturation and visibility catalyze *participation* as knowledge spreads beyond those with direct experience to include those who understand themselves as morally and politically involved. Participation also brings new attention to how bystanders are implicated in sexual violence and how they can relinquish complicity in favor of support. These elements converged rapidly in the #MeToo breakthrough, fueled by growing public awareness of survivors and informed by the feminist lineages on which they drew.

It is possible that many or even most breakthroughs share the conditions of emergence I have described. Some of these elements—saturation, visibility, participation—describe other cultural shifts, like the racial justice uprising following the killing of George Floyd by white police officer Derek Chauvin in the pandemic summer of 2020.[10] Lamenting the belatedness of white attention to police killings of Black people prior to George Floyd, *New Yorker* writer Jelani Cobb offered a cross-racial analogy, a trope familiar within feminist history and often used by white women analogizing legal marriage to slavery, a history I discuss in chapter 4.[11] Connecting the uprising for racial justice to the #MeToo movement, Cobb wrote: "As with men, who, upon seeing the scroll of #MeToo testimonies, asked their wives, daughters, sisters, and co-workers, 'Is it really that bad?,' the shock of revelation that attended the video of Floyd's death is itself a kind of inequality, a barometer of the extent to which one group of Americans have moved through life largely free from the burden of such terrible knowledge."[12] Recurrent tropes and narratives from the nineteenth century to the twenty-first through which the racial politics of sexual violence are figured do not stand outside the events they describe. Like sexual violence, racial violence saturates culture. Its harm is experienced and understood by millions of people in the United States and worldwide. It is thoroughly analyzed by scholars and other experts, and sits firmly on the agenda of policy advocates, religious organizations, sports leagues, and activists. Racial violence is not new, but many agree that expectations for justice shifted following George Floyd's murder. As with #MeToo, there was an opening between what happened and what changed in which many white people experienced a reorientation to a problem, even a cognitive restructuring that changed their expectations of fairness. White people saw and heard things that changed their default bias. How media covers a story, who is on the ground as an expert to frame the long view, who can witness and speak to the pain of many, and how advocates can drive lasting organizational change determine how much officially suppressed history can be incorporated into contemporary public memory.[13]

## SILENCE BREAKING AS NARRATIVE ACTIVISM

I have taken a long walk up to the #MeToo tweet in order to provide the context it did not have in its early weeks, and also to diminish its talismanic quality as "the" origin of a surge in survivor activism. With this in place, let's examine what Alyssa Milano tweeted in response to allegations about Weinstein's predatory sexual behavior (figure 3.1).

FIGURE 3.1. Tweet by Alyssa Milano, October 15, 2017.

Within hours, thousands responded with likes and retweets. While many retweeted Milano's message without adding a personal comment, other retweets included specific personal examples, swiftly assembling an archive of what sexual violence looks like in everyday life. The retweets visualized a call-and-response format, and, as public answers to the invitation accumulated, more survivors participated. Through participation, they created the #MeToo effect as a collective witness. As the tweet migrated across social media platforms, from Twitter to Facebook and Instagram, it joined a genealogy of feminist tweets from the recent past that expanded awareness of sexual violence. #YesAllWomen, #SurvivorPrivilege, #TheEmptyChair, #WhyIStayed, and #MeToo are online speech acts that attest to women's vulnerability to sexual violence. All are framed from a survivor perspective. Their proliferation demonstrates the capacity of the internet to host organic feminist publics in response to specific events and also within "a discernible genealogy that has important cultural resonances."[14] Sometimes the #MeToo tweets cited these hashtags, consciously acknowledging and further documenting an online feminist lineage.

As I have shown, the #MeToo hashtag was notable in that it cited an activist lineage outside social media and a specific source: Burke's "me too" movement.[15] Milano was unaware that she was quoting Burke. She simply resonated with the words "me too." But attached to the context of the breaking Weinstein story, and tweeted to millions by Milano, Burke's distillation of an intersectional feminist stance on empathy into a compact phrase went viral. At the same moment Burke saw her work validated by this uptake, her contribution to building a movement for survivors was eclipsed by the rush to tell a breaking story, even as it was buoyed by a genealogy of online feminist activism. Within forty-eight hours of the tweet, the world knew about Burke's role in #MeToo origin story. Burke and Milano appeared together on television and gave interviews. The initial displacement, however, represents the fits and starts that characterize breakthrough moments as multiple histories vie for narrative prominence in the very networks that have marginalized them.[16] It also shows that the work and witness of Black women is subject to displacement and theft.

Beyond offering an invitation to respond and share, actions common to all hashtag activism, the tweet aligned with Burke's movement because it proffered shared silence breaking as a form of activism, connected survivors to each other, and placed their knowledge at the center. The invitation to share "me too" felt collective and personal, affectively repositioning speaking out as a form of participatory testimony rather than a step in joining a legal process. Yet, like peeling an onion, the layers of quotation need to be pared away to discover how the source of "me too" emerges from unattributed citation. Milano's words come first: "If you've been sexually harassed or assaulted write 'me too' as a reply to this tweet." This call to action prefaces a Facebook post that activist Charlotte Clymer saw on the page of a friend. Clymer took a screenshot of the post and sent it to Milano. The post that Clymer saw also cites the anonymized "suggested by a friend" and includes the quotation that gives rise to Milano's tweet: "If all the women who have been sexually harassed or assaulted wrote 'Me too.' as a status, we might give people a sense of the magnitude of the problem."[17] Unattributed citation is common on social media, but the presence of quotation marks represents the trace, in this case, of an actual source.[18] Burke provided the framework to hold the outpouring that the breakthrough triggered. The multiple citations in the tweet demonstrate that her intersectional analysis enables saturation, visibility, and participation to merge.

How Burke's contribution was "forgotten" and belatedly acknowledged provides an opening into the history of forgetting sexual violence itself. There is a vast archive of officially forgotten experiences of sexual violence. Stories not told, to be sure, but also stories retold in ways that distort them. These include denying the centrality of rape by white men in the plantation economy or travestying it as romance, masking intimate partner violence as a "domestic disturbance" between similarly culpable people, and dismissing rape of students by other students and teachers as a problem with alcohol. The #MeToo effect enabled a reframing of the previously unheard stories now filling the public square as resurgent testimony. It contextualized speaking out about and in reference to Weinstein, whose fame guaranteed headlines and visibility, as an episode of narrative activism within a larger frame of feminist reference. I focus next on what the Weinstein story exposed about the silencing of survivors in the criminal-legal system and how the silence breakers responded, before turning to the long-stalled ushering of feminist narrative activism into the context of #MeToo.

## BREAKING THE WEINSTEIN STORY

On October 5, 2017, the *New York Times* ran a front page story entitled, "Harvey Weinstein Paid Off Sexual Harassment Accusers for Decades."[19] The story, which capped months of investigative reporting by Jodi Kantor and Megan Twohey, was the first time several of Weinstein's victims went on the record. Their collective evidence overwhelmed his denials. With so many suppressed witnesses coming forward, it was clear that Weinstein's continuous enactment of sexual abuse relied on a far-flung, coordinated network to dupe actresses into taking business meetings that were pretexts for sexual assault and cover up Weinstein's behavior.

In their book devoted to the investigation, *She Said: Breaking the Sexual Harassment Story*, Kantor and Twohey identified two key patterns in Weinstein's behavior.[20] The first was the sexual abuse of women who worked for, or sought work from, him, dating back to 1990. His behavior was so consistent that a "common narrative" emerged. Under the pretext of holding a professional meeting, Weinstein would introduce a reason to switch the meeting location to his hotel room. When a woman arrived, he would be wearing only a bathrobe, or change into one, and demand a massage, which she refused. From there, Weinstein would escalate to sexual assault or rape. The second pattern was the cover-up of this abuse waged through a network of employees and enablers, including private investigators, lawyers, and hotel staff, as well as Miramax and the Weinstein Group employees. Weinstein used nondisclosure agreements (NDAs) and financial settlements to silence victims, dating back decades and involving millions of dollars in payments that his lawyers negotiated and board of directors approved.

Used routinely in creative industries to protect intellectual property and as a feature of exit agreements involving financial settlements, non-disclosure agreements are, nonetheless, as abstruse to a general public as the credit default swaps that fueled the global financial crisis in 2008. NDAs are legal instruments, couched in technical jargon, that create confidentiality by binding one or both parties to secrecy. Sometimes they protect proprietary information or limit competition. In sexual harassment complaints, they are weaponized against victims because they reinforce the secrecy that protects abusers. NDAs and the settlements that accompany them represent neither an apology nor compensation for injury. For women, they often represent the best version of a bad bargain. Kim Masters, editor-at-large for the *Hollywood Reporter*, describes how NDAs made reporting on sexual harassment difficult. She had been writing stories critical of Miramax for years but was unable to persuade victims to do more than speak on background: "I'd heard really brutal allegations. We couldn't write about those, we couldn't get it on the record. I think [Weinstein] kind of believed, as he did with reason for years to come, that he was going to be untouchable."[21] *New Yorker* writer Ken Auletta also tried to break the Weinstein story. In 2002 he spoke with Zelda Perkins, who had moved to Guatemala after signing an agreement with Weinstein. She was terrified of what Weinstein would do if she talked so she declined to be interviewed, but Auletta confronted Weinstein with what he knew: "I wish I could have nailed the guy in 2002. The problem I had was that I couldn't prove it. Clearly, people knew or suspected that Harvey was a—was a predator, a sexual predator, and they kept their mouths shut."[22]

Kantor and Twohey focused on the abuse and settlements while Ronan Farrow, writing for the *New Yorker*, exposed the network that enabled Weinstein and the cover-up.[23] Farrow detailed the workings of a machine composed of agents who would book actresses to take hotel meetings with Weinstein, hotel staff who would deliver women to those meetings, and an assistant who injected Weinstein with erectile dysfunction medication prior to meetings. To ensure the silence of victims, Weinstein not only hired attorneys to pressure them to sign NDAs, he hired private detectives, some of whom previously worked for the

Israeli defense service Mossad, to harass them. Weinstein's network was abetted in its abuse by police departments and district attorneys who failed to charge him. He seemed invincible because for decades he was.[24]

Because magazines like *Hollywood Insider, Vanity Fair,* and the *New Yorker* under editor Tina Brown were publishing stories that crossed from celebrity profile into investigative journalism, reporters like Kim Masters and Ken Auletta often heard stories about sexual abuse and harassment. Yet when they submitted stories that high-profile figures did not like, editors often balked, preferring continued access to exposing the truth. Unfavorable material was trimmed, story lines were dropped, and editors denied the reasons. For example, Vicky Hill's reporting in *Vanity Fair* on Jeffrey Epstein's sexual assault of girls was excised at the direction of editor Graydon Carter. Nonetheless, reporting about Weinstein and Epstein revealed how girls and women were delivered to them under the pretext of giving massages to Epstein and auditioning for roles with Weinstein. Reporters began to understand how systems of procurers, including agents at Creative Artists Agency (CAA), lied to victims and covered for abusers, revealing complex relational networks in which many people had long ago abandoned the pretense of plausible deniability. Although reporters had tried and failed to provide adequate protections for women to come forward, the fact that so many stories had been reported out—from fact finding and interviewing to corroboration—meant that the breaking news in the *Times* and the *New Yorker* would be augmented by substantive reporting elsewhere.[25]

Between October 2017 and March 2018, over one hundred women came forward with allegations that Weinstein had sexually assaulted or raped them. Katherine Kendall, for example, who had just finished acting school in the early 1990s, went to a meeting with Weinstein at the Miramax office that her agent booked. The meeting went well. Weinstein exclaimed, "Welcome to the Miramax family!" and invited her to a film screening scheduled for later in the day. As soon as Weinstein picked her up, he started switching the details about the "screening," ultimately luring Kendall to his house, where he quickly changed into a bathrobe and demanded a massage. When she refused, "He left the room and he came back, and he was just fully naked. I thought, 'He's coming after me.' I just remember sort of darting back and forth and trying to get past him. You know in that moment that you may not make it."[26] Kendall did not speak to reporters until after #MeToo revived interest in Weinstein's history of abuse.

To counter decades of silencing and frustrated attempts at reporting, Kantor and Twohey crafted a trauma-informed strategy to persuade women to go on the record. Twohey conferred with a sexual violence survivor advocate who advised her that survivors are often motivated by civic duty and a desire to prevent future assaults. NDAs frustrate this ethical desire to protect others from harm. Twohey framed her request for attribution as a promise to tell the story honestly, expose Weinstein to the world, and prevent future assaults. The reporters' tactic walks a fine line between an appeal to moral virtue and gendered notions of sacrifice. Women are often instructed to think about others and act on their behalf, and they often do. In the absence of assurance that their claims will be treated fairly, how ethical is such a demand?[27] The lack of a fair process for hearing survivor testimony represents a structural disadvantage and, for some, a risk too reminiscent of the abuse itself. Some women who are asked to respond in this way risk whatever stability they have managed to create.

Yet Kantor and Twohey created an alternative for survivors to making a legal claim or relying on weak human resources departments or filling out reports in police departments. They offered a space for holding the testimony of survivors together: isolated by the abuse and silencing, they could not speak for themselves and expect to be heard; together, however, they created a collective witness. By aggregating their stories, they demonstrated a pattern over time, overwhelming Weinstein's exploitation of dynamics that favored him, including publicly asserting that all the assaults were consensual sexual activity.

The abundance of Weinstein's abuse meant that there were many witnesses. When they were heard in 2017 as a result of the #MeToo effect, Manhattan district attorney Cyrus Vance, Jr., charged Weinstein: "We had confidence in that, were we to take this to a jury, that the jurors

would be able to see through the myths that were thrown up about victims of sexual assaults, and listen to the women and, as the jurors did,
believe them."[28] At earlier moments in the timeline of Weinstein's criminal behavior, Vance's office declined to bring charges.[29] In 2015, for
example, Ambra Battilana Gutierrez, a twenty-two-year-old model and
actor from Italy, met with Weinstein to discuss her career. Shortly after
the meeting began, Weinstein groped her breasts, reached up her skirt,
and forcibly tried to kiss her. She fought him off and immediately went
to the New York police, who found her account credible. As a non-
American, she says she assumed this was the correct course of action
and expected her claim to be taken seriously. When she told the officer
that the man who assaulted her was Harvey Weinstein, she recalls the
officer saying, "Again?" which she took to mean that Weinstein was well
known to the NYPD for sexual assault. Instead of questioning Weinstein,
however, they insisted that Gutierrez strengthen her case by wearing a
wire and returning to confront him. Although understandably reluctant
to engage with him again, she agreed to invite him to meet at a hotel near
his office.

When Gutierrez confronted Weinstein, the audio recording captures
his increasingly aggressive tone as he bullies her, trying to get her into
his room. His intention, it seems, is to overwhelm and break her down,
to make his verbal demands so unbearable that she will go into the room
to make him stop. The transcript documents a conversation that is without preamble or development. Weinstein is laser-focused on maneuver-
ing Gutierrez into a position where he can assault her. His language is
directive: "I'm telling you right now. Get in here." Gone is the pretext of
the professional relationship. The words, "I'm going to take a shower. You
sit there and have a drink," tell Gutierrez that Weinstein is restart-
ing their encounter at the point she previously broke it off and went to
the police. Gutierrez asks, "Why yesterday you touch my breast?" Weinstein replies, "I'm used to that." Weinstein's menace is clearer in the
audiotape than on the page. He never stops talking, and she is clearly
frightened.

After Gutierrez receives Weinstein's admission that he groped her, she
returns to the police. His words, "I'm used to that," uttered while he

attempts to reenact the original assault, confirm her account. The police, she recalls, were "super happy and, like, saying, 'Wow, now this person is completely finished. You saved a lot of women.'" The NYPD determined the charges were worth pursuing because the accuser was credible, and they turned over the evidence to Vance, expecting they had met the burden necessary to charge Weinstein. Vance turned the case over to attorney Martha Bashford, head of the Sex Crimes unit, who treated Gutierrez from the outset as a tainted witness. According to Gutierrez, Bashford "interrogated me like I was the criminal, with questions like, 'Have you ever been a prostitute?' Or, 'Have you ever gotten gifts? Or, 'Have you ever asked for a movie role?' And I'm like, 'Did you hear the recordings?'"[30] In the meantime, Weinstein hired a team to smear Gutierrez, seeding the press with false information and innuendo that echo Bashford's hostile questioning. In both the court of public opinion and the Manhattan D.A.'s office, the smear campaign worked by tainting the witness and the potential jury pool. Vance declined to charge Weinstein.[31]

Although Gutierrez possessed an audiotaped admission of groping by Weinstein, Vance determined she lacked the credibility to support charging Weinstein. Words to name how women are discredited, from *mansplaining* to *gaslighting*, indicate a world of asymmetrical credibility. Gaslighting goes beyond lying and asserts control over the means of representation. It includes calling rape consensual sex, or sexual assault a job interview. It amounts to imposing another's will on the meaning of reality to say, "I control this, I control you." Legal proceedings are not immune. Doubting women, in effect, blurs the prosecution of male defendants with the cultural norm of believing men and protecting male authority and reputation. Doubt controls the reality imposed on women in the criminal-legal system. Weinstein evaded criminal charges, even as his numerous settlements and nondisclosure agreements document a pattern of sexual assault and threats of retaliation known to Manhattan law enforcement, his own attorneys, and the board of Miramax for decades, because he controlled reality.

Considering Weinstein's outsize role in its 2017 launch, it was reasonable to wonder how #MeToo would impact his trial in New York in

2020 on multiple counts of sexual abuse against Jessica Mann and Miriam Haley, even as presiding judge James M. Burke attempted to downplay its presence: "This trial is not a referendum on #MeToo or sexual harassment."[32] Because Weinstein's abuse and, importantly, the exposure of it were synonymous with #MeToo, the trial tested the strength of survivors to change the default narrative of women's unreliability. Weinstein tried to revive the pre-#MeToo norm as his defense. His attorney Donna Rotunno argued that Weinstein had the legal right to call rape "consensual sex." Likewise, that a single act of consensual sex with any woman meant all future sex with her would be consensual *no matter what she said.* "I am used to this," Weinstein's explanation to Ambra Gutierrez about why groped her, was his legal defense. His attorneys smeared the women testifying, while Weinstein refused to take the stand and submit to similar treatment. In rambling comments to the judge prior to sentencing, Weinstein continued to assert his power to name rape as consensual sex, casting his lot with victims of the McCarthy era and opining: "I'm worried there is a repeat of the blacklist there was in the 1950s when lots of men like myself, Dalton Trumbo, one of the great examples, did not work, went to jail because people thought they were communists. You know, there was a scare, and that is what happened, and I think that is what is happening now all over this country."[33]

The jury disagreed, and Weinstein was convicted in February 2020 on two charges and sentenced to twenty-three years in prison. Cyrus R. Vance, Jr., attributed the verdict to a new level of awareness and understanding about how men deny responsibility for sexual assault. In 2015, when Vance's office did not charge Weinstein with sexually assaulting Gutierrez, he said, "Our best lawyers looked at the case. . . . I, like they, was very disturbed by the contents of the tape. It's obviously sickening. But at the end of the day we operate in a courtroom of law, not the court of public opinion, and our sex crime prosecutors made a determination that this was not going to be a provable case."[34] He defended his previous decisions not to charge Weinstein because he did not think women's credibility could withstand the attacks routinely directed at rape victims before #MeToo. They were already tainted witnesses in the court of public opinion. After #MeToo, Vance asserted, juries are capable of understanding that women can say no to sex with someone they consented to have sex with on a previous occasion. By changing the court of public opinion, the #MeToo effect of collective credibility replaced some rape culture myths with knowledge of the realities of sexual violence.

The formation of a public witness to the Weinstein allegations masks the complicated temporalities of witness when an ongoing history is framed as a current event. Because so much past trauma—including generational trauma—was activated, memories were shaped by different narrators to reflect their experiences of losing and finding voice. Clare Hemmings notes that the stories we tell about feminism are conditioned by scripts (she identifies progress, loss, and return as key narratives). These represent the shaping of complex movements into a shareable form for specific audiences. The choice of how to narrate feminist history circulates political meaning across audiences. To narrate #MeToo as the dawning of a new era and thereby associate it with the attendant optimism that a restart will enable a better outcome for survivors is therefore a trap, if an understandable one. Who didn't hope survivors would become credible, abusers accountable, and institutions responsive? But whether police, district attorneys, judges, and juries will continue to find women credible remains an open question. Further, to believe #MeToo has made sexual harassment and assault unacceptable and empowered any survivor to speak out suggests that there *is* a good time for survivors to speak—now, not then. This is still a dangerous myth that masks a systemic refusal to listen.

## THE SILENCE BREAKERS

When *TIME* Magazine designated a varied group of survivors, including Tarana Burke, as its composite person of the year in 2017, naming them the "silence breakers," it shifted media focus from serial predators to a survivor-centered narrative activism. It also contributed visual images to the new framing of sexual violence (figure 3.2). The cover featured portraits of well-known actresses like Ashley Judd and Rose McGowan, as well as FOX News personality Megyn Kelly, but it also

**FIGURE 3.2.** *The Silence Breakers.* Photographs by Billy & Hells, reproduced with permission from the artists.

provided an opportunity to broaden the understanding of what sexual harassment looks like in specific workplaces by including male actors Blaise Lippman and Terry Crewes, and by interviewing academics, journalists, restaurant and hotel workers, and entrepreneurs.[35] Stephanie Zacharek, Eliana Dockterman, and Haley Sweetland Edwards reported and wrote the story. Women fact-checked the piece and also created and edited the video and photo design central to the presentation of survivors.[36] As a collective witness, 2017's "Person of the Year" would break many silences.

The silence breakers are styled by Berlin-based photographers Anke Linz and Andreas Oettinger to enhance their unity as a group. The cover image recalls other victims of disaster who are presented through visual strategies that establish relation and preserve individuality. The uniformity of the grid, for example, where each box is the same size and all the photographs are headshots, encodes the subjects as sharing experience. Blending the visual styles of documentary photorealism and fashion portraiture transforms a diverse group of silence breakers into iconic figures, united in suffering and in accusation, diverse in race and class. This choice of visual display demonstrated that a broad public was not only hearing survivors in a new way but also seeing them within an emergent iconography of collective witness. Inside the issue, photographs of more silence breakers accompanied stories that fleshed out a timeline preceding the October 2017 tweet. The range of profiles highlighted *TIME*'s understanding of the facts of sexual violence, especially its scale. It recognized that no one was protected from harm by fame, status, money, or white privilege, but that these factors shape how sexual violence is experienced and how justice is sought. As an effort at collective history, the profiles showed how isolating survivors from each other strips the context necessary for understanding patterns of abuse and silencing. Seeing them united as silence breakers is a corrective gesture.

The #MeToo effect enabled individual experiences to become legible as a critique of the structures that permit abuse. Multiple story lines revealed the time lags between experiencing and telling someone about sexual abuse, between sharing a story in private and making an account public. There were also accounts of multiple episodes of harassment, sometimes by the same abuser, but also by several abusers within the same university or company. Some victims kept silent in order not to be fired or risk other forms of retaliation, and others because they had no one to tell. More often, they detailed repeatedly thwarted attempts to be heard. As Ashley Judd notes, "I started talking about Harvey the minute that it happened. . . . Literally, I exited that hotel room at the Peninsula Hotel in 1997 and came straight downstairs to the lobby, where my dad was waiting for me, because he happened to be in Los Angeles from Kentucky, visiting me on the set."

*TIME* sought to broaden the story by pointing to industries beyond film and TV where sexual violence is endemic. A manager at a local Walmart or restaurant could coerce or punish women whose low wage jobs were at risk, just as in workplaces and labs with chronic sexual harassment problems, women are often bullied out of careers. In academic medicine and higher education, male gatekeepers control women's career prospects.[37] Threats of reputational destruction, economic ruin, and loss of career were levied by famous men who had such tools at their disposal, including those with massive popular followings like R. Kelly, Russell Simmons, Mario Batali, and Bill Cosby.[38] Many men in positions of relative power over women could also count on their supervisors siding with them and sacrificing women.

As a broad public gained a new perspective on the scale and impact of sexual violence, they also heard concrete descriptions of behavior they had previously minimized or excused. An indelible gallery of images now existed where a "gray area"—foggy, out of focus, capable of misinterpretation—once was: Weinstein lunging, naked in a gaping bathrobe, as Ashley Judd ran around a hotel room trying to reach a door to escape; Charlie Rose answering the door to his apartment naked after requiring interns to bring work over; Matt Lauer anally raping Brook Nevils, after which she bled for days.[39] It became harder not to imagine actual examples of injury when #MeToo was referenced. Silence breakers do not only add images and speech where none has been before, they create the conditions for hearing what has already being said.

Unlike whistleblowers, who are afforded the protection of anonymity by statute, women have been compelled to share information about abusers through whisper networks.[40] Whistleblowers are frequently associated with acting alone for the public good. The U.S. government has an interest in hearing from those who can expose wrongdoing and offers protection on this basis.[41] Yet protections for speaking out about sexual violence in workplaces, places of worship, or education are not nearly as robust as those afforded to whistleblowers. Because silence breakers are typically tracked into mediation, victims often have better luck in court bringing whistleblower complaints about workplace sexual harassment, pointing to climate and retaliation. Victims of sexual harm also fare better in civil court, where the lower burden of proof enables victims to overcome the imposition of doubt on their testimony, an unfair burden women face independent of the facts of the case. Whistleblowers more obviously seek a public audience, whereas whisperers seek to share context-specific advice to protect community members. Both represent how narrative activism is constrained by rules that restrict speech about danger, rules that bind those who speak out in ways that often protect those who do harm.

## #METOO GENRES: LETTERS OF SUPPORT, NONAPOLOGIES, CONFESSION, AND TESTIMONY

The letter of support is one of the genres central to #MeToo. The audience for letters of support can be public or private. Public letters are formal statements of support. Their authors intend them to influence and shift the formation of judgment in specific cases. Sometimes they take a cautionary tone and ask for reflection; other times they urge specific action. The letter of support typically features a roster of high-profile signatories, people whose credibility in their professions amplifies doubt directed at the survivor. There is also the public retraction of such support when the signatories are surprised by facts they had not considered or inquired into. Leaked letters of support addressed to decision makers in disciplinary processes reveal how powerful people wield influence in a genre that blurs an informal contribution to a formal process. Unless such letters are sought, or complainants have access to and may rebut them, or are given an equal opportunity to contribute similar letters, they lie outside due process. Inadvertently they expose the informal and extralegal routes routinely explored on behalf of those facing discipline. Authors and signatories of such letters may not intend to skirt due process or imagine they wield influence a complainant cannot match. They may, instead, feel righteously compelled to stand up for a colleague, an advisor and patron, or someone with whom they feel or seek a bond.[42]

When Professor Avital Ronell faced allegations from a male graduate student that she had sexually harassed him, powerful academics signed a letter in support, citing her academic credentials and their friendship with her, and insinuating that the graduate student could not be trusted. Once equipped with facts from the lawsuit filed against

Ronell, however, and in response to negative public reaction to the letter, many of the signatories withdrew their support. These two features, signing a letter in the absence of fact checking its assertions about specific allegations and recanting in the face of criticism, reveal that there are different notions of "the problem" when powerful people face allegations of abuse. In this balancing act, #MeToo itself was targeted as having gone too far and creating a space of judgment with chaotic rules of participation. Similarly, twenty-six women professors published a letter in the *Chronicle of Higher Education* in support of Junot Díaz condemning his treatment on social media, where allegations of his sexual misconduct circulated. They took pains not to disavow the women making those allegations, but targeted the #MeToo movement as too entangled with social media mobbing. By criticizing how the allegations about Díaz arose and circulated, the signatories created sympathy for him as someone in a terrible situation rather than someone who may have created one: "The issue at hand is not whether or not one believes Díaz, or his accusers, but whether one approves the use of media to violently make a spectacle out of a single person while at the same time cancelling out the possibility of disagreement about the facts at hand, or erasing a sustained attention to how the violence of racial hatred, structural poverty, and histories of colonialism extend into the most intimate spaces."[43]

This nuanced point about the reach of structural forces into intimate life is at the heart of an account by poet Shreerekha, a professor at the University of Houston at Clear Lake, identified as the lover "S" in Díaz's *New Yorker* essay about his own experience of sexual trauma. "In the Wake of His Damage," published in the *Rumpus* two days before the *Chronicle* letter, describes Shreerekha's complex feelings of erasure as she read a draft of the *New Yorker* essay Díaz shared with her, as well as what she describes as the racialized sexual dynamics at the core of their intimate relationship. Her account did not circulate primarily on Twitter, and it is grounded in a feminist decolonial critique of the epistemic privilege to name reality exerted, as she describes it, in her relationship with Díaz. She writes: "His privilege, even when it came to oppression, was far greater than mine, and he got to call the shots. It made sense why he had to keep finding new lovers; I did not fit the bill. In many ways, he loved me for my blackness and discarded me for the same. That is a mindfuck I have not fully recovered from even today."[44] The letter of support did not acknowledge the seriousness of allegations about Díaz. These were not limited to social media and involved intimate partners whom he referenced in print. The women who spoke out took pains to address the burden of publicizing their experience in racist contexts.

In addition to letters of support, narratives countering the #MeToo effect range from blanket denials to regretful statements about "changing standards." Sometimes alleged abusers acknowledge the general problem of sexual violence, the importance of listening to survivors, and the need for men to respect boundaries even as they sidestep accountability to specific victims and seemingly acknowledge that the allegations have merit. Díaz offered all the above. In a statement provided by his literary agent to the *New York Times* in response to initial allegations in May 2018 of forcible kissing, Díaz said: "I take responsibility for my past. That is the reason I made the decision to tell the truth of my rape and its damaging aftermath. This conversation is important and must continue. I am listening to and learning from women's stories in this essential and overdue cultural movement. We must continue to teach all men about consent and boundaries."[45] Subsequently, in a front-page story in July 2018 in the *Boston Globe*, he said he only appeared to apologize because he was "distressed," "confused," and "panicked" by the allegations, but now wanted to offer a full denial: "I was, like, 'Yo, this doesn't sound like anything that's in my life, anything that's me.'"[46]

The genre of the nonapology also emerged in Harvey Weinstein's initial response to reporting on multiple allegations of sexual assault. The nonapology is characterized by a humble, teachable stance on sexual violence rather than on specific allegations. It identifies misinterpretation as the problem—the victim's misinterpretation—and acknowledges that, yes, she got it wrong, but who could blame her? After all, times have changed, she was drunk, or "I'm used to that." The nonapology hijacks sympathy for the victim and transfers it to the abuser, who, through no fault or responsibility of his own, was, if you think about it, equally a victim of a misunderstanding. When Bill Cosby admitted to drugging and raping Andrea Constand, he said, "I don't hear her say anything.

And I don't feel her say anything. And so I continue and I go into the area that is somewhere between permission and rejection. I am not stopped."

The nonapology has been parodied as "I'm sorry if anyone was offended." It deflects responsibility, particularly legal responsibility, and is often crafted by legal teams to offer maximum deniability. From Weinstein's promise to "work on himself" to Charlie Rose's and Matt Lauer's "I'm sorry if anyone ever felt uncomfortable, that was not my intention" excuses, and even chef Mario Batali's sorry-not-sorry blog post that ended with a recipe for cinnamon rolls made out of pizza dough, there is ample evidence of how the nonapology reveals the banality of confession. We can think of the nonapology as confessional in the sense that Foucault regarded it: an attempt to gain absolution by spinning sex, including sexual violence, into discourse. Specifically, by recycling the myth that rape is sex gone wrong. Abusers exploit this false view when they apologize for having "consensual sex" that was misinterpreted as rape. The victim's misinterpretation is what they are sorry about. They repudiate their representation as someone who could do harm and disavow it as a psychic other: "Yo, this doesn't sound like anything that's in my life, anything that's me." "That doesn't sound like me" differs from "I did not do that" in that it seeks to turn the person who could be held accountable into a phantasm.

The nonapology encodes a fervent wish to put #MeToo behind us. Such a wish defines stories that seek to alter the temporality of a reckoning, which ends not with the ticking of the clock but with epistemic change, and fast forward to the return of abusers. Narratives set in the imagined calm of "after" shift to retrospection about #MeToo rather than engage with it so that we can move ahead. Instead of asking how institutions will determine whether processes are working or what kinds of trauma-informed research on sexual violence will guide policy, post-#MeToo narratives ask, instead, "What about the men?" I want to explore this question as part of a larger trend in which efforts to place #MeToo in the past seek most obviously to restore sympathy to the victims we are trained to care about: men. Not the largely fictional construct of the falsely accused ones, but the ones whose abuses have been exposed and, to varying degrees, acknowledged.[47] The genres of the nonapology, the letter of support, and reputational salvage represented by "What about the men?" tap into the discourse of confession. They depart in important, even surprising, ways from survivor narratives that draw on a testimonial lineage of truth-telling. But the focus on survivor testimony is frequently hijacked by these neoconfessional genres.

Confession and testimony are not binary. Rather, they exist as repertoires of truth-telling that subjects exercise degrees of agency and creativity in accessing. Sometimes they flip-flop, as they do in the #MeToo movement, with confession being a mode of the abuser and testimony a mode of the accuser who has found her or his voice and an adequate witness. Why does the distinction between confession and testimony matter? Confession pits a subject who is required to humble themselves before authority, admit error, do penance, and seek atonement against a subject who bears witness to harm and seeks justice. #MeToo stories seem confessional because they are associated with sex and shame, but the #MeToo effect offered group credibility to those most vulnerable to the judgments associated with confession by framing them as testimony. Drawing a distinction between confession and testimony helps to highlight how #MeToo stories are not in search of absolution. They rely on the salutary benefit of collective speech rather than an appeal to a specific authority. If we read testimony as if it were confession, then we are already in a narrative that frames sexual violence from the perspective of the abuser and sees it as sex gone wrong. This is a category error, fueled by cultural myth and the normalization of a status quo. It also feels "right" because it speaks to accountability. It does so, however, by wrenching responsibility away from the person who authors it and sticking it elsewhere: onto a victim, their clothing, or alcohol as some general "evil" that hurts both parties equally.

Foucault theorized that sex becomes discourse through its expression in specific forms of speech, like the confession. Religious and legal confession associate sex, as the "privileged theme of confession," with sin, shame, and secrecy.[48] In the #MeToo moment, abuser apologies consistently replaced violence with sex in order that those accused might confess to sex from an empowered position. They describe harassment, assault, and even rape as consensual sex the victim mis-understands. They apologize for that interpretation, rather than their actions. As a confessing ritual, the abuser apology insists that men and not the targets of violence have the power to name it. Abusers cast doubt both on those they mistreat and on the interpretation of their own behavior. They perform penitence to profess innocence. They meant no harm. When the abuser apology collided with #MeToo, the rising credibility of survivors exposed its false show of regret as a parody of accountability.

An apology carries an admission of fault, so it is not a small thing. When someone's truthful account is denied, they are cut off from the authority of their experience and from the context in which their testimony makes sense. When testimony is refuted by an alleged rapist who says that the acts were consensual, and that false narrative circulates, it becomes part of a larger narrative over which the survivor does not have control. An apology directly addresses this injury. It is an example of discursive justice that restores the reality and credibility of survivor testimony. Discursive justice, as John Frow defines it, is a form of ethical responsiveness that "recognizes a duty to the story of the other."[49] Silence breaking requires a witness. Survivor testimony has a dual address. It speaks to the survivors and witnesses that ethical responsiveness requires, and it addresses the powerful, calling out their violence, demanding a hearing, and refusing to appease.

In his final lecture course in 1981, Foucault followed his earlier work on confession with a focus on the problem of truth-telling. He traced a history of truth-telling as avowal, defined as direct and open assertion, from ancient Greece to the present. Foucault's theme is the inexorable association of avowal with veridiction and the juridical. Not, that is, with the independent truth so much as the institutions and entities empowered to judge it, where the juridical represents an arrangement of power. Foucault held out one form that carried the strongest imprint of independent truth: *parrhesia*, defined as frank and fearless speech. In addition to the prophet, teacher, and sage, the *parrhesia*, from Plato's *Apology* through Christian thought, is defined by courage, risk, and, perhaps surprisingly, the "generosity at the heart of the moral obligation."[50] The identification of generosity and moral obligation in *parrhesia* illuminates the competing forms of avowal in #MeToo.

The core of *parrhesia*, for Foucault, is risk, which describes the position from which survivors speak. *Parrhesia* names the willingness of survivors to sever relationships that depend on silencing: to shift from victim to "accuser," for example, exposes survivors to reputational harm, job loss, and precarity in family and social relations. Sara Ahmed characterizes the moral and political courage of survivor testimony as willfulness, which she defines as "a style of politics when we are not willing to go with the flow; when we are willing to cause obstruction."[51] Those in power (kings and tyrants for Foucault) who offer fake apologies and pretend the "problem" of sexual violence is that a victim misunderstood cannot be *parrhesiastes*. They risk nothing. Nor do they address themselves directly to those they harmed, or, with sincerity, to any authority that might bind them. Instead, they conjure an "anyone" who might have been offended and seek to evade repercussions for their actions. Yet, generosity infuses survivor advocacy, as Alison Turkos, a survivor suing the rideshare company Lyft, emphasized: "Accountability is an act of love" (August 22, 2021).

Testimonial moments are vulnerable to being derailed when new subjects encounter old judgments. When Black Lives Matter protestors are called "terrorists" and protests demanding accountability for police violence in the wake of the murder of George Floyd are labeled "riots," when student survivors of the mass killing in Parkland, Florida, are called "crisis actors" and survivors are accused of fomenting a sex panic, violating due process, or overreacting, we witness older forms of veridiction—stereotype and longstanding patterns of doubt—animated to tamp down insurgent social justice movements. Although the #MeToo effect owes a debt to the impact of the election of Trump, #MeToo did not derive from a single cause. The breakthrough elements of saturation, visibility, and participation converged when the longstanding problem of sexual violence was reframed from the perspective of survivors. It was as if gravity reversed: from impunity to accountability for abusers, from silencing to speech for survivors, and from the power of abusers and the institutions to the collective credibility created by the #MeToo effect within an intersectional lineage of truth-tellers. Tarana Burke is not, therefore, simply a figure to cite to get the #MeToo origin story right. Burke shows how "me too" exemplifies narrative activism—storytelling in the service of social change—rather than confession—the public exposure of private pain in order to appeal to an authority for expiation or atonement.

# 4

## BACKDROP

Antirape Lineage from Harriet Jacobs to Tarana Burke

*My master had power and law on his side; I had a*
*determined will. There is might in each.*

—HARRIET JACOBS, *INCIDENTS IN THE LIFE OF A SLAVE GIRL*

Silence breaking begs the question: Why is no one listening to stories of sexual violence? Uttered *and* unheard, where *is* an account before it is on the record? What archive holds the unacknowledged testimony of sexual violence? In her pivotal essay, "Mama's Baby, Papa's Maybe: An American Grammar Book," Hortense Spillers offers the notion of the vestibule to theorize the immanent quality of halted speech.[1] Spillers names a location—offstage—and an activity—waiting—to capture the sense in which testimony incubates before Black women craft strategies to step out of roles assigned through stereotype to say, "I." Just how hard it would be for the work of Black women and antirape activists to transition from the vestibule onto the mainstage of history surfaced immediately as a range of commentators sidestepped the intersectionality represented by Tarana Burke and proffered other framings for #MeToo from recent feminist history.

When #MeToo was denounced as a sex panic that threatened the return of regressive tropes such as the sexual predator and a conservative clampdown most likely to harm queer people, it recalled the sex wars of the 1980s, a time of divisive debate about pornography and legal efforts to restrict it. This focus fractured the participants at the Barnard conference in 1982. In some ways, the imposition of this framing—a censorious, antiqueer, antisex #MeToo versus a sex-positive feminist left that is also conservative in its view of the law and due process—suggested that feminists had unfinished business from those clashes. But framing #MeToo as a return to the antipornography activism of feminist law professor Catherine MacKinnon and Andrea Dworkin rather than as an episode of narrative activism in an intersectional feminist lineage overstated the role of law in solving the problem. Due process advocates worried that the law would not be respected while the #MeToo effect shifted the conversation about accountability and justice outside the courts where it had stalled.[2] These warnings were leveled in print and other public forums as both cautionary tales and predictions about how #MeToo would fail. Framing #MeToo as a revival of the 1980s sex wars placed it within a history that made speaking out about sexual violence retrograde.

Historian Darlene Clark Hine observed in 1989 that one "of the most remarked upon but least analyzed themes in Black women's history deals with Black women's sexual vulnerability and powerlessness as victims of rape and domestic violence."[3] Hazel Carby, too, noted that the "institutionalized rape of black women has never been as powerful a symbol of black oppression as the spectacle of lynching. Rape has always involved patriarchal notions of women being, at best, not entirely unwilling accomplices, if not outwardly inviting a sexual attack."[4] Hine and Carby point out how the "links between black women and illicit sexuality consolidated during the antebellum years had powerful ideological consequences for the next hundred and fifty years."[5] Hine argues that Black women responded to the prevalence of sexual violence in two ways. One entailed migration as women left the American South in search of economic freedom and freedom from sexual violence. The other response to rape and threats of rape was "the development of a culture of dissemblance among Black women." Here Hine offers a theorization of the vestibule as a space canny self-representation incubates: "By dissemblance I mean the behavior and attitudes of Black women that created the appearance of openness and disclosure but actually shielded the truth of their inner lives and selves from their oppressors." This assertion of Black privacy at the site of testimony about rape is woven throughout literature, reflected in contemporary Black women's writing, and reaches back to nineteenth-century slave narratives by women, including Harriet Jacobs's *Incidents in the Life of a Slave Girl*, published in 1861.

Harriet Jacobs stands at the beginning of a lineage Burke embodies. Like Burke, she cast a light on sexual violence by telling her own story as one of shared exploitation. More than raise awareness, Jacobs fosters empathy and identification with readers by recounting stories of her girlhood and family life.[6] Jacobs calls for a universal witness to the testimony she offers on behalf of all enslaved women and forges an abolitionist appeal grounded in the experience of rape within slavery. She wrote under a pseudonym to protect her relatives, free and enslaved, from the coercions of the Fugitive Slave Act to which she and they could be subjected. At the same time, her use of a pseudonym amplified the collective quality of her narrative.

*Incidents* is a slave narrative, a nonfiction genre that confers the authority of the eyewitness on the one who writes. It is a testimonial genre written to expose and explain violence. Grounded in the first-person "I," slave narratives, like other testimonial life writing, offer a first-person account to represent a collective experience. Testimony indicts systems of oppression through the experience and perspective of a specific, real person. Its various examples often evince a shared pattern with other autobiographical accounts: stories of childhood and family fill the early pages, followed by experiences of violence and the development of political consciousness that ground an appeal to readers. The specificity of individual experience gives shape to the representation of larger social harm. Kwame Anthony Appiah calls the slave narrative "the first African American literary genre," Henry Louis Gates defines the genre as "a communal utterance, a collective tale, more than merely an individual's autobiography," and commenting specifically on the theme of sexual violence in *Incidents*, Hortense Spillers adds that the location from which Jacobs writes, "the other side of freedom," is a complex "aftermath" of remembering and reliving a trauma that never stays in the past.[7]

Often, authors of slave narratives are well known to contemporary audiences. They speak to gatherings of abolitionists, they publish articles and books, and their work is known in transatlantic political and publishing circles. They are the protagonists of their own narratives. Sometimes Black authors relied on the assistance of white scribes, editors, or publishers to reach readers. For Jacobs, however, there was no scribe. Although she was assisted by white women Quakers Amy Post and Lydia Maria Child on the path to publication, the narrative, as the subtitle avows, is "Written by Herself." In fact, the publication history includes several twists and turns ably navigated by Jacobs.[8] For example, she traveled to London to pitch her book and later found a new publisher at the eleventh hour when the original publisher went out of business. After the civil war, Jacobs reunited with her family and traveled again to London. She was known by contemporary writers, including Harriet Beecher Stowe, with whom she had a tense relationship, and *Incidents* was widely credited as Jacobs's autobiography. Between her death and the middle of the twentieth century, however, its undisputed status as testimonial nonfiction with Jacobs as its author was replaced by the myth that Lydia Maria Child herself was the pseudonymous author.[9]

As with Milano's tweet, the title page of *Incidents* requires "interrogation" to hear its multiple voices.[10] Following the title, in the place one would find the author's name are the words "Written by Herself." A quotation from within the narrative serves as an epigraph and is attributed to "A Woman of North Carolina," which locates the author in the South but still does not name her. The title page lists only the editor's name, L. Maria Child, and ends with a third reference to the unnamed Jacobs: "Published for the Author." Child is clearly designated as editor, not author, and the multiple references to Jacobs are placeholders for her name. A preface by the author is signed with a pseudonym, Linda Brent, and Child's introduction attests to the identity and authorship of an actual person. Even with this documentation in place, along with the contemporaneous knowledge of Jacobs's identity, readers by the mid-twentieth century assumed Child was the author of a well-made abolitionist narrative and that Linda Brent was a fiction, a composite perhaps, but not the author.

Jacobs pointedly exposes the sexual violence at the core of slavery. Her ability to communicate shivery disgust with the malignancy of white men and to implicate white women in sexual abuse delivers a potent abolitionist argument to a northern public accustomed to grounding its politics in its own moral virtue. Jacobs's appeal speaks to more than an individual story. She connects Dr. James Norcom's (Dr. Flint in the narrative) threats of rape to a larger pattern faced by all enslaved women. She describes the limited agency she exerted when she maneuvered out of Norcom's grasp and agreed, instead, to a sexual relationship with Samuel Tredwell Sawyer (Mr. Sands in the narrative), a white slaveholder with whom Jacobs had two children. The limitations on agency then and now do not mean that women should be held accountable for the conditions within which they maneuver away from greater violations. Rather, her choice of Sawyer represents a way to exercise some agency when the choice is between survival or annihilation.

In exposing the full gamut of sexual violence within slavery, Jacobs indicts an entire system and the white men, women, and children who benefited from it. White women in the person of "Mrs. Flint" are represented as debased: they are jealous and vengeful, but also libidinally entangled in the sexual violation slavery cannot exist separate from. Jacobs describes how Norcom begins to pour poison in her ear when she is fourteen years old, whispering the degrading things he plans to do to her. "Mrs. Flint" joins him in sexual harassment by brooding threateningly over Jacobs as she sleeps in encounters that Hortense Spillers notes are "so charged with elements of sexual frisson and the mishaps of ecstasy that we are led to believe that the wife is invigilating the young woman in her own behalf" (35): "Sometimes I woke up, and found her bending over me. At other times she whispered in my ear, as though it were her husband who was speaking to me, and listened to hear what I would answer. If she startled me, on such occasion, she would glide stealthily away; and the next morning she would tell me 1 had been talking in my sleep, and ask who I was talking to. At last, I began to be fearful for my life" (33). White women like "Mrs. Flint' ventriloquize the white husband's speech. They act in his place in order to reproduce sexual violence. They do not stand apart from it, as this image shows.

The role of the fully implicated white "mistress" joins a gallery of complicit white women recounted in the narrative: from the "benevolent" woman who owned Jacobs's mother and promised but never got around to freeing her to the white women who bequeathed ownership of enslaved girls like Jacobs to their daughters as a generational transfer of wealth, the role of complicit white women must have struck the "white women of the north" whom Jacobs directly addresses as a clear call to separate themselves from white women in the South. Yet if white women readers did not see themselves in "Mrs. Flint," were they able to recognize themselves in Jacobs's portrayal of the well-intentioned woman who failed to secure her mother's manumission? Jacobs holds white women to account by compelling them to look at how the actions of other white women perpetuate slavery. This adds another layer to the message and the frames of witness, as does Jacobs's use of white women helpers Amy Post and Lydia Maria Child to deliver an indictment of white women to white women.

The authorship of *Incidents* was erased in the decades after Jacobs's death. By the time Jacob's biographer Jean Fagan Yellin was studying slave narratives in graduate school in the 1970s, the scholarly consensus was that Child wrote the narrative. Only a massive archival undertaking restored what had previously been common knowledge because the work of Black women to expose and end sexual violence is not woven into official history. The forgetting of this background as the lineage behind Tarana Burke's "me too" speaks to the racial politics of sexual violence. Historian Catherine Jacquet, for example, argues that anti-rape campaigns by racial justice activists had a continuous history from mid-nineteenth to the twentieth century but waned in the 1960s as the focus of Black activism turned to civil rights. At the moment many white feminists began organizing rape hotlines, crisis centers, and self-defense training in the 1970s, Jacquet notes, "many believed that their work in speaking out on behalf of victims was unprecedented.

Most were wholly unaware of the history that preceded them."[11] In the mid-1970s, feminist antirape activist Susan Brownmiller wrote, "That women should organize to combat rape was a woman's movement invention."[12] Feminist movements diverged around civil rights even as most feminists continued to organize against sexual violence.

The antipathy toward marriage and the consistent reference to slavery provided an opening for Jacobs to address white feminists on the topic of a right, marriage, about which they were ambivalent. Legal marriage, Jacobs wrote, permits white men to rape enslaved women. White women are fully implicated in the institutional collaboration between legal marriage and slavery. They benefit economically and politically from it. They are aware of rape and forced reproduction, including children their husbands father through rape. They can inherit and own enslaved people. In other words, they are similarly positioned as white men. However, given their avowed critique of sexual coercion as a real harm in their own lives, they should understand that Black women share similar feelings about chastity, virtue, and sexual autonomy and therefore about rape as white women, an argument Jacobs presses.

White feminists in the nineteenth century had varied interests, including suffrage, free love, and abolition, that appear to be at odds with similarly situated men. Despite this appearance, white feminist interests centered on political, educational, sexual, and economic freedom, where they understood their goals as the achievement of citizenship rights equal to men's. They saw themselves in the lineage of Mary Wollstonecraft, who argued that girls and women must be educated in order to take up their rightful position as citizens alongside men of their class. Liberal feminists of the 1970s are the most obvious heirs of this legacy, but it extends into the present with Sheryl Sandberg's "lean-in feminism," a current example of the demand for gender equality within an elite.

In contrast, the Combahee River Collective, a Black feminist organization active in Boston from 1974 to 1980, argued for a Marxist, lesbian stance on community solidarity and an anticarceral and antisexist response to sexual harassment and assault. They did not embrace the separatism they associated with white radical lesbians, and they wrote critically about the hypermasculinity of the Black Panther movement. They challenged white feminists on racism and Black men on sexism through a critique of the violence of white supremacy. The feminist lineage of intersectionality, a term coined by law professor Kimberlé Crenshaw, demonstrates how self-reflexive positioning provides a specific stance on sexual violence. The CRC offers insights into how subjects are entangled with each other through white supremacy and patriarchy. They explain the necessity of shielding men of color from racist violence and also holding them accountable for sexual violence, and insist on protecting Black and brown trans women from transphobia and what Moya Bailey calls *misogynoir*.[13] This is a lineage that was left at the threshold in the rush to report on the "unprecedented" #MeToo story.

Crenshaw's analysis of the cultural politics of law explains how both sexual violence and violence directed at people of color are often legally permissible. In the legal case central to Crenshaw's introduction of the term "intersectionality," Black women sought standing to sue an employer for discrimination on the basis of race and gender. Although they faced barriers of gender *and* race, they could neither join a class action with Black men nor sue the same employer on the basis of gender because the white women in their job category were not discriminated against.[14] When they sought relief for intersecting forms of discrimination, they were without recourse through Title VII. In 1986 Mechelle Vinson, a Black woman, won the first successful Title VII sexual harassment claim before the U.S. Supreme Court, which ruled unanimously that sexual harassment in the workplace is a federal crime. Vinson was hired as a bank teller when she was nineteen years old and supervised by Sidney Taylor, who had worked his way up at the bank from janitor to manager and vice president. What Vinson initially believed to be a mentoring relationship devolved into four years of constant sexual harassment, including multiple rapes, once on the floor of the bank vault. In *Meritor Savings Bank v. Vinson*, the Court expanded its understanding of Title VII to include verbal harassment, sexual assault, and rape in its definition of workplace sexual harassment.

Intersectional feminist experience, analysis, and activism prepared the way for the #MeToo effect: from abolitionist writing in the nineteenth century to Anna Julia Cooper and Ida B. Wells, whose work spanned Reconstruction to civil rights, to the Combahee River Collective in the 1970s, to Title VII's focus on the reality of sexual violence and racism in the 1980s, and Anita Hill's testimony in 1991. The interlocking forms of testimony they offered—legal, extralegal, political, essayistic—worked together both to enable a widespread wrong to be witnessed and understood by a public that had previously granted itself plausible deniability for its own passivity and, in the moment of attention, to equip it with a full-fledged analysis.

Despite this powerful genealogy of intersectional feminism, as Vrushali Patil and Jyoti Puri argue, the initial and even movement-defining #MeToo cases, with the exception of Lupita Nyong'o and Salma Hayek, were about white women, showcasing the limits of sympathy in a global movement. The outpouring of speech supporting white women was accompanied by the halted testimony of women of color. Patel and Puri note how hard it is to break through colorblindness: "Even as the #MeToo movement trails these entwined histories of sexual harassment, race, and media representations, it also emerges in a different cultural and political moment—one dominated by a changing media landscape, networked feminist counterpublics, and the persistence of colorblind racial ideologies."[15] In noting the significance of Darlene Clark Hine's "culture of dissemblance," Shoniqua Roach argues that "black women's quest for privacy" exists in a context where stereotypes distort sexuality, agency, and violence. Roach identifies the complexities of vestibular testimony: "This implicit call to honor black privacy while carefully locating black agency, to apprehend the gendered and sexual specificities of antiblack violence while shielding black (female) subjects from the inevitable harm of the white (institutional) gaze, embodies a black feminist care ethic that we continue to grapple with in the age of #BlackLivesMatter, #SayHerName, #MeToo, and persistent social, political, and economic precarity."[16] The lineage of Black feminist thought argues that the conditions in which survivors gain justice must be continuously re-created.

# 5

## #METOO STRESS TEST

The Kavanaugh Hearings

*Let me explain again.*

*Indelible in the hippocampus is the laughter.*

This chapter takes Anita Hill's testimony as a starting point for examining how #MeToo forced a new hearing for many stories from the past but ultimately exposed how disadvantaged survivors remain within the hostile processes that host their testimony. Hill's testimony resurged into public memory when Christine Blasey Ford testified that Supreme Court nominee Brett Kavanaugh sexually assaulted her when they were teenagers. Hill's testimony that Clarence Thomas sexually harassed her when she worked for him at the Equal Employment Opportunity Commission riveted a national audience during three days of televised testimony in October 1991. When Hill, a Black law professor, faced the white, all-male Senate Judiciary Committee, Republican members accused her of fabricating lurid tales drawn from pornography rather than take seriously her careful and consistent allegations about Thomas's behavior. The hearing showed how vulnerable she was to being smeared in the only formal process available to her.

Let's return to that hearing to recall how allegations of sexual misconduct about a Supreme Court nominee were handled. No experts provided testimony about sexual harassment to inform the male senators who openly doubted its impact. Without a context to analyze power and sexism, stereotype reigned. Hill was caricatured as a "little bit nutty and a little bit slutty," a "scorned woman" who either invented what Thomas did to her, encouraged it, or failed to stop it. Republicans were not interested in determining whether Thomas had abused his power and what this meant for his future on the court. They accepted his refusal to engage Hill's allegations and directed their allotted time to smearing her. Committee chair Joseph Biden refused to call Angela Wright to corroborate the pattern of abuse by Thomas that Hill alleged. Senator Ted Kennedy was muted in response toward his colleagues' treatment of Hill because, like Thomas, his own behavior had diminished his standing. His nephew, William Kennedy Smith, was about to stand trial for rape, and Ted Kennedy was scheduled to be called as a witness because he had been present on the night and instigated a midnight outing for drinks where his nephew met the woman who claimed he raped her. Even as sexist attacks against Hill went unchallenged, the committee members strove not to appear racist toward Thomas.

The judicial forum shape-shifted into political spectacle as Republican members heaped acrimony on Hill, belittling her and her claims. In addition to accusing Hill of exaggerating or inventing Thomas's actions and their impact, the Republicans on the committee and their allies launched a frenzied campaign characterized by wild false accusations. Senator John Danforth, an ordained Episcopal priest, led the charge in soliciting false affidavits from anyone who might be persuaded to throw dirt at Hill. Her testimony, as she writes in her recent memoir, catalyzed a #MeToo-style outpouring as "traumatic stories in letters and calls continued flooding my mailbox and telephone, filling file cabinet after file cabinet in my office. Some who contacted me sought legal representation, but most were just determined to tell someone what had happened to them, many for the first time."[1] She became their adequate witness, and they addressed their gratitude for her courage and accounts of their pain to her. This part of the story did not break through; instead, it incubated until these accounts could be shared, as so many of them were, in the public testimonial context created by #MeToo.

During Blasey Ford's testimony in the Kavanaugh confirmation hearings, the Senate Judiciary Committee reenacted the dynamics of the Hill-Thomas hearings, alternately resisting and referencing the #MeToo movement as the context for understanding the risks survivors take in coming forward, the processes in which their claims can be heard, and the appropriate response to allegations of sexual misconduct by nominees. With Democrats calling for accountability and Republicans seeking a return to the tactics of 1991, the hearings fractured into parallel processes: the Republicans staged a rape defense for Kavanaugh, which meant Ford would be put on trial, and the Democrats insisted "this is not a trial."[2] Less a do-over than a grim replay, the hearings enabled Kavanaugh's aggrieved self-defense to overshadow Ford's claim to civic duty.

Ford acted as survivors often do: she spoke out to prevent others from experiencing a harm she had suffered. She wanted to warn America about Kavanaugh. She described how Kavanaugh and his friend Mike Judge forced her into an upstairs bedroom at a house party, locked the door, and turned up the music to cover her screams, while Kavanaugh pinned her to the bed and sexually assaulted her. She believed he intended to rape her and feared that he might accidentally kill her when he covered her mouth with his hand to silence her. Although Republican control of the White House, Senate, and the House rendered Kavanaugh's confirmation a foregone conclusion, the emergence of her account within the framing of #MeToo and the shift toward accountability for some powerful men raised expectations that her testimony would be taken seriously, Kavanaugh would not advance, and the wrong Anita Hill experienced when she testified would be righted. This did not happen. Instead, as in the 1991 hearings, survivor testimony became the occasion for the reputational destruction of the accuser rather than the accused. The #MeToo effect, voluble in the court of public opinion, was muted as Republicans sought to convey the impression that Blasey Ford was on trial.

## WITNESS ON TRIAL

Although hearings are not trials, they resemble them.[3] When the setting looks like a trial, women who testify will be forced to pay the rising cost of doubt while nominees like Thomas and Kavanaugh will be protected by the presumption of innocence and the benefit of the doubt, both of which are artifacts of a criminal trial. This disparity offers further evidence of how women are placed at a structural disadvantage within the law: even the resemblance of the hearings to a trial places *their* testimony under suspicion. During the Kavanaugh hearings, the Republican-led Senate Judiciary Committee adopted several tactics to enhance the trial-like qualities of the hearing as they attempted to stuff the #MeToo genie back into the "he said / she said" bottle. They restricted the investigation of Blasey Ford's allegations to a rerun of Kavanaugh's previous FBI background check even as the Democrats on the committee insisted that the precedent of Anita Hill's mistreatment and the context of the #MeToo movement demanded they do better. What resulted, in effect, were two processes unfolding in the same time frame and location with radically different purposes. Under questioning by Republicans, Blasey Ford was on trial. In contrast, the Democrats insisted, she was not. Because Democrats were the minority party, they were not positioned to prevent the Republicans from exaggerating the trial-like qualities of the proceedings nor to hold Kavanaugh accountable for his outlandish behavior during questioning had it truly been a trial. Like Anita Hill, Blasey Ford spoke about sexual misconduct in a setting that made it impossible from the outset for her to receive justice.

Memories of the Hill-Thomas hearings remained vivid. Remarkably, still seated on the committee were Democrat Patrick Leahy and Republicans Chuck Grassley and Orrin Hatch. Hatch had promoted the bizarre hypothesis that Hill drew on *The Exorcist* and pornography to describe Thomas's behavior. Senator Grassley now chaired the committee. Senator Leahy was so exasperated in 1991 by the extraordinary leeway Republicans were given to slander Hill that he memorably asked, "What are the rules?" He could have raised the question again in 2017. The familiar faces as well as the process made 1991 feel very close. So did the presence of Clarence Thomas on the court, and the demonstrable success of the Republican strategy to replace Thurgood Marshall with a Black candidate who would provide a reliably anti–civil rights vote on the court. That strategy was epitomized by the autobiographical narrative Thomas offered in lieu of a substantive discussion of his judicial philosophy. Similarly, Kavanaugh would use his personal story to cloak his opposition to abortion rights, obscuring his willingness to overturn *Roe* with his record of hiring women and law clerks and coaching girls' sports.

In the wake of Robert Bork's failed nomination to the court in 1987, handlers crafted life narratives for nominees to serve as political messaging about how they would rule.[4] Thomas used the up-by-the-bootstraps narrative to describe his rise from poverty to stand on his own feet through education and hard work. With a twist. He assured conservative supporters that no hardship in his young life—not poverty, paternal abandonment, or racism—had harmed him as much or as lastingly as affirmative action. The signal was clear: he could be counted on as a conservative, anti–civil rights vote on the court.[5] Kavanaugh played the golden boy, presenting himself as destined for greatness. He attended Yale Law, after which he clerked for Judge Ken Starr, whom he followed to the Office of Independent Counsel, where he assisted on President Bill Clinton's impeachment trial. He drafted the Starr report recommending impeachment and notably insisted that Starr ask Clinton sexually explicit questions. Kavanaugh worked on the Florida recount for the George W. Bush campaign and advised Bush on judicial nominees. Like Thomas, Kavanaugh established himself as a reliably conservative political figure. This is not the story he told the committee. Instead, he emphasized his support for women and commitment to diversity. He was a privileged white man who hardly needed to make his case. He was already taking a victory lap.

Yet when Blasey Ford's testimony interrupted Kavanaugh's story, his confident affect changed dramatically. As with Thomas before him, Kavanaugh angrily repudiated his accuser. Both declared themselves victims of conspiracy. They expressed outrage that proceedings they saw as designed to elevate them to the high court and cover them in glory had been used to injure them personally. Thomas memorably decried his treatment as a "high-tech lynching for uppity-blacks," while Kavanaugh, less majestically aggrieved than Thomas, whined that he "liked beer." Neither was sober as a judge.

Even when survivor testimony broke through in 1991 and again in 2017, it could not compete with the packaged life stories of the nominees. Hill's and Blasey Ford's testimony demonstrate that women's life stories alone cannot overcome the refusal to hear them. Context matters. When women speak out in settings that invite disclosure but are neither fair nor transparent, they do not enjoy an expectation of credibility; instead, they are exposed to doubt and erasure. As Hill's testimony and the expansion of #MeToo showed, for women and girls of color in particular, testimonial sites and rituals can be locations of epistemic violence.[6] While Thomas and Kavanaugh could rely on audiences to believe them before they were accused and, *even when they found Hill and Blasey Ford credible*, to defend them after, survivor testimony has no such audience. Even when it does not press a legal claim, it can be made to seem to. And the appearance of a legal forum assembling around it places survivor testimony at risk.

I define *survivor testimony* as an account of sexual abuse offered by the victim in which harm is understood as a past wrong and an ongoing injustice that demands a reckoning. It reframes four elements: (1) identity: the one who speaks out often shifts through testimony from victim to self-defined survivor; (2) acts and events: sexual violence is represented from the survivor's perspective, taking it as traumatic rather than trivial; (3) temporality: acts committed in the past are understood to have lasting negative effects that deserve and require a proportional response and, as such, statutes of limitations fail to account for trauma and the suppression of survivor speech; and (4) justice: survivor demands for justice do not necessarily reduce to a carceral response but are not ready made. This definition of survivor testimony thus fits with a rhetorical understanding of narrative: somebody (the survivor) tells somebody else in the present (an audience charged with assessing her telling) that something happened to her (somebody assaulted her in the past), and she does so for the purpose of seeking redress and otherwise influencing the future.[7] Neither Blasey Ford nor Hill pressed a legal claim, filed a complaint, or suggested Thomas or Kavanaugh should be charged, tried, or sentenced. Instead, a survivor's sense of justice required them to advise the Senate Judiciary Committee about a man whose past behavior made him unfit to be a Supreme Court justice and whose future influence over women's lives would be enormous. Their method was testimonial: they told the truth in public.

Once Blasey Ford was called to testify, the hearings transformed, as they had in 1991, from a nomination process into a trial. The parallels reveal how little had changed. As Hill did when she came forward, Blasey Ford asked for anonymity. Yet both had their identities leaked to the press and saw their intention to advise the committee turn into a public trial in which they were accused of conspiracy and characterized as delusional. Neither was permitted a basic guarantee at trial: the right to have corroborating witnesses offer testimony. As with Thomas, testimony about Kavanaugh incubated in what Hortense Spillers theorizes as the vestibule, the offstage space where stories and tellers are held without a hearing. Deborah Ramirez was not permitted to testify about his alleged sexually abusive behavior toward her in college. No expert witnesses were called to discuss workplace sexual harassment in 1991, nor any to explain the reasons trauma victims delay reporting in 2018. Maine Republican Susan Collins made the most overt attempt to turn the hearings into a trial in a September 18 letter to Grassley: "I respectfully recommend that you invite the attorneys retained by Dr. Ford and Judge Kavanaugh to pose questions during the hearing." "Dr. Ford's attorney would be permitted to question Judge Kavanaugh, and Judge Kavanaugh's attorney would question Dr. Ford. Each would be permitted equal time to do so before Senators began their round of questions."[8] In other words, Collins urged that Kavanaugh's legal team be allowed to improvise a rape defense in the midst of a nomination hearing in order to attack the testimony of a woman alleging attempted rape.

The protections of a trial were omitted even as its trappings were swiftly assembled in order to disadvantage Hill and Blasey Ford. These included the format of testimony and interrogation in an adversarial mode (with Democrats acting as defense and Republicans as prosecution), the presence of attorneys flanking the witness, and the anomalous introduction of Rachel Mitchell, a criminal prosecutor hired by Republican senators as their proxy to question Blasey Ford. Rachel Mitchell's presence encouraged a framing of Blasey Ford as an accuser in a criminal proceeding and Kavanaugh as a defendant, to whom would be owed presumption of innocence, due process, and the burden of proof in a criminal proceeding: guilt beyond a reasonable doubt. As with Anita Hill's testimony, this impression would extend the benefit of the doubt to Kavanaugh as energetically as it was denied to Blasey Ford, turning her from what even Trump called a "very credible witness" into a tainted one under the relentless denigration of her testimony.[9] The hearings showed how a tainted witness is not who someone *is*, but what someone can *become* in the process of bringing an account into the public sphere.[10] The ease with which the hearings came to resemble a trial exploited the vulnerability victims of sexual violence face in the forums of judgment in which they bear witness and seek justice.

The misrepresentation of the hearings as a trial exposed Blasey Ford to disproportionate scrutiny and benefited Kavanaugh by enabling him to improvise a performance that would not have been permitted in court. He lashed out at Democratic senators, interrupted, and threw their questions back at them. He asked Senator Amy Klobuchar if she had ever blacked out after drinking. Because it was more theater than courtroom, Kavanaugh was able to frame himself as a backlash culture invention: the falsely accused (white) man. As to Blasey Ford's identity in the proceedings? Although initially listed in the transcript as WITNESS, she is referred to subsequently as KAVANAUGH ACCUSER. As she loses the assignation of "witness," she is no longer framed in relation as an advisor to the committee's process. Instead, she is framed as Kavanaugh's antagonist.

## PARALLEL HEARINGS

*I did my best to suppress memories of the assault because*
*recounting the details caused me to relive the experience,*
*and caused panic attacks and anxiety.*

—CHRISTINE BLASEY FORD, BRETT KAVANAUGH SUPREME
COURT NOMINATION HEARINGS

*"What happens at Georgetown Prep stays at Georgetown*
*Prep." That's been a good thing for all of us, I think.*

—BRETT KAVANAUGH, CATHOLIC UNIVERSITY'S COLUMBUS SCHOOL OF LAW, 2015

From the outset, two jurisdictions vied for authority—one offered by
Senator Grassley as chair, the other by Senator Feinstein, ranking Democrat on the committee. In Grassley's jurisdiction, obstructionist
Democrats were using Blasey Ford as a pawn in a complicated political
attack on Brett Kavanaugh. In Feinstein's, Blasey Ford was a courageous
citizen and survivor whose testimony would be treated with respect.
Given the structure of the hearings, in which Democratic and Republican senators took turns addressing Blasey Ford, the competing jurisdictions would alternate throughout the hearings but never mesh. In his
opening statement, Grassley spoke at length about how Blasey Ford's
allegations reached him. When it was Feinstein's turn, she reframed the
transit of Blasey Ford's allegations, effectively making a second beginning. As a temporal sequence, Feinstein's forum should supplant Grassley's in the logic of seriality. Instead, the two continued to speak as if
each were chairing a different hearing, establishing side-by-side contexts
for hearing the testimony.

In Grassley's trial, Blasey Ford is accused of sending a "secret letter,"
a mischaracterization that will hang over the hearings. Grassley describes
Feinstein's agreement to maintain confidentiality as laying a trap for an
eleventh-hour ambush and asserts that if Feinstein had acted in good
faith, "These allegations could have been investigated in a way that main-
tained the confidentiality that Dr. Ford requested." He blames her for
harming her own case, encouraging a view of her as both self-injuring

and threatening to Kavanaugh. Accused of bad faith and bad timing, Blasey Ford is out of order from the beginning. To cement the charge of bad timing, Grassley conjures an alternative temporality in which such a report could have been made, and thus a confidential forum in which the witness could have been heard. This time has passed. Instead, in the time of her actual testimony, she cannot be heard. But what is the good timing of survivor testimony? Trauma fractures time into before and after. Some formal processes impose this injury to time on the witness. The most obvious examples of this are statutes of limitations and waiting periods for reporting. But the refusal to hear survivor testimony *at all* means Blasey Ford is construed as permanently at temporal odds with what can be heard and when. She is always either too soon or too late, either rushing the process or derailing it. Both of which are her fault. Grassley's casting of her testimony as permanently untimely underlines that no process exists in which to hear survivor testimony that is ordered by and for survivors. The only injury Grassley will acknowledge Blasey Ford has suffered is the one Senator Feinstein inflicted on her by honoring her request for confidentiality, a request breached by the press: "And that's where Dr. Ford was mistreated."

When Blasey Ford testifies, she is reluctant but determined: "I am here today not because I want to be. I am terrified. I am here because I believe it is my civic duty to tell you what happened to me while Brett Kavanaugh and I were in high school." It can take a very long time to transform a hurt into words. The lag between the injury and the telling can lengthen to decades. The challenge to find the words is inseparable from the search for an adequate witness.[11] Blasey Ford's opening statement is direct, as are all her answers to the committee's and Rachel Mitchell's questions. She does not back track or contradict herself. She represents both the girl who was sexually assaulted, through her close description of the events, and her adult self, as she offers expert testimony on trauma, her field of professional expertise. Her testimony highlights the complex temporality of trauma. She can speak from her perspective at the time of the assault and from her perspective at the time of her testimony. The time of the assault is always present, ready to irrupt into the present. When she responds to Leahy's question about what stays with her from the assault, the full temporality of the survivor speaks: "Indelible in the hippocampus is the laughter." The adult gives voice to what the terrorized girl can never forget.

Blasey Ford's opening statement carefully contextualizes her girlhood in a scene of deceptively safe suburban affluence, a location where girls are blamed for what boys do to them:

> **Blasey Ford**: I grew up in the suburbs of Washington, D.C. I attended the Holton-Arms School in Bethesda, Maryland, from 1980 to 1984. . . . During my time at the school, girls at Holton-Arms frequently met and became friendly with boys from all-boys schools in the area, including Landon School, Georgetown Prep, Gonzaga High School, country clubs, and other places where kids and their families socialized. This is how I met Brett Kavanaugh, the boy who sexually assaulted me.

The committee is urged to understand that Blasey Ford and Kavanaugh are peers. They live in the same wealthy neighborhood, attend single-sex private high schools, and are known to each other as "girls" and "boys." This locution risks exposing Blasey Ford to the kinds of judgments girls often face who accuse privileged boys of sexual assault and activating the "boys will be boys" defense of the casual misogyny and drunken partying she is about to describe. But she also tests the committee's ability to discern how the past lingers, how trauma can interrupt a girl's life, and haunt her thereafter. Blasey Ford conjures versions of herself and Kavanaugh not as a research professor from Palo Alto and a Supreme Court nominee, but as teenagers. Not as Professor Blasey and Judge Kavanaugh, but as Christie and Brett.[12] In 1982 psychologist Carol Gilligan's best-selling book on the moral development of girls, *In a Different Voice*, theorized that white adolescent girls lost their voices because they were bombarded with cultural messages telling them to become smaller and quieter to fit into the confines of femininity.[13] Her work explains why Christie would have been the one in trouble had she told her parents what Brett did to her.

Blasey Ford, the adult, supplies a context for understanding the assault and her reaction to it. She can vividly remember some aspects of the house party, but others have receded, a description of traumatic memory well known to her from her research.

> **Blasey Ford**: I truly wish I could provide detailed answers to all of the questions that have been and will be asked about how I got to the party, where it took place, and so forth. I don't have all the answers, and I don't remember as much as I would like to. But the details about that night that bring me here today are ones I will never forget. They have been seared into my memory and have haunted me episodically as an adult.

The details she remembers are of a scene frozen in time, a party with a few people drinking beer in a living room, followed by a chaotic assault in which she fights two older drunk boys, one of whom is trying to tear her clothes off.

> **Blasey Ford**: Brett groped me and tried to take off my clothes. He had a hard time because he was so drunk, and because I was wearing a one-piece bathing suit under my clothes. I believed he was going to rape me. I tried to yell for help. When I did, Brett put his hand over my mouth to stop me from screaming. This was what terrified me the most, and has had the most lasting impact on my life. It was hard for me to breathe, and I thought that Brett was accidentally going to kill me.

Blasey Ford testifies that she was able to flee when Mike jumped on Brett and they both fell off her. She locks herself in a bathroom until she hears Brett and Mike "pin balling" down the stairs. With this word, Blasey Ford indicates how the memory of trauma migrates from sight to sound. The boys careen down the stairs like weighted metal balls, unpredictable in their velocity and destination, flung by impersonal flippers. It's an unmenacing word for their flight from the locked room. The word "pin balling" turns the scene into an arcade, a place for adolescents to hang out, where boys shout "score!" and a girl's life tilts. About her own flight down the stairs and out of the house, she says she "ran," limp with relief to find herself in the street and alone.

Their lives diverged. Kavanaugh would go on to joke about his drunkenness in high school, while Blasey Ford attempted to suppress the memory in order not to relive it in panic attacks. Kavanaugh would be portrayed by his "powerful allies as a champion of women's rights and empowerment."[14] He was not traumatized by assaulting Blasey Ford. In fact, by all accounts, he thrived. Because he bears no trace of the violence he inflicted, *for him* the past is past. Trauma, however, represents a lasting injury. Suppressed memory is not the same as gradual forgetting or the diminishment of pain over time. The prominence of #MeToo contributed a new level of awareness about sexual violence and traumatic memory to the cultural context for hearing Blasey Ford's testimony. More people understood her explanation of trauma's lasting effects than had a ready language for sexual harassment when Hill testified because the public square has been filled with survivor testimony in the intervening years. Many people now know about cases of powerful men being fired, as well as cover-ups lasting years and even decades, nondisclosure agreements, and threats of retaliation. Anita Hill is not only a powerful figure in memory, but a current law professor who also works on sexual harassment policy. The mutating jurisdiction of the hearings, controlled by the Republicans to put Blasey Ford on trial, tested the penetration of #MeToo into the Senate Judiciary Committee, even as the movement was culturally prominent.

The hearings refocused public attention on the forum itself and demonstrated how very little had changed in twenty-seven years in the nomination process, even as so much had changed in one year of #MeToo. So much and so little change. Progress and backlash describe coevolving forces: on one hand, the rising credibility of women and, indeed, all survivor accounts of sexual violence, and, on the other, the mechanisms, motive, and means for discrediting them. That Blasey Ford would testify in a new era of #MeToo is demonstrably true. That this new era exists during patriarchy is equally true. As Anita Hill has said about what she calls the "tragedy" of the Kavanaugh confirmation: "The deception of a pretext of fairness is almost as damning" as the outright silencing of victims.[15]

Blasey Ford's testimony was amplified by survivors outside the hearings who massed in Washington to protest the nomination. Two survivors, Ana Maria Archila and Maria Gallagher, confronted Republican committee member Jeff Flake as he stood in the elevator that took him from his office to the hearings. Archila demanded that Flake listen: "What you're doing is allowing someone who actually violated a woman to sit in the Supreme Court. This is not tolerable. You have children in your family. Think about them. I have two children. I cannot imagine that for the next 50 years they will have to have someone in the Supreme Court who has been accused of violating a young girl. What are you doing, sir?" The confrontation is recorded on a cellphone, as Flake stares at the ground, waiting for the elevator doors to close. Archila presses: "I didn't tell anyone [about being sexually assaulted], and you're telling all women that they don't matter, that they should just stay quiet because if they tell you what happened to them, you're going to ignore them. . . . Look at me when I'm talking to you. You're telling me that my assault doesn't matter."[16] She draws the focus to her framing of his actions: you are doing this, you are doing that. She demands he recognize the role his silence plays.

At the conclusion of the hearings, Kavanaugh was confirmed by one of the slimmest margins in history: 50–48. Republican surrogate Rachel Mitchell wrote a five-page memo follow-up that had no bearing on the vote.[17] Mitchell's memo states that because Blasey Ford can remember some details and not others, she is not credible. She can remember the bathroom where she hid, and that it was across the hall from the bedroom where she was assaulted, but not the street address of the house. Mitchell accuses Ford of a discrepancy—a loaded word in ascertaining the credibility of testimony—for describing her age as "late teens" when she was fifteen. Mitchell concludes that Ford is not credible because she can remember drinking "one beer" and that she was not taking medication when she cannot recall the street address of the house where she was assaulted, despite the consistency of Blasey Ford's memories with trauma. Her top-line conclusion is that she, Rachel Mitchell, sex crimes prosecutor in Arizona, would not bring charges against Brett Kavanaugh today based on Blasey Ford's inability to remember the street address of the house where the attack occurred. Yet, surely, one can only imagine her "finding" as part of another trial-like process in which she, Rachel Mitchell, interrogated Blasey Ford as if she were a sex crimes prosecutor determined not to charge Kavanaugh. In so doing, Mitchell demonstrated how hard it is for victims to be heard. How elements related to traumatic memory—the heightened awareness of the scene of the attack, the gaps in memory immediately following the attack—can be used to attack the credibility of the witness. Mitchell used trauma against Blasey Ford.

## WHY TWO TRIALS MATTER

When a single jurisdiction hosts two competing versions of justice, it displays who may be sacrificed by power and who will be protected. In the hearings, Thomas and Kavanaugh were shown considerable deference as they displayed a range of emotions that did not diminish their credibility or bar their promotion to the court. From anger and self-aggrandizement to self-pity and intimations of future payback, both men acted out in ways that were off-limits to the women who exercised levels of self-control and professionalism the nominees abandoned. How the nominees and their accusers testified revealed a difference in their status, too, as legal subjects. Neither Hill nor Blasey Ford refused to answer questions. Neither openly mocked, derided, or accused committee members of subjecting them to gender-based harassment for insinuating that they had been the ones inflicting harm because they threatened a man's career. Had they done so, they would not have been any more off base than Thomas or Kavanaugh. They alone were disadvantaged as the hearings morphed into a trial. The contrast was sharp. The only agency the women could exercise was to stop participating. They had no leverage on how they entered the process, could not find a fair hearing once it started, and failed to gain the outcome they sought. Their ethical decision to advise the committee was publicly mocked, they were harassed as they were questioned, and their lives were upended. Thomas and Kavanaugh both enjoy lifetime appointments to the court.

If we think of the hearings as a kind of trial, perhaps the stakes are best understood in terms of whose stories cannot be given a fair hearing and whose lives need to be sacrificed in order not to disrupt the smooth functioning of patriarchal power. As a display of expendability, the hearings show that women who speak out are a threat. Because survivor testimony halts perpetrators in their rise to or maintenance of power and reputation, judges and criminal defenses often bemoan the damage a rapist faces at the hands of the law in sentencing. His future, especially when he is white, privileged, and young, counts heavily in calculations to preserve gender hierarchy and the sovereignty of white men.

Susan Collins held outsize power in this decision. She read a statement announcing her decision to support Kavanaugh, an expected outcome given that she is a Republican and the hearings were schematically partisan. Although she could have used her platform to rehabilitate Kavanaugh's badly tarnished reputation, she attacked Blasey Ford in a textbook case of gaslighting. Yes, Collins opined, Blasey Ford was traumatized, someone must have hurt her, but it wasn't Kavanaugh. Asserting her power to rename reality, Collins identified the blameworthy person as Blasey Ford: she failed to remember, she came forward, and she hurt herself. Collins did everything except demand that Blasey Ford apologize. The hearings let America have it both ways: she is both credible and did this to herself; he is both to blame and the victim. Both frameworks were preserved in the hearings: the seeming openness to survivor testimony unfolded in parallel with the mechanisms that prevented it from being heard. As an example of gaslighting, Collins renamed the problem as a woman speaking out, which works even in the #MeToo era. Framed as part of a #MeToo-fueled reckoning with past wrongs, Christine Blasey Ford's testimony demonstrated the obstacles to holding men accountable for sexual assault. Her testimony and the feminist outcry around it clearly affiliated Blasey Ford with the rising expectation of testimonial justice that defines the #MeToo effect; yet the confirmation vote sent a message: your testimony can set you free *and* it will also be used to destroy you. This is the paradox of speaking out about gendered violence in proceedings freighted with gendered doubt.

# II

## NARRATIVE JUSTICE AND SURVIVOR READING

# 6

## READING LIKE A SURVIVOR

*One wants a teller in a time like this*

—GWENDOLYN BROOKS

**W**hat do survivors want? Although there is no single answer, the worry that #MeToo would become a recipe for revenge finds little support in the actions survivors take or views they express. While some survivors seek punishment, especially where rape is a weapon of war—and perhaps more might advocate for punishment if they believed such views would be tolerated—most survivors say they come forward out of a sense of duty and the desire to prevent future harm. They seek, variously, to engage in processes of community reconciliation, to remove abusers from positions of authority and hold them accountable, and to replace the structures that enable abuse.[1] While survivor organizations do advocate for proportional penalties, they rarely demand *more* policing or carceral solutions. More typically, they work for social change through education and understanding alongside changes in law and policy.[2] Even organizations like the National Women's Law Center that explicitly interface with the law focus on achieving gender justice by protecting Title IX, advancing reproductive justice, and ensuring workplace protections for sexual harassment rather than increased punishment within the criminal justice system. Survivors and their advocates seek to be addressable and audible as telling the truth. They want the right to be heard. This chapter shows how narrative activism provides a blueprint for the kind of justice that survivors seek. It identifies the need to create the conditions for speaking, listening, and acting, a process I call *survivor reading*, a critical practice that enables witnesses to understand trauma, consent, agency, and justice as if they themselves were survivors. Critical practices that build up doubt and direct it at survivors have taught generations to look at sexual violence as an ancillary part of a grand historical narrative that places men on center stage and relegates women to the wings. I propose instead that we read testimony-in-waiting as an ongoing conversation among survivors and that we dissolve the agreement that it matters less.

## NARRATIVE JUSTICE: THE RIGHT TO BE HEARD

The barriers to being heard are imposed by the experience of trauma and amplified by cultural practices of silencing. Victims of sexual violence are taught to blame themselves, to feel shame about being hurt, and to remain silent to prevent more harm to themselves and their families. They are dismissed as angry, crazy, slutty, and worthless. The drumbeat instilled in victims is that they are lucky to be alive, and, according to an accounting that balances their supposed worthlessness against someone else's definition of injury, to conclude that what they suffered is not *that bad*. The theme of minimizing trauma runs through the essays in a collection edited by Roxane Gay, *Not That Bad: Dispatches from Rape Culture* (2018).[3] Jill Christman writes about reading the feminist classic *I Never Called It Rape* (1994) and recognizing her own experience. She describes her self-defense instructor's advice to replace the conditioned polite response to sexual violence, "What will he think of me?"—if she refuses, if she fights, if she tells—with "What do I think of *him*?" as paradigm-shifting: "The simple rearrangement of pronouns flipped something in my brain. Forever."[4] From this perspective, Vanessa Mártir also writes about shifting the balance from "not that bad," a calculation to reduce the abuser's responsibility, to "It was bad enough."[5]

As the essays in *Not That Bad* attest, #MeToo prompts a form of auto-biographical storytelling that transforms shared pain into testimonial agency: the power to tell one's own story. When the #MeToo effect exposed histories of oppression and shifted shame from the abused to abusers, it cleared space for new forms of listening and understanding to emerge. Personal testimony enables survivors to represent the psychic and embodied impact of sexual violence. But as the essayists also argue, the lack of a shared language about sexual violence impedes narrative activism, and our capacity to bear witness to these too-common stories is severely uneven. Gayatri Spivak calls the silencing of marginalized groups "epistemic violence."[6] Philosopher Miranda Fricker identifies the harm inflicted on someone in their capacity as a knower when hearers refuse to meet them halfway as "epistemic injustice."[7] In the context of sexual violence, epistemic violence and epistemic injustice are tools of abuse woven into institutions through doubt and silencing.

To better understand what testimonial justice looks like for survivors, consider the testimonial injustice it seeks to replace. Kristie Dotson identifies two forms of testimonial injustice especially relevant to an analysis of #MeToo: testimonial quieting and testimonial smothering.[8] Testimonial quieting prevents survivors from speaking out *at all*. Shame places a metaphorical hand over a survivor's mouth. Doubt ensures it stays there. Abusers ensure victims' silence by telling them no one will believe them. They threaten to harm children or family members. Victims stay silent as the clock ticks on statutes of limitations, which favors abusers. Abusers use gaslighting to distort reality, striking at the capacity to name one's own experience and inflicting long-lasting harm. At a cultural level, "commonsense" myths about sexual violence contribute to testimonial quieting and allow assailants to shift blame for sexual assault onto victims, a form of injustice that strikes at women's right to be heard.

Testimonial smothering discredits survivors when they do speak. It takes their words out of context, twisting the threads of meaning until they break. Testimonial injustice is inflicted within the same systems that survivors are required to turn to for protection, like policing. Police often sympathize with abusers, not because sexual violence is rare, but because police officers themselves are often accused of it.[9] Police target women of color for sexual abuse, and trans women of color face the highest rates of abuse.[10] Sex workers, who are more exposed to policing, report being coerced to exchange sex to avoid arrest.[11] In 2015 serial rapist and Oklahoma City police officer Daniel Holtzclaw —who would pick up women, threaten them with arrest, and demand sex—was convicted of raping thirteen Black women, one of whom was handcuffed to a hospital bed when he assaulted her.[12] In New York it was not illegal for a police officer to have coerced sex with someone in custody until a recent case forced a change in the law.[13] Anna Chambers, a teenager at the time, was picked up by two police officers, placed in a van, handcuffed, and raped. The two officers claimed that this rape-in-custody was consensual sex.[14] They were tried and received no jail time. As a form of epistemic violence, calling rape in police custody "consensual sex," as the accused did and the media repeated, represents gaslighting at a cultural scale. These failures of listening and the silencing they enact form the connective tissue of testimonial injustice.[15] Both testimonial quieting and testimonial smothering answer the question, "Why didn't you tell anyone?"

Sometimes testimonial quieting and smothering are so much a part of everyday speech that they circulate without much notice. Consider how insidiously euphemisms sentimentalize sexual abuse, shaping how we imagine and understand it. Euphemisms to describe sexual assault are often borrowed from the lexicon of romance or nurturance. This is especially common when the abuser and victim know each other, and when the victim is young. Using a verb that means to caress or pat like "fondle" to describe sexual battery, often of a child, suggests a refusal to reckon with violation at a deeper level than vocabulary. Describing sexual violence euphemistically enables it to be shielded from shared knowledge. It disables the capacity to see something and call it by its name. It diminishes our ethical agency when language makes violence indistinguishable from care.

In the context of medical training, the gender stereotypes that connect euphemistic language to disinformation are so normalized they escape notice. In her classic essay on how medical textbooks recycle the language of heterosexual romance and stereotypes about women and aging to describe menstruation and menopause, Emily Martin decried how misogyny and metaphor work together to teach medical students that the egg waits passively like a fairy tale princess in a tower for a sperm to succeed in its active masculine quest to fertilize her.[16] Menstruation produces "debris" and "decay," and menstrual flow is characterized as the womb weeping for its fertility failure. Menopause is the withering into uselessness of the female synecdoche of value: the uterus. Martin urges readers to wake up the sleeping metaphors, and her advice applies equally to the language of sexual violence in law, media, and everyday use. Euphemism conditions hearers to minimize the harm of sexual violence and is a form of epistemic violence because it downgrades survivor credibility.

The #MeToo effect is an example of how narrative activism aims to create testimonial justice and its promise of the right to be heard. *Witness* has a twofold meaning: it refers to one who speaks and one who listens.[17] On one side, survivors forge language that enables them to speak out about their experience and, by providing courage and empathy to others, encourages more speech. On the other side is reception: one learns to listen. Together they form a collective witness, which I use as a general concept here to indicate how survivors were able to benefit from the credibility that arises from shared experience, including patterns of abuse, trauma-related disruptions, and structural disadvantage in the law. Rather than isolating and dismissing survivors one at a time, their collective witness replaces routine epistemic violence with testimonial justice. The form through which this is enacted is survivor storytelling. In the context of #MeToo as a storytelling practice, narrative activism drives narrative justice. A broad public became engaged in narrative justice through two reorientations to the common sense of sexual violence: learning to hear #MeToo stories as credible and, from that baseline, engaging with survivors as silence breakers, truth-tellers, and justice-seekers. By focusing on collective witness as a compact among survivors and a method for accessing narrative justice, we move beyond any single abuser to a focus on global movements to end sexual violence, including labor activism focused on workplace sexual harassment.

The formation of a collective witness to sexual violence enabled #MeToo to succeed by two key measures where previous awareness-raising campaigns and legal reforms faltered. First, social media lowered the bar to participation. People could share "me too" without naming names, specifying anything about abuse, or taking part in an official complaint. This open invitation enabled millions to self-identify.[18] Second, and surprisingly, this sharing led to a surge in accountability as some men's previous impunity evaporated. When first-person accounts appearing on social media, and in interviews, essays, and visual media like comics spurred the #MeToo effect, testimony broke out of its containment in courts and institutional processes notorious for minimizing it. Narrative activism offered an alternative jurisdiction to courts and shifted the primary stance toward survivor testimony from judgment to solidarity.[19]

The extralegal quality of #MeToo exposed anew the strictures placed on survivors and the challenges they face in accessing a right to be heard. For example, a survivor's story must be repeated without variance if she is to be credible in court, and her own words can be used against her, even if her memory sharpens over time. Philosopher Susan Brison writes in her memoir *Aftermath* about how her report of rape was shaped by police who interviewed her in the hospital after an assailant left her for dead. Brison had been walking when she was attacked by a stranger. Rather than allow that this is something a woman may do without qualification, police supply a justification—*comme je suis sportive* (because I am athletic)—as if walking while female required a defense.[20] Once her testimony is taken, it becomes the standard against which her credibility will be measured. Trials may drag on for years, and during this time survivors are required to seal themselves inside their initial traumatic narrative and speak from it on the court's timetable. Tanya Serisier argues that survivors are prevented from asserting "a selfhood that exceeded the experience of victimization" when their narratives are judged according to how well they conform to dominant meanings about abuse in order to gain credibility. Further, Serisier shows that this narrative strategy restricts survivors to the role of "injured victims" rather than "political claimants."[21]

Many survivors whose initial statements about abuse are taken close to the time of an assault describe how the timeliness of their testimony is used against them. These statements have evidentiary significance, in part, because details are fresh. But the survivor is traumatized and often does not understand how their initial accounts will become the standard by which their own truthfulness is measured. Dylan Farrow, who was interviewed as a seven-year-old child about alleged sexual abuse by her father Woody Allen, was consistently found to be a credible witness. Her language describing the abuse was age appropriate, which weakened Allen's contention that she was coached by her mother Mia Farrow, and she used the same language over the course of many interviews. In an interview in the HBO docuseries *Allen v. Farrow*, Dylan Farrow commented on how the continual probing of her story made her language seem like the problem rather than the abuse she described: "The more I was asked the same question over and over, the more I started to wonder, what do they want from me? And feeling like the more I said the same thing, that it was the wrong answer. That I was being treated like I was lying. If I change a word here, they say I'm being inconsistent. If I use exactly the same words that I used every other time, I was coached."[22]

From the moment a victim of sexual assault, intimate partner violence, or rape begins to tell her story to police, if she goes to the police, she will be asked questions designed to test whether she is credible, whether her words carry enough weight to support bringing a charge. Whether she is injured and how badly will count for less than she might imagine. If she has an advocate present, she may be advised about the processes she will encounter and shielded from some hostility and insult. If her case advances to court, which is rare, her testimony will be shaped by another set of rules that offer a range of advantages to the accused. In this context, anyone feels licensed to dismiss or demean victims, including people to whom they turn as they try to navigate formal reporting processes. Narrative justice for survivors requires a new framework and agenda, one that rejects statutes of limitations and the diminished status of victims (all of whom as women, children, queer, nonbinary, and trans people, Indigenous, Black, and people of color are seen as less credible in court than cisgender white men).

Survivors often find that telling their stories—in their own words, to empathetic listeners, in contexts of credibility—can enable healing. As Susan Brison observes, a person who has suffered rape has been stripped of autonomy, a key feature of selfhood. Regaining autonomy after sexual violence depends on the help of other people.[23] They must listen to survivors narrate traumatic memory and, in listening, enable survivors to move beyond the judgment that they are not credible because they are traumatized. Life writing offers survivors a narrative form that exceeds the confines of criminal-legal systems in which they are doubted. It allows them to reenter time, to reflect on and represent trauma, and to offer new terms for understanding that produce autonomy in relation to others. In life writing, survivors can show how testimonial quieting and smothering overlap, how they are leveraged against them in different ways over time, as Lacy Crawford did in her memoir *Notes on a Silencing* (2020).[24] As an adult, Crawford returns to the memory and story of her rape at boarding school after she learns, much later, how the boys who assaulted her were protected by the full power of an elite school.

In October 1990 Crawford, then a fifteen-year-old junior at St. Paul's in New Hampshire, was lured to the room of a student, an eighteen-year-old senior whom she knew because she had helped his friends in math class. When he telephoned, he was crying, saying something about his mother, and that he urgently needed Crawford's help. She was flattered and wanted to help, so she crossed campus to his dorm and crawled through the window. She discovered he was not alone. There were two boys, both naked, and they held her down and raped her. Crawford begins the narrative in the third person: "Four hands on her, she said, 'Just don't have sex with me.' Instead, they took turns laying their hips across her face. Their cocks penetrated her throat past her pharynx and poked the soft back of her esophagus, so she had to concentrate to breathe" (5). Before Crawford is able to name the experience for her-self, the boys talk immediately. They brag about having a "threesome." Crawford counters: it was rape; "cruelty exacted in domination and shame" (8). The assault occurred a year before Anita Hill's televised tes-timony at which Clarence Thomas and his defenders publicly demon-strated how slander is used to taint a witness so that nothing she says, including the truth, will be heard. St. Paul's managed some of their silencing behind the scenes, but they did not hesitate, at the highest lev-els of responsibility, to blame the victim.[25]

As an adult delving into her case, Crawford confronts the patchwork of state laws about rape. In New Hampshire law in the 1990s, the men committed felonious sexual assault (because she was under sixteen) and aggravated felonious sexual assault (because she was restrained). These laws ought to have been well known to adults at St. Paul's. As a board-ing school, they acted in loco parentis for minors and also had a duty to turn over evidence to police. Instead, the school administration closed ranks against Crawford. She contracted herpes as a result of the rape, a case so severe that she was sent from the infirmary to a doctor in town, chosen by St. Paul's, who did not forward the medical information to her family, pediatrician, or local police. None of the medical personnel associated with St. Paul's told Crawford her diagnosis. In 1991 a pedia-trician diagnosed her when she was at home, and, as a mandated reporter, informed the police that Crawford was the victim of sexual assault. Any of the authorities at St. Paul's or the doctor they sent Crawford to could and should have contacted police. Instead, their cover-up was so success-ful that Crawford discovered it only when she was approached in 2017 by police investigating her rape in connection with other sexual assaults at St. Paul's.

The rhetorical and metaphorical elements that characterize Craw-ford's memoir as narrative activism involve voice. She observes that not all talk about the rape is banned. The boys are free to spread gossip throughout the school, and both teachers and members of the adminis-tration slander her. Only she is silenced. Their speech attempts to dis-place and supplant hers in a perfect example of testimonial smothering. Crawford places silence and voice within the domain of shame and its refusal. She draws on Maggie Nelson's memoir *The Argonauts* to assert, as Megan Twohey and Jodi Kantor did, that speech is a solvent for shame: "I told you I wanted to live in a world in which the antidote to shame is not honor, but honesty." Crawford aims to resettle shame where it belongs. She refuses to keep the school's secrets, protect the boys' reputations (she names them and the responsible male leaders in the school), or remain silent. Crawford asserts that when St. Paul's deprived her of speech and wrote her story themselves, they engaged in testimonial quieting. *Notes on a Silencing* traces how the school protected itself by shielding the boys and blaming her for the assault. The school contends that because Crawford broke a rule when she went to the boy's room, she was as responsible as they were. The headmaster, Bill Matthews, tells Crawford's father, "She's not a good girl, Jim. You don't want to go there, Jim" (378). The priest at St. Paul's delivers the same message to her mother: "Oh, no, this is on Lacy. This is really Lacy's doing" (379). Crawford's memoir documents silencing as a comprehensive strategy that compounds sexual violence with epistemic violence, extending the locations of harm beyond the school and purposefully lengthening the duration of trauma by interfering with the police investigation. The initial injury is the rape, compounded in the immediate aftermath and over decades by an epistemic injury to her status as a knower and a teller.

Memoirists who narrate traumatic experiences from their youth often become detectives, sifting through documents to find the truth. Crawford is assisted in discovering the extent of her silencing by police, but as the investigation homes in on St. Paul's culpability, it is mysteriously curtailed. The detectives, furious and frustrated, are barred from telling Crawford why they were called off, how close they got, and who shut down the investigation. They are reassigned, and Crawford confronts the inadequacy of evidence to force accountability: "Fool girl, I had trusted that documents and perpetrator admissions and the fullness of time would suffice" (376). Crawford concludes her book with an accounting. She has settled the debt with the rapists, told their names, what they did, and that they even admitted it when confronted as adults.

But St. Paul's refuses responsibility: "First, they refused to believe me. Then they shamed me. Then they silenced me. On balance, if this is a girl's trajectory from dignity to disappearance, I say it is better to be a slut than to be silent." Speaking out is what makes you a slut at St. Paul's. Crawford critiques the tropes of silence to argue that "the slur *slut* carries within it Trojan-horse style, silence as its true intent. That the opposite of *slut* is not virtue but voice" (382).

The #MeToo effect enabled memoirs like Crawford's to further narrative activism, by fusing them together as a collective form of witnessing rather than isolated accounts. Memoir becomes a vehicle for retelling traumatic memory and establishing the authority of the self as eyewitness and narrator. A memoirist can describe her younger self's experience of sexual abuse in the language she gained access to only as an adult, a change over time Crawford highlights. Storytellers can control narrative form in ways witnesses in court cannot. Extralegal genres offer an opportunity to narrate the experience in ways that are not retraumatizing. In contrast, when survivors testify in court, or to audiences that are hostile, or before they have received adequate support, you can hear them struggle against shame and silence. They appear to return to the trauma in retelling it, struggling through the gates of dissociation and fear sealed in their bodies and unlocked through their words. When Jeffrey Epstein's accusers describe the abuse, for example, they use language they might have at fourteen or fifteen.[26] They do not risk language their younger selves would not have known because it might indict them as older or more experienced than they were. These stories are sealed away, as if not telling them or telling them to only a few trusted interlocutors can enable the victim to survive when the cost of telling is so high. When the witness fears that she will not be deemed credible, when her testimony alone proves inadequate, then silence is less a refuge than a judgment about her relative worth. #MeToo offers an opportunity to recalibrate norms around sexual violence by uncoupling the unheard testimony of survivors from the disclaimers that reinforce male entitlement. Together, they cocreate doubt and credibility. Disentangled, they enable survivors to be heard.

## READING LIKE A SURVIVOR:
## FROM *ANTIGONE* TO #METOO

The question before us now is: How do we read these stories? I am arguing that we recognize the demand they urge on us as testimony: they speak from the position of the "I" who has experience and authority. Although this "I" has spoken many times—in private and in court, in doctors' and teachers' offices, in published writing and in whisper networks, in bodily evidence of bruises and in depressive withdrawal—it has not been heard. At least not in a way that adequately provides a witness who will hold the pieces together as they emerge from trauma, as the #MeToo effect does with sexual violence. In literary criticism, scholars have offered an alternative to the "hermeneutics of suspicion" that encourages a skeptical stance toward a text and posited in its place practices better attuned to trauma texts and posttraumatic readers.[27] Following Donald Winnicott's notion of the "good enough mother," I have described the adequate witness as one who will hold the survivor's testimony and listen without deforming it through the imposition of terms that are not the survivor's. We owe survivors something better than suspicion. We owe them a hearing. To that end, I offer survivor reading as a critical practice drawing on feminist theory, literary criticism, and care to fashion that "something better." Survivor reading acknowledges that people and stories come to us in pieces and that our attention is necessary to restore them. While listening more and better might seem like modest goals, consider how much better suited such stances are to the certainty that "we" already know that women who accuse men of sexual violence are not credible. Survivor reading offers the possibility of hearing something true without assuming the form that truth will take or where it will lead.

From classical references to sexual violence in Ovid, Greek tragedy, and Shakespeare to contemporary memoirs, the trauma of suffering or witnessing sexual violence in literary narratives raises questions about obligation and justice. Sexual violence, a demonstrable theme from Ovid forward, belongs to a larger representational project about who can speak and be heard animating a range of literary, testimonial, and popular forms. Often tugging at the edges of awareness in the form of minor characters, or those who have been relegated to that status, lies the drama of how to attend to what is right in front of us, even when it mirrors our experience, when we are told it means something else. We need a form of reading that moves with testimony across multiple media, texts, and contexts. A form of reading as mobile as testimony itself so that we may become the witness such testimony seeks. Survivor testimony demands the unlearning of the ready-made script for denying women's credibility. Audre Lorde's insight "that the master's tools will never dismantle the master's house" reminds us that to call for the replacement of doubt with "believe all women" mistakes doubt as the origin of sexual violence instead of a practice through which patriarchy is perpetuated. The subordination and silencing of women is as old an issue as the struggle to maintain male supremacy, and the theme of men hurting women regularly appears in literature from antiquity on. And yet much in the literature by and about women comes to us in pieces. From the fragments of Sappho's poetry to the representations of sexual violence in Ovid, something is happening to women that leaves blanks in the record, blanks like partial archives and lost records, but also those made over time by the sedimented certainties of reception.

Models of resistance to patriarchy represented by groupings of female characters, sometimes as friends and sometimes as sisters, also stalk the literary imagination. A tradition of female figures in sororal pairings is tied together by themes of testimonial unreliability and violence. High school students in English class are introduced to the concept of the unreliable narrator through the male narrators of *Catcher in the Rye* and *The Great Gatsby*, but a focus on the female characters shows how their unreliability is linked to their not being heard rather than to their evasive or partial speech. This notion is important to survivor reading because it places responsibilities for attention on the reader. In *The Great Gatsby*, Daisy Buchanan, cousin of Nick Carraway and former-and-soon-to-be-current lover of Jay Gatsby, is introduced along with friend and somewhat shady golfer Jordan Baker, in a scene in which everything is lifted as if by whispers. Breezes waft, curtains billow, dresses float: "The only completely stationary object in the room was an enormous couch on which two young women were buoyed up as though upon an anchored balloon. They were both in white and their dresses were rippling and uttering as if they had just been blown back in after a short flight around the house" (10). The ambient airiness suggests the breath-form of conspiracy as Daisy and Jordan practically hover in the scene of their introduction. What are they talking about? Daisy has more secrets than she can share, and they are not all about Gatsby. At the moment Nick greets Daisy, she is trying to tell anyone that Tom hurts her. She brandishes an injured finger as evidence of her husband's violence and no one bothers to deny it (15). Although Daisy is "somebody telling somebody else on some occasion and for some purpose(s) that something happened" (Phelan), they refuse to hear it in a way that would compel anyone to respond.

Whether female friendship billows forth from subplot or commands narratorial attention, as in the fiction of Toni Morrison, it generates a testimonial space for readers to bear witness to the complexity of female agency in the couplings of lovers, sisters, and friends. In Morrison's *Sula*, girlhood friends Nel and Sula share a terrible secret. Their lives diverge and reconverge over the decades as the secret incubates within their bond. They hold the narrative together. So, too, Elena Ferrante's Neapolitan quartet, focused on the passionate, rivalrous, and life-defining friendship between Elena and Lila, gives full attention through the narrative voice of Elena to the primacy of female friendship. The novels demonstrate how literature can focus on the complexities of female pairing and create a form of attentiveness to them. Yet throughout literature, such attention has been intermittent. Often unrecognized as a model of dissent or resistance, or described through its failure, sisterhood represents an incomplete model of political subjectivity. How can characters with a minimal toehold on sovereignty, after all, leverage their power to overthrow injustice? And how can survivor reading offer an adequate witness to their struggle? I turn to a classic play, *Antigone*, to examine how sisterhood offers a model of survivorship attuned to real-world precarity.

Consider the form this takes in *Antigone*, a play written by Sophocles in the fifth century BCE and continuously revived for its relevance to crises of authoritarianism. Confronted with the implication that his edict against burying one brother slain in battle and not the other is unjust, the new king, Creon, worries that changing his mind about punishing Antigone for breaking his law will cause them to change genders. What he stands to lose is what she would gain. "Assuredly now," he says, "I indeed am not a man, but she is a man, if this victory shall accrue to her without hurt" (T. W. C. Edwards translation). Anne Carson, in her contemporary and flexible translation entitled *Antigonick*, puts it this way: "You think you are iron / but I am the man here / I can bend you."[28] Creon's panic at the prospect is barely contained by the armor he has donned to harden his masculine authority. The play asks how much he is willing to hurt Antigone in order not to switch genders with her.

There is a scholarly tradition that sidesteps a focus on Creon's fear of becoming unfixed from masculine gender by noticing how similar Creon and Antigone are. As characters who similarly refuse to bend or yield, they are said to mirror each other, and yet Virginia Woolf's observation about how women are made to mirror men clarifies that what Creon and Antigone are afraid of losing is not the same. In *A Room of One's Own*, Woolf observes that women "have served all these centuries as looking glasses possessing the magic and delicious power of reflecting the figure of man at twice its natural size."[29] A scale seems a more apt metaphor for the kind of comparison *Antigone* is making. Creon worries that if Antigone will not be the (lesser) woman to his (greater) manliness, the scales will tip. For the scales to balance for Creon, he must be worth more than Antigone. Following this inexorable accounting, she must be worth less. To ensure that this remains so, he sends her to her death.

*Antigone* is a legalistic play from beginning to end. When Eteocles refuses to turn over power to his brother Polyneices as their prior agreement requires, Polyneices's assault on Thebes is a military response to the legal problem of succession. When Creon announces that Polyneices must be left unburied, his edict is backed by threat of capital punishment, the law's lethal instrument. The play's trial and trial-like confrontations propel the action down fatal paths. In his role of regent, the legalistic elements gather within the character of Creon, compelling those around him to engage him on these terms. After she has buried

Polyneices, Antigone is brought before Creon. Although she readily admits her responsibility, Creon convenes a trial, demands that she confess, and hastens to impose punishment. Foucault sees the play as a "perfectly clear judicial paradigm organized around the question of how to discover the guilty party whose crime has been established but whose identity remains unknown."[30] Yet this describes just one version of the play: the trial over which Creon presides. In a parallel play, also unfolding within the judicial paradigm, Antigone elaborates an alternative: an extrajudicial paradigm within which her testimony overleaps the confines of the trial to reach the Chorus.

Although Creon hastens to convict the guilty party as soon as Antigone's identity is confirmed, the play pauses precisely at this point to introduce a competing extrajudicial paradigm in the form of Antigone's explanation. That Creon does not want to hear her reveals the limits of testimonial justice in his mode. She does not wish to argue the facts, but to persuade the Chorus and the audience that they are listening to a truth-telling *parrhesiaste*, one who risks all to confront power, and not a criminal. In the alternative jurisdiction created by her speech, Creon represents a danger to the city. The proof will come as Creon in rapid succession becomes responsible for the deaths of his son Haemon, by suicide after a dispute with his father, his wife Eurydice, another suicide after she learns of her son's death, and Antigone, the third suicide, as she accelerates the fate to which she is sentenced. Antigone was responsible for performing forbidden funerary rites, but Creon's actions precipitate the need for three more burials. His mode is annihilation and hers is avowal, but in its shifting of the juridical and extrajuridical frames another position emerges in the figure of Ismene, the one who survives.

In the scholarly and performance history of *Antigone*, Ismene refuses Antigone's invitation to join her in offering funerary rites to their disgraced brother and argues that, as women, they will be destroyed if they disobey Creon. Read as either a simp who accepts her subordinate status within the household and the state or a nonentity, she has been relegated to the status of an afterthought. Yet in a new reading of the play, Bonnie Honig argues that for millennia an obvious interpretation has been hiding in plain sight: Ismene and Antigone worked toward the same end, and committed the same offense.[31] When Creon demands to know who buried Polyneices, Ismene answers, "I did it." Honig says we should believe her and move the sisters' conspiracy to the center of our reading of the play's stance on politics, resistance, and justice. We should note, moreover, the consequences of mishearing Ismene's declaration as a lie. That women speaking alone or together might amplify their message requires conditions for them to be heard.

Ismene, as a political strategist without resources to command, in other words, a survivor, analyzes the sisters' plight: "as women" they are outmatched. Together, they are likely to be seen as interchangeable, hence equally at risk. Creon's disregard for their separateness impels him to call for the death of both sisters until the Chorus reminds him that only Antigone is charged with burying her brother. Alone, they cannot conspire and strategize for their survival. However, if the play is staged with Antigone and Ismene together, in proximity for communication, we can imagine they are on the verge of speaking what the hearing otherwise has no ear for. Such an opportunity is lost when Antigone and Creon square off like gladiators and Ismene drifts out of view. More nuanced than a focus on either Antigone's defiance or Ismene's surrender, looking at the sisters together reveals their relationship as a resource for survival. Literature abounds with women who are trying to speak or threatening to speak, whose speech must be silenced or distorted at any cost and is unhearable until it is heard by another woman, often a sister like Ismene.[32]

One more example shows us how difficult it is for women alone to construct the conditions of hearing. Consider, in contrast, the representation of active collaboration in the story of Philomela, the girl whose rapist cuts out her tongue to prevent her from naming the man who harmed her, whose story traces a bloody path from Ovid through Shakespeare to the contemporary essay. Philomela, who is raped by her sister Procne's husband Tereus, weaves a tapestry to attest to the crime and lay blame. Together, Philomela and Procne undertake revenge on Tereus. Procne kills Itys, her and Tereus's son, boils, and serves him as a meal to Tereus. After Tereus has eaten, the sisters show him Itys's head so he, too, can read the wordless evidence of prior violence.

From weaving to cooking, Ovid maintains the testimonial and retributive acts as domestic and feminine. Tereus takes an axe and pursues the sisters. When it appears that he will catch them, the sisters appeal to the gods, who transform them into birds: Procne becomes a swallow, Philomela a nightingale, and Tereus a hoopoe. Their shared metamorphosis obscures that they are caught up in a frenzy of vengeance because of Tereus's original act of violence.

Shakespeare updates the myth of Philomela through the figure of Lavinia in *Titus Andronicus*, a bloody account of revenge and, as in *Antigone*, survival for those cast out of power by a change in rule. Lavinia is introduced with one other woman onstage, Tamora the captive queen, as part of an exchange of the spoils of war. Lavinia is handed over—with her agreement—to Bassianus, but the deal is upended when she is "seized" by Saturninus. Now both women are captives. The surprises continue as Tamora is offered marriage to Saturninus and the option to switch her status from Queen of the Goths to Empress of Rome. In an assertion of the right to name, Lavinia's capture is deemed lawful, and her return to her betrothed would be a rape. Such semantic wrangling will give way to her actual rape by Tamora's sons, Demetrius and Chiron. After they rape her, they cut her hands off and her tongue out. They taunt her, too, telling her to go home and wash her hands. They say they'd kill themselves if they were her, but too bad, she can't tie a noose. They replace her means of speech with their mockery; put themselves in her place to annihilate her.

Overall, *Titus* has been infrequently produced, but it is more accurate to say it has had periods of revived interest followed by lengthy production droughts. The elements are gruesome: the rape and mutilation of Lavinia, the revenge scheme to murder her rapists and serve them up as dinner to their mother, and the execution of Lavinia by her father when his revenge is complete. When theater companies return to *Titus*, what do they want audiences to see in this tragedy? In Peter Brooks's production starring Laurence Olivier as Titus and Vivien Leigh as Lavinia, the famous married couple brought star power to the stage. Brooks created an aural atmosphere to soothe and manage the horror unfolding onstage. One reviewer balked at Brooks's transformation of *Titus* into a "romantic play," pointedly asking:

> Who could forget the return of the ravishers with Lavinia? They bring her through the leafy arch that was the central pillar and leave her standing there, right arm outstretched and head drooping away from it, left arm crooked with the wrist at her mouth. Her hair falls in disorder over face and shoulders, and from wrist-and-mouth trail scarlet streamers, symbols of her mutilation. The two assassins retreat from her, step by step, looking back at her, on either side of the stage. Their taunts fall softly, lingeringly, as if they themselves were in a daze at the horror of their deed; and the air tingles and reverberates with the slow plucking of harp-strings.[33]

Perhaps with some deference to Vivien Leigh, the "mutilation was not insisted upon."[34]

Lavinia is led away to an ominous soundtrack and returned to her father's house. What strikes me is the construction of her rapists as boys who seem not to know what they have done: "as if they themselves were in a daze at the horror of their deed." They detach from responsibility, look on the evidence of their crime—Lavinia—and back away. As if in leaving her, they could leave behind their involvement. Her body has absorbed their violence and she alone bears it. These fictional representations map onto real life. In 2012 Daisy Coleman was raped by a classmate when she was fourteen years old and dumped on her front lawn in freezing weather. In the summer of the same year, high school football players in Steubenville, Ohio, loaded an unconscious sixteen year old into their car, where they filmed themselves raping her as they transported her from party to party.[35] The boys shared the crime on social media and in text messages with classmates. The community rallied to defend the boys, young and drunk, but also young and promising. Both victims were smeared in the press. All of which seems to repeat the stage directions for *Titus*: "Their taunts fall softly, lingeringly, as if they themselves were in a daze at the horror of their deed;

and the air tingles and reverberates with the slow plucking of harp-strings."

Three issues connect Lavinia and the fictional women I have been discussing within the new context for #MeToo I am tracing. First, she appears in relation to another woman, Tamora, as do the sisters Antigone and Ismene and Philomela and Procne, but she is set against her, too, in ways that expose her to extreme harm (rape for Philomela and a death sentence for Antigone). Second, what she has to say cannot be heard. Her literal speech is stopped, and her means for communicating delayed. Third, as she struggles to communicate, her crisis to speak stages a crisis of interpretation. Why did no one take seriously Ismene's claim? Philomela makes art of her claim, weaving the scene of her rape and the identity of her rapist into a tapestry she shows her sister. Everyone tries to interpret Lavinia, but they can't figure it out. Finally, she gets hold of young Lucius's copy of Ovid's *Metamorphosis* and flips to the story of Philomela. Marcus Andronicus offers her his staff, and Lavinia, in the stage directions, *"takes the staff in her mouth, and guides it with her stumps, and writes* the names of Chiron and Demetrius in the dust."

Why is it so hard to give women a hearing? Why do the consequences of this refusal result in the unleashing of such violence? Certainly those who assert agency by acting or speaking out run a risk, but women are exposed to an excess of violence in the absence of speech, too. Publics are conditioned to think of women and girls as subagentic, as lacking credibility even when they tell the truth. This mostly succeeds by isolating and silencing them. Less accident than ubiquitous cultural training, the construction of girls and women as outside the body politic proffers a theory of personhood and unequal justice specific to patriarchy: the refusal to hear women. Women transform this cultural gag order by breaking a prohibition on speaking to one another.

*Antigone* is often revived in periods of crisis when individuals appeal to moral law rather than the state. In South African playwright Athol Fugard's *Robben Island*, African National Congress members imprisoned for defying the apartheid regime stage *Antigone* for the guards as a way to confront them under the permissible cover of performing a play.

More recently, *Antigone in Ferguson* adapts the play to comment on the killing of Michael Brown in August 2014 and the ensuing uprising that was violently suppressed by a militarized police force. This adaptation uses the play to address issues about racism, police violence, misogyny, and community. It begins with a staged reading by four actors who are backed by a contemporary gospel choir that acts as the Chorus. *Antigone in Ferguson* speaks powerfully about the resonance between the classic tragedy and the events in Ferguson. After Michael Brown was killed, police left his body to lie in the street for hours in the August heat. People came to witness, pray, sing, read poems, and grieve. By evening, they were confronted by police. The desecration of the body, Brown's and Polyneices's; the violence of state power, wielded by the police and Creon; and the violation of natural law, decried by Antigone, Ismene, and ultimately the Chorus and the Black community in Ferguson, powerfully tie the past to the present. The staged reading is followed by a town hall–style discussion about racial justice, community care, and the power of art to host discussions fueled by frustration, fury, trauma, and hope.

The singular girl hero Antigone, as resonant as she is as a testimonial agent, is not the only figure in the #MeToo story. The sisters who speak and act together and the Chorus who is slow to defend Antigone flesh out the scene of witness. The Chorus represents the failure of bystanders to become participants in a timely way. Their belated support accelerates Antigone's tragic end. The Chorus is late to urge a change of heart and action for Creon. In Anne Carson's *Antigonick*, the Chorus aligns Creon with timeliness. They say he arrives in the "nick of time" to confront Antigone, who has been caught and handed over for trial. Creon's arrival onstage puts their own actions—to intervene, to speak out, to change the headlong rush to judgment—on hold. Carson presents the Chorus as a representative of the law. The Chorus asks: "How is a Greek chorus like a lawyer / they're both in the business of searching for a precedent / finding an analogy / locating a prior example / so as to be able to say / this terrible thing we're witnessing now is / not unique / you know it happened before / or something much like it / we're not at a loss how to think about this / we're not without guidance / there is a pattern / we can find an historically parallel case / and file it away under / ANTIGONE."

They try to read the present crisis as the repetition of a prior pattern in order to contain it, a stance that prevents them from responding to a crisis in the present. The play ends with a warning. Although it is directed at Creon and the audience, it is equally self-admonishing: "last word / *wisdom*: better get some / even too late."[36]

As if taking up the position advocated by these words, survivors emerged and formed a new and substantive body of shared experience through the #MeToo effect, drawing power and authority from assembling together. When they spoke of their own experience, they were heard in the context of others, as knowledge about sexual violence added up. There were patterns and themes to abuse: who does it, where, and how they evade responsibility for it; who is protected or sacrificed; who is silenced or covered up for; how damage carries over generationally; and who benefits when survival is enabled or thwarted by institutions. When a broad public adopted "the #MeToo era" as common reference, it indicated both a temporal and an epistemic shift and identified "now" as the time to listen and act.

The classical past of myth and literature, read in this way, enables an engagement with sexual trauma that reopens a perspective on how survivors bear witness in earlier literature. It also shows how a collective witness can emerge, guided by #MeToo, to read with empathy and patience for what has not been adequately heard. Such a reading practice means that we listen to victims and also to what victims hear in the voices of sexual harassers like Trump, Weinstein, and their enablers. It means we snap out of the daze that permits rapists to dump the bodies of victims and leave us staring at the women while the rapists simply walk away, turning back into sons, husbands, and fathers whom we love and learn how to hold them accountable. It also means returning to the texts of Ovid, Sophocles, and Shakespeare to see how survivors are abandoned to violence through habits of reading. There are more rapes and attempted rapes in Ovid's *Metamorphoses* than you remember. There is Philomela's, of course. Hades rapes Persephone after he has abducted and dragged her to the underworld. Apollo tries to rape Daphne. Zeus rapes Leda. He also rapes Io, whom he turns into a cow. Emily Ogden reminds us that although the myth of Narcissus does not mention it, "just before the story starts, he had been raped by one of the gods. Such things are not uncommon, after all."[37] The myths are about many things, but they consistently show that rape changes people. The transformations—laurel tree Daphne, bovine Io, nightingale Philomela—suggest that sexual violence is a kind of blighted begetting. None can speak "after," but they are eloquent figures we must learn to read. Yet, Ovidian rapists have leeway in their shape-shifting. They turn back into themselves. The victims, however, are changed forever. Even Persephone, whose mother Demeter barters her probation, must return annually to the rapist. Although cast at the limits of language through extreme acts of silencing, survivors embody what has been done to them and speak of it in the language they can access.

A recent biographer proved to be such a witness to Emma Gatewood, who is famous for her hiking feats.[38] Gatewood is the first woman to through-hike the Appalachian Trail, which she did twice, the first time at age sixty-seven. She section-hiked it a third time, and she also pioneered ultralight hiking. When asked what motivated her, her routine answer was: "I thought it would be a nice lark." Biographer Ben Montgomery does not accept Gatewood's answer as an example of modesty or homespun quirkiness. Instead, he reads in it an assertion of agency and privacy from a woman who might well have been drawn to the freedom of hiking after suffering twenty years of physical and sexual abuse by her husband. As Montgomery documents, Gatewood said she was raped three to four times a day for twenty years, including throughout eleven pregnancies. Most commentators focus on the heroism of Gatewood's hiking, but few have mentioned the sexual violence her husband inflicted. Narratives of heroism often include overcoming and resilience, physical courage, resolve, and sacrifice, all of which are in ample supply in Gatewood's story, but how does marital rape fit into this script? For the admiring throngs who learned about Gatewood contemporaneously, her comment that it would be "a lark" placed her in the rhetorical company of explorers noted for similarly terse public comments about complex motives, a version of Sir Edmund Hillary's "it was there." How do we read when "it" is trauma?

Gatewood's biography raises the question of how to engage with sexual violence in the archive of history. How, that is, to overcome the bias that we lack evidence rather than the will to confront it. Demonstrably, when victims speak out about sexual violence, their language is often coded as unreliable, unheard, and unactionable. It was not hard for Gatewood's biographer to learn about her violent husband, but an adequate legal and social apparatus for contending with survivor speech was lacking. Sometimes, for survivor testimony to break through, we must rewind history and restore a connection between survivor speech like Gatewood's and trusted listeners. The archive is riddled with gaps, purposefully created by nondisclosure agreements and statutes of limitations to leave blanks where accusation and accountability might otherwise lodge. The limitations are intertwined with victim blaming. Survivors are tasked with making their testimony hearable. Think, instead, of listening to a woman and hearing her as potentially reliable and persuasive, of mutually tasking listeners and hearers with bearing witness. Whether readers agree that gender, race, and violence are stuck together in such a way that men (notably white men) can rely on impunity and women cannot access credibility depends on how aware they are of the persistence of these constellated meanings.

The notion of the unreliable narrator has migrated from rhetoric and literary studies into the public domain, where it attaches readily to victims of sexual assault. Readers carry assumptions about unreliability from literary texts and nonfiction into real life. Received meanings about literature influence how they will interpret the representation of violence. When listeners routinely refuse to grant tellers a baseline of reliability about the truth of their testimony about sexual violence, they make it hard for any survivor to gain a hearing. Yet Tarana Burke's emphasis on empathy and identification is right at home in a discussion of literature because those impulses lead readers to recognize themselves in new characters and settings. They turn us down new paths, including away from what is familiar. Readers care about characters, derive consolation from literary language, and enter complex ethical terrain where questions about what we owe one another are refracted through multiple points of view.[39] Readers process the unsettling emotions stirred by representations of sexual violence that reverberate long after the time of reading. Burke points toward a model of survivor reading based in shared knowledge about trauma, who can be believed, what needs to happen "after," as well as "next." It is a model of mutual care that does not dissolve specificity—experience differs, survivors differ—but, as with the ways that we read literary texts, asserts that knowledge and care can be connected. Rather than disavowal or aversion, hearers (in philosophy), readers (in literature), and publics (in political theory) can apply survivor knowledge to cases of sexual violence. They can see survivors as credible rather than unreliable by default. They can attend to the edges of the frame, to who is pushed out, rendered unhearable. And from this reorientation, they can develop a new apparatus of witnessing.

# 7

## #METOO STORYTELLING

*Language is the first site of loss and our first
defense against it.*

—PAISLEY REKDAL, "NIGHTINGALE: A GLOSS"

*Stories suture up our parts against the
primordial awareness that.
we are in pieces.*

—EMILY OGDEN, "HOW TO HOLD IT TOGETHER"

#MeToo has produced a wave of storytelling about sexual violence in multiple genres. Often through direct reference within a book, for example, or highlighted in publicity materials, the focus on survivor testimony, credibility, and accountability places a broad range of texts and their audiences within the #MeToo paradigm. Reviews frequently announce that certain films belong to the #MeToo era. Docuseries including *Athlete A* about the abuse of gymnasts by Dr. Larry Nassar, *Jeffrey Epstein: Filthy Rich*, *Surviving R. Kelly*, and *Allen v. Farrow* testify to the significance of #MeToo as event and framework. When exploitative representations of sexual violence appear in film now, the trope is likely to draw derision for its laziness as well as its contribution to rape culture.[1] Instead of remaining separated from one another by genre, memoirs like Michelle Bowdler's *Is Rape A Crime?*, Alexander Chee's *How to Write an Autobiographical Novel*, Crawford's *Notes on a Silencing*, Roxane Gay's *Hunger*, and Chanel Miller's *Know My Name* are seen as connected to the HBO series *I May Destroy You*, the Netflix adaptation of the book about Marie Adler, *Unbelievable*, the poetry collection *Nightingale*, by Paisley Rekdal, and essay anthologies *Indelible in the Hippocampus* and *Not That Bad* as examples of #MeToo storytelling across genres.[2] By carrying the representation of survivors across the borders of separate genres and media and by reaching a public increasingly likely to understand the #MeToo reference, the #MeToo effect continues to collectivize survivor credibility. Authors write about experiences of sexual violence, filmmakers focus on survivors as compelling central figures, documentarians return to cases in which victims were smeared to make the case anew, publishers and producers in all media back these projects, and audiences embrace them. This does not happen universally or automatically, of course, but it is more likely following #MeToo that it might.

Survivors figure centrally in these works. Through a focus on them, myths about rape are replaced by new knowledge about consent, agency, and obligation. I turn to how two memoirs, both of which enjoyed critical and popular success, raised the question of how to tell a rape story from a survivor's perspective decades before #MeToo: Maya Angelou's *I Know Why the Caged Bird Sings* and Maxine Hong Kingston's *The Woman Warrior*.[3] Maya Angelou was already a well-known performer and activist when *I Know Why the Caged Bird Sings* was published in 1969. Her narrative is framed by two events: at age three, Angelou and her brother Bailey are sent to live with their grandmother (Momma) and Uncle Willie in Stamps, Arkansas, and at age sixteen, Angelou becomes a mother. Momma and Uncle Willie are the relatively prosperous owners of the general store in Stamps. Referred to locally with a capital "S," the Store stocked "food staples, a good variety of colored thread, mash for hogs, corn for chickens, coal oil for lamps, light bulbs for the wealthy, shoestrings, balloons, and flower seeds. Anything not visible had only to be ordered" (5). The phrase "anything not visible" lingers over the opening chapters. Angelou's loving descriptions of the peace and orderliness of the Store, the satisfaction of chores like feeding animals and tending vegetable gardens, and the academic success of the intelligent siblings recall Harriet Jacobs's evocation of girlhood, the love between her parents, the prosperity of her free grandmother, the joys of family and place for Black folks asserted against the horror of slavery. "Anything not visible" speaks to the protection of Black children from whom the worst of racism is hidden as long and as well as possible by loving families and community. But the menace breaks through because it is everywhere present. In a chilling example, white neighbors warn the family that the Klan intends to lynch Black men that night and to keep Uncle Willie "hidden." He will literally become part of the Store's "not visible" contents as he is loaded into a vegetable bin while they keep a tense vigil.

The visible and hidden are related to sin and virtue in Angelou's upbringing. She is given strict lessons in female piety filled with euphemism and shame about her body and the parts to keep hidden. In a scene she describes as "the most painful and confusing experience I had ever had with my grandmother" (14), "powhitetrash" teenage girls taunt Momma in an escalating display of disrespect. They call her by her first name, imitate her body posture to mock her, and, to young Maya's eyes, show such grievous disrespect that she is certain some form of punishment is coming their way. The scene appears to be on the verge of turning to violence as the oldest girl reaches down, perhaps to pick up a stone to throw. Instead, she does a handstand: "Her dirty bare feet and long legs went straight for the sky. Her dress fell down around her shoulders, and she had on no drawers. The slick pubic hair made a brown triangle where her legs came together. She hung in the vacuum of that lifeless morning for only a few seconds, then wavered and tumbled" (25–26). Maya is shocked by the display of what she has been taught must always stay hidden and utterly confused by her grandmother's response. Momma begins to sing a hymn, and when the girls leave the yard, she acknowledges them by name, "'Bye, Miz Helen, 'bye Miz Ruth, 'bye Miz Eloise" (15), including a term of respect they pointedly neglect. That is not the end of the scene, though. With the girls gone, Maya sees her grandmother is smiling, her face streaked with tears because they have survived this racist and gendered aggression: "Whatever the contest had been out front, I knew Momma had won" (27).

Adult Angelou describes the routes of Black migration out of the South to explain her mother's relocation to St. Louis, a context she lacked as a child to explain her surprise when her father returned to Stamps to take Maya and Bailey to live with their mother in St. Louis: "Years later I discovered that the United States had been crossed thousands of times by frightened Black children traveling alone to their newly affluent parents in Northern cities, or back to grandmothers in southern towns when the urban North reneged on its economic promises" (4). In St. Louis, Maya and Bailey move in with their mother, who lives with a boyfriend the children are taught to call "Mr. Freeman." He is nice enough to the kids at first, but once he can be alone with Maya, he begins to sexually assault her. The shock of him masturbating while he gropes her genitals is compounded by the warnings she received from her grandmother never to let anyone touch her unnamed and shameful private parts. Mr. Freeman hardly needed to threaten to kill Bailey if she told anyone what he was doing to her. She has no language for sexual abuse.

After months of regular molestation, the abuse pauses. Angelou forgets about it, she writes, or allows a gap in her awareness to form around an experience she cannot name. The adult writer's perspective on the child's experience of traumatic memory shows how sexual abuse fractures the child's sense of time. It is not only that she does not know if the sexual abuse has truly stopped as abruptly as it began and if her childhood has restarted, or if her life now permanently consists of unpredictable periods of sexual violence. The violence does resume. Freeman rapes Maya, harming her so badly that she must be hospitalized. The family knows what happened, but they don't know who did it. When Bailey visits her in the hospital, he persuades Maya to name the rapist. When she is silent, he urges her to speak out to prevent him from hurting another little girl. The belief that a victim can stop a rapist by naming him appeals to young Maya, but her fear for Bailey's safety is stronger. When Bailey assures her no one can kill him, she believes him and names Freeman.

Angelou remains in the hospital, a refuge of routines and calm, until she testifies at Freeman's trial, where eight-year-old Maya's age offers her no protection from hostile questioning:

> "What was the defendant wearing?" That was Mr. Freeman's lawyer.
> "I don't know."
> "You mean to say this man raped you and you don't know what he was wearing?" He snickered as if I had raped Mr. Freeman. "Do you know if you were raped?" (70)

There is laughter in the courtroom, but Maya is determined to identify Freeman. He is convicted and, despite being sentenced to a year and a day, released immediately. Later that day, Freeman is found dead, presumably at the hands of Angelou's uncles. Freeman's death returns Angelou to his original threat: don't tell anyone. She decides that the only action she can control is speaking. Anything beyond her silence risks consequences she can neither control nor comprehend. Her family begins to worry as Angelou's silence lengthens, and her mother sends her and Bailey back to Stamps. With the support of a kind teacher and the consolations of literary language, Angelou finds her voice.

*Caged Bird* was controversial because it depicted the rape of a child in a coming-of-age narrative. Librarians, parents, and teachers debated whether it would harm or help young readers.[4] It also sparked controversy about genre because it blended storytelling techniques associated more with novels than with autobiographies by famous white politicians, whose style scanted characterization and description, relied on chronology for its organization, and stuck to the public record. Undeniably, it raised the question: How do you tell a story you have been forbidden to utter, a story that has a lethal power? How do you tell a rape story so that it stops violence? In 1976, a few years after *Caged Bird* was nominated for a National Book Award and Angelou had published her third autobiography, Chinese American author Maxine Hong Kingston published

*The Woman Warrior: Memoirs of a Girlhood Among Ghosts*, a coming-of-age narrative centered on Kingston's powerful mother and the oral tradition of talk-story. Like *Caged Bird*, it is a bildungsroman of a writer focused on the dynamics through which a personal voice emerges. And it, too, is centered on a fundamental aesthetic, moral, and political question: How do you tell a rape story so that it breaks silence and halts further violence? Is that possible?

The memoir addresses this question in the first chapter, entitled "No Name Woman." Ostensibly, this is a cautionary tale Kingston's mother offers to mark her daughter's first period: "'You must not tell anyone,' my mother said, 'what I am about to tell you. In China your father had a sister who killed herself. She jumped into the family well. We say that your father had all brothers because it is as if she had never been born" (3). The villagers punished her pregnant aunt with a violent raid on the family home because the father was unknown. The message is clear to young Kingston: now that she is menstruating, this could happen to her. Using her mother's story as a prompt, however, Kingston imagines different versions of her aunt's life, testing how the few facts she has been given fit into the genres for narrating a woman's life. Was this a romance? Did her aunt have a lover? Were they kept apart by fate, but tied through love? Or was this a melodrama? A discovered affair, a jealous wife, a mob rallied to vengeance? Kingston tries to tell the story so that it offers generational continuity: "Unless I see her life branching into mine, she gives me no ancestral help" (8). After trying on different possibilities, Kingston discards the ones that would give a young woman unimaginable agency either to choose a lover or refuse sex. She concludes that this is a story about rape and how women are punished for it.

The first chapter establishes lineage, narrative, and rape as the key themes through which sexual violence is patterned into talk-story, tempering narrative into a tool for protection. Kingston's memoir is filled with mythic feminist avatars who avenge their villages in epic style, but for her aunt, there can be only Kington's refusal to participate in generational shaming. She interrupts the cycle by offering her aunt narrative care. Kingston accompanies her aunt imaginatively through her final hours. She pictures her hiding from the villagers and vengeful ancestors in the family pigsty, sheltering there to give birth. She imagines the child is a daughter, her gender binding her fate to her mother's suicide because "there is some hope of forgiveness for boys" (15). She follows her aunt to the family well and worries about incurring the wrath of a "spite suicide" as "I alone devote pages of paper to her" (16). When Kingston imagines revenge in the context of a rape story, it's not about settling scores with the rapist or the villagers. For Kingston, the scene of injury and redress have shifted to narrative. She will risk breaking silence because "the telling is the revenge" (32, 167).

Beginning in the mid-1990s, a memoir boom brought the self-representation of trauma, including sexual violence, to new audiences interested in nonfiction and autobiographical fiction.[5] *Prozac Nation*, by Elizabeth Wurtzel (1994) and *Liar's Club*, by Mary Karr (1995) were among the best-selling books that replaced autobiography's previous focus on the public careers of well-known white men with memoirs that pulled back the curtain on private life with all its messy complications.[6] Following *Caged Bird* and *Woman Warrior*, memoirs by women in the 1990s, like *Liar's Club*, navigated the complexities of silence breaking about sexual abuse. Like Angelou, Karr balances what she understood as a girl about sex and violence with what she knows as an adult about the structural aspects of abuse. Like Kingston, telling the story of rape is connected to finding her voice and subject as an author, and to situating it within a lineage of storytelling: for Kingston, talk-story; for Karr, the "liar's club" confab of her Texas father and his drinking buddies.

In *Liar's Club*, published in 1995, Karr writes about the teenage boy who rapes her when she is seven years old. According to her school records, Karr weighed about fifty pounds at the time: "Think of two good-sized Smithfield hams—that's roughly how big I was. Then think of a newly erect teenaged boy on top of that and pumping between my legs" (66). "Think of" her, Karr instructs us, then "think of" him. The injunction is not so much visual as moral; less "picture" this and more "take this in." She is talking to us, establishing a shared ethical bond of witnessing. With this in place, she addresses the rapist, now grown up: "I picture you now reading this" (66). She shifts from implied direct address to the reader—(you) picture this—to direct address of the rapist reading this account. She places him in the present, makes him real both then and now. Like Angelou and Kingston, the rapist's threat is fully integrated into the lessons of gendered childhood, including the messages that girls and women are to blame for rape and are primarily valued for their virginity and chastity. Karr notes: "He didn't even have to threaten me to keep me quiet. I knew what I would be if he told" (68).

When women wrote about sexual abuse during the memoir boom, reviewers often participated in testimonial smothering. Kathryn Harrison's memoir about father-daughter incest, *The Kiss* (1997), drew harsh, gendered criticism along with praise.[7] Harrison's parents split up when she was young. Her mother returned home, leaving Kathryn to be raised primarily by her well-to-do white grandparents. Her father reappears in her life when she is in college, and he initiates a sexual relationship that will almost destroy Harrison. The memoir addresses the impossibility of consent in incest; her adulthood offers her no power to stop her father. Some reviewers overlooked those themes to condemn Harrison as a bad person. She was accused of exaggerating the abuse in order to profit from her pain. She was called a bad mother for writing about the experience at all. One reviewer distilled the negative chorus to its essence and told Harrison to "hush up." But what made her unsympathetic? The fault lay in breaking her silence.

The theme of silence breaking in memoir coupled with the prevalence of testimonial silencing in reviews establishes the memoir boom of the mid-1990s as a relevant context for #MeToo storytelling, placing both in the lineage of memoirists like Angelou and Kingston twenty years prior and heralded by Harriet Jacobs's *Incidents* in the nineteenth century. This intersectional tradition of life writing about sexual violence prefigured the themes of writers in the #MeToo era, including rhetorical strategies and creative decisions about disclosing sexual violence, to what audiences, and from what perspective. Roxane Gay was already an established writer of fiction and essays when she published *Hunger: A Memoir of (My) Body* (2017). Gay had written about being fat in complex ways, about stigma and accommodations, but also about joy, sex, and power. Until *Hunger*, she had not identified the trauma of being gang raped with gaining weight. Even the title, *"A Memoir of (My) Body,"* with its shielding of "my" within a parenthetical enclosure, creates a protected space for a body subjected to the unwelcome gaze and touch of others. Gay describes herself as a shy and studious girl before the assault. She is the daughter of Haitian immigrants and her family is loving and prosperous. The parents value education, church, and their daughter. When she is twelve, Gay is gang raped by boys, one of whom is a boy she liked. The complexities of coming-of-age she had begun to experience, along with her relationship to her body, shift into the time of trauma. She writes: "What you need to know is that my life is split in two, cleaved not so neatly. There is the before and the after. Before I gained weight. After I gained weight. Before I was raped. After I was raped."[8] The path "after" includes reading feminist books like *The Courage to Heal* and gaining access to a feminist analysis of consent and sexual violence that assured her she was not to blame.[9] It will take years to claim this knowledge for herself.

Terese Marie Mailhot's *Heart Berries* (2018) is an elliptical memoir begun in the mental institution she checked herself into for suicidal depression. Mailhot grew up on Seabird Reservation in British Columbia and currently lives and teaches creative writing in the United States. Her memoir traces a personal story in relation to settler colonialism and histories of Indigenous removal in the Americas, all of which inform her experience of generational trauma, including sexual violence. Mailhot's self-representation as a survivor resonates with Gerald Vizenor's definition of Native survival stories: "renunciations of dominance, detractions, obtrusions, the unbearable sentiments of tragedy, and the legacy of victimry." Storytelling as matriarchal Indigenous practice, survival skill, and literary art is at the heart of this memoir. Like Jacobs's *Incidents*, *Heart Berries* walks a razor's edge of frank self-revelation about mental health, domestic violence, and racism for a diverse audience drawn to memoir. Of some aspects of her experience, Mailhot chooses strategic silence: "It's too ugly—to speak this story."[10]

The memoir is crafted as a series of letters written during treatment and addressed to Casey Gray, her creative writing professor and future husband. They begin when Mailhot checks herself into an institution as memories of childhood sexual abuse by her father surface and the loss of custody of her son overwhelms her. The short chapters offer no easy toeholds of chronology. She is stuck within the temporality of trauma and the specific violence directed at women: "It's almost funny because, yeah—there is nothing new about what they do to us. We can write about it in new ways, but what value are we placing on newness? Familiarity is boring, but these people—they keep hurting us in the same ways." Echoing Kingston's observation that the telling is the revenge, Mailhot writes: "I can name my pain so well that people are afraid of the consequences and power" (119). Mailhot questions how violence ends, not only in specific relationships, but across generations of settler colonialism and its violent reproduction in the everyday lives of family and community. In Mailhot's memoir, many of the concerns of #MeToo about coercion, consent, agency, and structural violence find expression as she confronts a legacy of silence and shame about those who have hurt her, especially when she has been taught to protect them with her silence.

During her testimony about being sexually assaulted by a drunken, teenage Brett Kavanaugh, Christine Blasey Ford was asked by Senator Patrick Leahy what stayed with her from the attack. She replied, "Indelible in the hippocampus is the laughter." This memorable line provides the title for a collection of #MeToo poetry, essays, and fiction edited by Shelly Oria. *Indelible in the Hippocampus* provides an archive of material that, unlike Kantor and Twohey's *She Said* and Farrow's *Catch and Kill*, or even Blasey Ford's testimony, has not been filtered through reporting or shaped by legal proceedings.[11] Instead, the work often documents, and immerses readers in, the aftermath of trauma, as survivors feel exiled from a sense of time moving forward, untethered from the routines and rhythms of daily life. The host of posttraumatic symptoms, from hypervigilance to flashbacks, nightmares, and depression, not only make these texts feel haunted by violence and memory but evoke what it feels like to be stuck inside them. As the poetry, creative nonfiction, essays, and fiction in *Indelible* demonstrate, the posttraumatic temporality of sexual violence means that "after" and "next" do not unfold linearly. Unlike neoliberal life narratives that tout resilient and upbeat narrators, whose personal grit enables them to overcome obstacles once and for all, survivor accounts often offer fractured timelines, document disruptions in relationships and work, and record the toll on physical and mental health that trauma exacts.[12]

Anthologies have the built-in benefit of supplying context through aggregation. Many readers are accustomed to following individual cases of sexual violence in the news, as with the Weinstein story, or of reading an essay or two by survivors. But *Indelible in the Hippocampus*—just like the viral trending of #MeToo on social media—provides evidence of the scale of the problem. Editor Shelly Oria offers a trauma-informed introduction to the volume that affirms the power of telling your story in community. In one essay, "Nightingale: A Gloss," Paisley Rekdal intercuts her account of being sexually assaulted in 1992 with reflections about sexual assault in Ovid and Shakespeare depicted through Philomela and Lavinia. Rekdal asks what readers are willing to hear about sexual violence as a way to gauge what they can bear. Because "what" happened is not limited to the time of the assault. It does not end when the attacker stops or leaves. "After" names the time of trauma, which Rekdal transforms through analogy to lyric time. "Traumatic time," she explains, "works like lyric time: the now of terror repeatedly breaking back through the crust of one's consciousness."[13] Caitlin Donohue steps back into the river of time to pen "Letter to Myself Upon Entering College," offering a warning while also promising resilience. And in "Linger," Gabrielle Bellot navigates how the #MeToo movement falls short in failing to include her as a trans woman. If the #MeToo effect allowed isolated stories to be heard as one story, #MeToo storytelling insists those stories are not the same. *Indelible* helps us to ask why we require optimism of autobiographers when survival should be enough. What if readers can allow women to be angry, and even embrace anger as an affect we have barely fathomed the complexities of? What if we do not have to approve of, relate to, or sympathize with women to engage with them? If we do not have to shush or shame them, but can instead witness the messiness that patriarchy imposes, we might be able to imagine new endings for trauma.

In *The Reckonings: Essays on Justice for the Twenty-First Century* (2018), Lacy M. Johnson picks up a key trope of the #MeToo movement: reckoning. Through essays that blend autobiography and feminist analysis, Johnson surveys the wide swath of sexual violence that cuts through the lives of women and girls and asks what would make it end. She observes that sexual violence "is so unthinkable, so unfathomable, so taboo, as to render it unspeakable."[14] It contradicts the myth that women are protected and girls cherished, and that rape is a rare and terrible aberration. Women are silenced through this denial. They must tell something people do not believe is true and do not want to hear. Girls and women live with the experience of violence and the very real threat of retribution for saying anything about it. Yet because silence does not end sexual violence, #MeToo is a charged site of utterance. It breaks a taboo as it breaks silence. It also asks what happens after a survivor speaks. What changes for listeners? How do they bear witness?

Johnson survives kidnapping and rape by the man she lives with. When she begins to write and speak publicly about her experience, listeners struggle with their responses. They ask what happened to the man: "I explain how he got away, how he is a fugitive living in Venezuela, raising a new family." There is no justice for him in this scenario. He has fled and reconstituted his life elsewhere. But what about justice for Lacy Johnson? Not just for his crime, but for her suffering. What will balance the scales? "Usually it is a woman who asks the question—always the same question . . . 'What do you want to have happen to him?' . . . 'I mean, you probably want him dead, right?'" (1). His evasion of the law does not end the violence. Nor would her revenge make an ending. For Johnson, justice for sexual violence entails telling the story of rape so that a public and truthful account will replace the lies and myths that foster its perpetuation. This is not always what people want to hear. But for her, narrative justice is the most comprehensive response. It requires public truth-telling and apology as a means to end suffering. *Lex talionis*, or the law of retribution, imagines that justice can be found by matching a punishment to an injury: an eye for an eye. Narrative justice offers something other than a punitive or carceral response, although accountability would surely entail both in some circumstances.

#MeToo storytelling grapples with questions of justice and, specifically, with what narrative justice offers survivors and communities fractured by sexual violence. It identifies the crime as a location of injury and the telling as redress. It asks us to weigh the cost of sexual violence and the cost of doubt in order to consider how doubt perpetuates harm. Literature enables us to imagine how the impact of sexual violence spreads across the lives of characters, limits their horizons, and shapes their relationships. It can offer nuanced examples of sexual manipulation, grooming, and deception. It can play with revenge fantasies or imagine new ways to tell the story of old pain. Readers took up two works of fiction, the short story "Cat Person," by Kristen Roupenian, and Mary Gordon's novel *Payback*, as examples of #MeToo storytelling.

In December 2017, two months into the #MeToo movement, "Cat Person" was published in the *New Yorker* and went viral online.[15] Narrated in third person, it provided readers with a puzzle about consent that played with our shifting sympathy and evolving knowledge about the main characters: college student Margot and the older Robert, whom she dates. Their relationship unfolds primarily by texting. Both are skilled at creating an experience of intimacy, and their texting styles are self-assured. Their in-person encounters, however, are marked by miscommunication and tinged with menace, an intuition that Margot resists. She senses something is off but continues to see Robert. She enjoys their texting relationship and, intermittently, takes pleasure in their physical connection. On the date when she goes home with Robert, she is initially open to the prospect of having sex. As the encounter unfolds, too many things don't feel right. He is clumsy and aggressive. She redirects him, but he pouts. Although she doesn't want to have sex with him and begins to dissociate to get through it, she decides it would be too hard to tell him to stop.[16]

Reading, unlike life, not only allows us to pause, it requires us to continue. The different temporalities of experience and reading provide a check on the sense that an action is inevitable. We can pause to ask why Margot believes it is easier to absorb the experience of unwanted sex than risk Robert's reaction to her desire to stop. The reader is led to understand Margot's confusion between "texting Robert," whom she enjoys, and "embodied Robert," with whom she is frequently uncomfortable. Texting Robert has a life that includes two cats, Mu and Yan, about whom he and Margot create an elaborate narrative. Yet when she goes to his house, she is surprised that embodied Robert lives alone. More discrepancies slowly reveal a pattern of deception. Margot's gut feelings of danger arose early in their acquaintance and never disappeared, but their easy text banter creates a parallel Robert whom she likes. Because authors allow readers to know more than the characters do, we can see how their age difference, Margot's inexperience, and gendered dating norms put her at a disadvantage. The short story asks us to understand that he keeps her off-balance because it benefits him: he is grooming her for a sexual relationship by creating a persona via text she can trust and enjoy. His creepiness emerges whenever their interaction is sexual. A switch is flipped, and Margot finds she cannot translate between the Roberts in the moment. She freezes. Margot ends the relationship after the experience of dissociating when they have sex. Seeing her paralysis, her roommate sends Robert a breakup text from Margot's phone and Margot avoids any contact with him.

Readers are likely to have mixed feelings about Robert. Margot does. But the more haunting ambivalence is about Margot's agency and desire. Without access to Robert's intentions about having sex with Margot, can we call Robert a rapist? Is that the right word for an older man who seeks a sexual relationship with a younger, inexperienced woman, deceives her about his life and intentions, and has sex with her while she is immobile, unspeaking, and otherwise nonresponsive? Consent hardly seems like the best word to describe Margot's acquiescence to sex with Robert. She is dissociating through it, imagining herself at a safe remove in the future, and narrating this as a story that does not hurt her to a future boyfriend. Is Margot's inability to say "stop," which is what she wants to do, the same as saying "yes"? In court, such ambiguity is not an option for victims, where even the most obviously nonconsenting victim—those who are unconscious, those who are trafficked—can be said by the defense to have consented. Coming to a new understanding of how one has been coerced and manipulated into sex is not, as some conservative critics would have it, a matter of falsifying regretted sex as sexual violence. It is a more accurate way to think about how women are punished for their desire, including by themselves, and how literature helps us navigate the edges of desire, coercion, shame, and abuse.

Roupenian has a gut punch in store for the conclusion. After Margot has broken up with Robert, she sees him at a bar in town. Later that night he starts texting her, and she experiences the return of texting Robert: he's warm, but good about boundaries, says he's happy to see her, and hopes she's happy. But embodied Robert, real Robert, emerges when she does not resume her part in the text exchange, and he voices the menace she always felt in increasingly accusatory and misogynist texts about the male friends she's with that conclude with him calling her "whore." That word shines a klieg light on the "gray area" of consent the short story has so deftly presented, and we see, as Margot does, that Robert was never concerned with her consent, but only with sexual access to her, animated by violence, and expressed as ownership of her.

Mary Gordon's novel *Payback* (2020) is set in a girls' boarding school in Rhode Island in 1972 where a young art history teacher, Agnes, tries to mentor an isolated and brooding teen, Heidi.[17] Although Agnes's young colleagues find Heidi more surly than forlorn and warn Agnes about becoming involved, Agnes presses on. She pairs Heidi with another student for a joint project that, she hopes, will foster a friendship between the girls. Heidi reluctantly agrees to her part of the project: a visit to the Museum of Modern Art in New York City. While she is there, Heidi is picked up by an older man. He flatters and charms her, persuades her to come to his apartment, then rapes her. Heidi manages to take the train back to school, find Agnes, who lives with her parents, and tell her: "I was raped, I went to the lecture in New York and I met this man and he invited me to his apartment for lunch and then he raped me." Agnes is unprepared for Heidi's visit or her disclosure and immediately regrets the first words out of her mouth: "How could you have let that happen?" (95).

Heidi disappears, and Agnes is undone by her betrayal of the girl. She resigns from the school, moves to Italy, makes a new life for herself, but never forgives herself. Heidi, too, undertakes a transformation, re-creating herself as Quin Archer, the host of the reality show "Payback" that engineers confrontations between those who have been hurt, whom she calls "the owed," and those who must pay, "the owers." Quin Archer is especially vicious when "the owers" express regret, offer explanations or sympathy, or say they want to make amends. She cuts them off with her signature dismissal, "Well *boo hoo hoo* and *blah blah blah*," mocking the scene of potential accountability as failed from the outset. Heidi/Quin's views of language as meaningless and emotion as fake are taken directly from her vain and cruel mother. The TV show revels in the shock of the confrontation and the thrill of revenge, but just as frequently, the guests disappoint her: they want to make amends, apologize, and figure out how to move on. Quin Archer, however, can only imagine traumatic reenactment, a cycle Lacy Johnson describes as "more pain creates more sorrow" (11). The novel builds to Quin's plan to confront Agnes on an episode of her show.

*Payback* does not imagine justice for the crime of rape. Heidi knows the rapist's name and address: she saw his business card in the apartment he lured her to. Over the decades in which she transforms herself into an avenger, she directs her fury only at Agnes and the scene of her failed response when Heidi disclosed the assault. She seeks revenge for the testimonial injustice she felt when Agnes did not hear her. Heidi is an unsympathetic character in the novel. Gordon makes Heidi prickly and sullen as a teen. She lays it on thick by giving her an Ayn Rand obsession. As Quin, she becomes imperious, cruel, and very much like her terrible mother. *Payback* is about a world where girls and women are judged on their looks and held responsible for rape. The trauma does not end for Quin when she confronts Agnes because Agnes agrees that her words were a betrayal, that she was at fault, and that she deserves to be punished. With her acceptance of Quin's judgment and the subsequent support of her family and friends, Agnes's decades of suffering end. She tells the truth, apologizes without defensiveness on Quin's TV show, and even acquiesces to the "payback": Quin buys the house across the street from Agnes and cuts down the two old trees, promising insults to come.

*Payback* imagines how hard it is to gain justice for sexual violence. It distinguishes two injuries—the rape and the doubt—and two sites—embodied and testimonial—where the survivor suffers. As an example of #MeToo storytelling, it pushes back against rape myths and story lines. Heidi is not at fault for wanting to be kissed or trusting a manipulative older man. She could not, in fact, imagine that lunch would end with rape. Her youth makes her vulnerable to deception and predation. Had Heidi imagined rape as an outcome, she would hardly have risked it. *Payback* examines the slipperiness of blame, especially the way it slides off the rapist and attaches to Agnes. As it does in representations of sexual violence, from the classics to contemporary fiction and memoirs, #MeToo storytelling foregrounds a lineage of witnessing as it raises questions about obligation and justice from the perspective of survivors. It seeks narrative justice through telling these stories and interpreting them.

In this context, "me too" represents a plea to share the story rather than repeat the trauma. It is a gift that survivors give each other and a debt they demand be acknowledged, often stretching back generations, in recorded history, erased lives, and unheard testimony. Literature is especially suited to conveying how trauma restructures interiority in a lasting way, how even when no one seems to notice the stilled stories and diminished lives, they live on. Readers may be confused about the literary representation of sexual violence for the same reasons they blame and doubt victims, sympathize with those who harm them, and shrug off the pervasiveness of sexual assault by naturalizing it in everyday life: because they practice not hearing or seeing it in such a way that centers its complexity, relegating it, instead, to subplot or recurrent trope. #MeToo storytelling asks, "What happens next?," which is a question about justice. It grapples with how to tell the story of sexual violence so that the story can change. It settles debts through new story lines and new storytellers. It imagines narrative justice. One test for whether a text is part of #MeToo storytelling, rather than simply about sexual violence, could be that it represents sexual violence within the context of a full life and offers story lines that amplify survivor credibility in all its complexity.

# 8

## CONSENT BEFORE AND
## AFTER #METOO

*Regretting drinking is not the same as regretting sexual
assault. We were both drunk, the difference is I did not
take off your pants and underwear, touch you
inappropriately, and run away. That's the difference.*

—CHANEL MILLER, *KNOW MY NAME*

There is no consensus about consent. Its meaning has shifted as the rising demand for women to be free from sexual violence has forced changes in rape laws. In cultural conversations, and especially in educational settings, consent has moved to the fore as a conceptual framework for understanding bodily autonomy and sex. Many activists and advocates hope that consent will provide a shared baseline that guarantees everyone will have the right to say no. This hope—motivated by the desire to prevent sexual violence—confronts obstacles in law and culture. In the law, consent is often up for debate. A victim's testimony that she did not consent too easily ends up on the "she said" side of the scale. In cultural debates, where legal meanings migrate to diminish survivor credibility, consent is hardly a panacea for the power imbalance and violence that motivate rape. Whether consent is a necessary baseline a hopeless muddle, or the "least-bad standard available for sexual assault law," it establishes a floor, not a ceiling, for ensuring sexual agency.[1] The #MeToo effect made consent into a narrative genre about the right of the survivor to tell the story of "no."

The meanings of consent arise in two distinct locations: intimate life, where it can be a tool for understanding and enacting sexual agency, and law, where consent can be rewritten as "she said." Consent as a legal term is about argument: two people dispute what happened and who has the right to interpret it. In practice, consent does not guarantee that sex will produce feelings of connection and intimacy, or even be satisfying, only that those involved were willing. Nor can consent, as Katherine Angel writes, "miraculously displace the imbalances of power that operate in our every interaction."[2] We need consent because of these power imbalances. We act within limits when we say "yes" to anything, including sex, but for a yes to be meaningful, we must be able to say no. In rape investigations and legal defenses, this choice is rendered meaningless when "he said" it was consensual and "she said" it was rape is seen as a stalemate. The meaning of consent has shifted after #MeToo, but it remains an artifact of systemic bias refashioned with variable success into a tool through which to assert sexual autonomy. By looking at examples that originate in the #MeToo buildup and find their largest public audience after its breakthrough, this chapter examines the role of consent in high-stakes battles over accountability in formal structures.

Debates about consent that neglect the actual conditions in which women negotiate both safety and sex ring hollow, and yet the law often treats consent abstractly when it mentions it at all. The Moral Penal Code of 1962 addressing the adjudication of rape and related sexual offenses does not mention consent. Since then, states have updated rape laws, but the history of how the law imagines rape persists. Michelle Anderson identifies a "classic rape paradigm" central to the law: it involves a sinister stranger and a woman who fights valiantly to preserve her virtue.[3] She reports the crime to police, who believe her. The narrative elements differ starkly from rapes in which the victim knows the abuser, but the classic story informs the legal definition of rape and the understanding of its harm. Marital rape was not criminalized nationwide until 1993 in the United States, though some states, like Nebraska and Oregon, updated their laws in the 1970s. Wives were understood as having permanently consented. Neither the typical relationship (not strangers) nor the understanding of its harm ("merely a domestic dispute") fit the rape paradigm, which was heavily racialized and used as a tool both by the criminal-legal system and in extralegal vigilantism. Legal storytelling about rape offers no agentic "I" for survivors. It is not their story to tell.

The conditions in which those who do not want sex can be said to "negotiate" with potential rapists are also defined by power imbalances. The relative positions of those "negotiating" consent, as if the struggle to fight off a rapist is an argument to win or lose, is created through law. To return to *Incidents*, Harriet Jacobs describes the conditions in which she negotiated her desire to marry in the context of slavery and the threat of rape.[4] After James Norcom had begun his campaign of sexual harassment, Jacobs fell in love with a free Black man. Norcom refused to allow him to purchase Jacobs's freedom and the relationship ended, as Norcom stepped up his threats to sell Jacobs and her family members. When he revealed his plan to build a house and keep Jacobs in it, she understood he intended to make her his prisoner. The prospect propelled her to "plunge into the abyss," and she made a "desperate" plan that filled her with "sorrow and shame" (145–46). As she describes the plan, she initiates a negotiation with white women readers about identification and empathy. She asks them to put themselves in her place, despite their circumstances, and to understand how her extreme coercion shapes her actions: "But, O, ye happy women, whose purity has been sheltered from childhood, who have been free to choose the objects of your affection, whose homes are protected by law, do not judge the poor desolate slave girl too severely!" (147). She traces how slavery and Norcom have blocked all paths to choose her partner and entrapped her: "If slavery had been abolished, I, also, could have married the man of my choice; I could have had a home shielded by the laws; and I should have been spared the painful task of confessing what I am now about to relate; but all my prospects had been blighted by slavery." To the extent that this is an argument, she is making her case: "I wanted to keep myself pure," but she has no escape (147). Her desperation leads her to a fraught transaction.

Gossip about Norcom reached a white neighbor, Samuel Tredwell Sawyer, who knew Jacobs's grandmother and Jacobs well enough to speak to her about the situation and say he wanted to "aid" her: "He constantly sought opportunities to see me, and wrote to me frequently." Their differing positions are clear from the outset. He is "a white unmarried gentleman" and she a "poor slave girl, only fifteen years old." When he proposes a sexual relationship, she agrees: "It seems less degrading to give one's self, than to submit to compulsion." Jacobs articulates a real world standard for negotiating sex and safety in conditions of powerlessness: "There is something akin to freedom in having a lover who has no control over you, except that which he gains by kindness and attachment" (148). Not freedom, but something akin to freedom. In these conditions, choosing against a worse situation when her marriage was denied, her relationship with Sawyer and pregnancies, as she hoped, provided her some protection from Norcom. Her arrangement with Sawyer enabled her to exercise limited agency in conditions of extreme threat and coercion, an approximation that is less degrading, akin to freedom. The distance is measured against the freedom she seeks and the man she wishes to marry. Writing her autobiography in later life, Jacobs gives Sawyer the pseudonym Mr. Sands, suggesting something of the trap he represented for her and the shiftiness of the lover who promised to manumit their two children and refused to.

Over a century later, and with rape laws stuck in the past, radical feminists in the 1980s questioned whether consent was useful in distinguishing between sex and rape when women's sexual autonomy is routinely discounted. Catherine MacKinnon disputed whether women can consent given that they have little right to define their sexual desires, are dependent on men economically, and exist in a culture that is saturated with pornography.[5] More recently, consent has been touted as an important tool to help young people develop awareness around agency and intimacy, and to provide vocabulary for practicing how to integrate desires and boundaries. Rather than pretending that "yes" or "no" are equally sayable or hearable by most people in most situations, I propose we define consent as a *knowing* and *volitional* response to sex. Let's take each part separately: consent entails understanding what you are saying yes to. One standard for measuring whether someone can knowingly consent to sex is if they understand what "yes" entails at least as well as the person(s) with whom they agree to have sex. Otherwise, the attribution of consent to all sorts of people in all sorts of situations amplifies the power imbalance that muddles sexual violence by handing over the right to define it to abusers. Young people, including children, and intoxicated, anesthetized, or otherwise incapacitated people cannot consent given this definition. Their ability to prevent abuse must be present for consent to be possible. Now the second part of the definition: stipulating that consent entails volition centers agency and desire as a precondition. To be knowing and willing. That is all. To be able to say "no" and have it count reflects that willingness and knowledge can change, even abruptly. When we look at who is enabled to define consent, we more clearly see that the testimonial and legal crises swirling around it obscure a more fundamental point: who is empowered to consent *at all*.[6]

In an allegation of rape, when there is agreement that sexual intercourse occurred, the legal question turns to consent, transforming scenes of violation into disputes about interpretation after the fact. She said it was rape; he said it was consensual. Given the credibility imbalance, the emphasis on consent does more to confuse than to clarify when the victim's word is considered inadequate as evidence. Without corroborating witnesses, as I have shown, the investigation often stops there. Force and consent are tied together in rape law, with evidence of physical force giving credence to the victim's testimony. Sometimes broken bones, bruises, or genital injuries persuade a jury the victim did not consent. But not always. Those accused of rape often shift blame onto the victim by claiming that force was part of rough sex, where that is claimed to be consensual.[7] Forensic researchers argue that physical evidence of rape is complex and that the absence of force injuries does not mean an act was consensual. Terrorized or restrained victims cannot offer consent but may have no visible injuries. Yet courts can use lack of injury to raise doubt about consent. If she is not injured enough, then she did not resist enough.

U.S. law retains the notion from English common law that physical force is required to prove lack of consent, a vestige of seeing women as property and assessing the crime of sexual violence as one might check an object for signs of damage.[8] Force is a standard ill-suited to the realities of coercion and degrades both victim and the moral force of law. Spanish law differentiates the crimes of sexual violence not only by presence but by the degree of force a rapist uses. When the perpetrators of a gang rape who dubbed themselves the "Wolf Pack" cornered an eighteen-year-old woman in an alcove during Pamplona's San Fermín festival in 2016, filmed themselves gang raping her, and celebrated by sharing their cellphone videos on WhatsApp, their defense was that the victim "consented" because she was motionless and her eyes were closed.[9] The jury agreed and convicted the men of the lesser charge of sexual assault rather than rape. Too often the law requires the kind of injuries men receive in fistfights to prove a woman did not consent.

It would seem lack of consent should be easy to recognize in at least one situation: when someone is obviously unable to participate willingly in sex because they are unconscious. Yet in 2021 the Minnesota State Supreme Court ruled that a man could not be charged with felony rape of an unconscious victim who drank alcohol voluntarily.[10] Unless victims are forced to drink or otherwise become incapacitated against their will, they are responsible for the rapist's actions. Research indicates that men who sexually violate unconscious people know that they do so without consent.[11] Survivor testimony shows that the confusion baked into consent represents a category error. It applies the language of sexual desire and agency—the "yes" that accompanies willing participation—to the problem of sexual violence. In so doing, it pretends that the language that helps you navigate intimacy—saying yes or no and having that count—could also protect you from rape. Consenting to sex does not guarantee that sex will be great or even good, only that it is voluntary. This line in the sand, however, does not prevent consent from being used against women.

A series of cases helps to demonstrate how consent provides dubious protection for those who are targets of sexual abuse. It fails to protect girls and women from assault, and it hands a tool to courts and abusers with which to implicate victims in those assaults. Consent can be used to distort and misrepresent any moment in which a woman exercises volition, recasting her decision to go to a party, for example, as equivalent to consenting to sex later that night. The rape trial of Brock Turner in California discussed in chapter 2, the sexual assault at a New England boarding school discussed in chapter 6, the rape trial of Belfast rugby players and the recent outcry about age of consent and incest in France addressed in this chapter show how consent offers abusers a script that raises doubt, confers false agency on victims, and rewrites coercion as seduction.[12] It also shows that we cannot abandon consent because it has been used against survivors, even when that history complicates its repurposing.

## CONSENT AS A GRAY AREA

Consent for sex lies in a so-called gray area, complicated by norms of male impunity, men's access to and control over women's sexuality, and women's relatively late entry into legal subjectivity. But the gray area also has to do with the murkiness of desire, with the mismatch between legal language about decision making and the unfolding of a sexual encounter in which ambivalence may not indicate unwillingness, precisely. To acknowledge this psychic suppleness may help us to better understand the work of recovery that follows a sexual assault because it reminds us that our desires do not implicate us in the crimes others commit. It serves less well, I would argue, to describe actual sexual assault. Our psyches are filled with gray areas, but it is part of the cultural mythology of gender to insist that women are responsible through their own actions for sexual violence. The gray area names a conceptual space of mixed meanings that are undecidable. Applied to sexual violence, the claim of undecidability (she said it is rape/he said it isn't) represents a refusal to hold abusers accountable masked as sophisticated acknowledgment that desire is complicated. The resulting mismatch in evidentiary norms—gray areas in the psyche versus in sexual assault—does little to advance legal or cultural understandings.

Some of the confusion about consent derives from its legal history. Consent is about more than sex, of course; it is foundational to the emergence of liberal democracies. John Locke established the "consent of the governed" as a bedrock of legitimate government, distinguishing it from the divine right of kings to rule. Consent appears early in the commentaries of Blackstone on law. Much of consent as a legal term emphasizes what cannot be taken from you without your permission, such as land or other property, which cannot be seized by the state without compensation. In shifting consent onto citizens and the social contract, Blackstone recognizes that consent is about competing interests and the conflicts they give rise to. For consent to function meaningfully, it must offer leverage in bargaining *and* a path toward redress when consent is abused. Unsurprisingly, consent does not appear in Locke in relation to sexual violence, nor does he include women. The closest he comes is to say that persons have inherent rights to their own bodies, but those persons are gendered male. Within this liberal tradition, Carole Pateman argued in the 1980s that Locke demotes women to mere subjects of contract rather than parties to them.[13]

In *Redefining Rape*, Estelle Freedman examines how this legacy informs rape laws.[14] Freedman argues that changing definitions of rape and citizenship are connected. More than a legal term, rape is a social and political concept developed and enforced by a ruling class of white men to support male and white supremacy. Citizenship confers the right to consent. Those excluded from the category or relegated to a second-class version of it stand little chance of gaining legal protection or recourse in cases of rape by claiming they did not consent. Married white women could be raped by their husbands because they had no right to withhold consent. Enslaved women had no legal standing to refuse sex with anyone. When marginalized persons, including women, appeal to the structures that offer them diminished personhood as an entry point for participation, they find themselves subordinated to privileged persons within those structures. This can be catastrophic for victims.

Courts interpret consent inconsistently, and laws vary from state to state. Some localities require a victim to verbally withdraw consent for sexual contact—that is, to say "no"—for that contact to qualify as a sexual assault. Yet even when there is no dispute about whether someone utters an audible "no," if the victim can speak, words are vulnerable to misinterpretation. The joint testimonial and legal crises—that the law is unclear about what consent is and "no" does not prevent or stop a sexual assault or prevail as evidence in a rape trial—raise the following questions: Why does the law understand sexual violence as something women must verbally opt out of? Why does it place the burden on women to stop sexual violence through their speech when it frequently disregards their testimony in court?[15] Why does the law place such importance on the speech act of a subject whose testimony it is predisposed to doubt? Related and troubling, too, is the law's ambivalence about a victim's silence: not only the silence of a victim who is speechless out of shock or terror, but one who is unconscious or semiconscious. What protection does the law offer someone who cannot consent for those reasons? Excluding women from access to the full power of consent while men retain it sets up the mismatch—legal and testimonial—that #MeToo exposes.

## BELFAST RUGBY RAPE TRIAL

*What happened last night was not consensual.*

—WITNESS, BELFAST RAPE TRIAL

In 2016, the same year Brock Turner was convicted in California on three counts of felony sexual assault, a sexual assault case in Belfast, Northern Ireland, highlighted the limits of consent to prevent violence against women in life and court. On a June evening, a twenty-year-old woman went with friends to a club to celebrate finishing exams.[16] The scene was lively. In addition to students, some members of the Northern Ireland football team were in the club, including those who would be tried in connection with the alleged rape: Paddy Jackson, Stuart Olding, Blane McIlroy, and Rory Harrison. A friend suggested they go to an after-party, and the woman agreed, getting into a taxi with three other women and

Paddy Jackson. The party was low key, a few people were drinking and dancing, and the woman went upstairs with Jackson to his bedroom, where they kissed consensually. When he tried to take her pants off, she refused and left the room. He followed her downstairs, where the mood of the party had shifted, she testified. McIlroy was taking pictures of women, and she decided to leave. She had left her bag in Jackson's bedroom and went to retrieve it.

What follows is her testimony of gang rape. Jackson followed her to his room, grabbed her from behind, and pulled her pants down. They were tight and got stuck around her knees, immobilizing her. Jackson raped her. Olding walked in. The two got her pants off and Jackson raped her vaginally while Olding raped her orally. A woman walked in and the victim feared she would be filmed, but the woman left. Jackson tried to force his hand into the victim's vagina. She testified that she was bleeding heavily. McIlroy entered the room, holding his penis in his hand. She was able to grab her clothes and escape. She testified that McIlroy said, "You fucked the other guys, why won't you fuck me?" and she replied, "How many times does it take for a girl to say no for it to sink in?"[17] Rory Harrison followed as she ran outside the house and took her home in a taxi. The taxi driver testified that the victim was profoundly upset. "Stroke-crying," as he described her. He also testified that Harrison called someone (McIlroy, it was later confirmed) and seemed to be speaking "in code": "She is with me now. She is not good. I'll call you in the morning." When the driver dropped the woman off, he saw that her white pants were stained with blood. Harrison texted the woman to "keep her chin up." She texted back: "what happened last night was not consensual." Meanwhile, the defendants sent texts like this to each other and friends: "pumped a bird with Jacko last night, roasted her."

One anomaly of the trial was that all four defendants had separate counsel. Four sets of barristers, all men, were permitted not only to call their own expert witnesses, but to vigorously cross-examine the victim, which they all did. She spent eight days in the witness box. They passed around her bloody underwear for inspection. The trial was a topic of national interest, not only because the accused were celebrity athletes, but because their own derogatory texts about and behavior toward the victim occurred amid a public conversation about "consent and male entitlement."[18] The law defines rape as penetration by force. The most common defense is to raise doubt about consent: "the majority of rape accused accept they had sex with the complainant but contend it was consensual."[19] A medical witness for the defense, Dr. Janet Hall, tried to place responsibility anywhere but on the men: "Drink can lead to people making ill-judged decisions which give them pleasure, Dr. Hall said. She further agreed it can reduce inhibition and create arousal as well as leading to feelings of regret and remorse."[20] In the end, the jury deliberated only four hours. The not guilty verdict was unanimous.

The verdicts in 2018 met with support from many but also prompted an outcry by women about the treatment of the victim. Buoyed by the #MeToo movement, women took to the streets in Belfast to protest. They shared stories of abuse, humiliation, and sexual violence. Evidence of the young men's attitudes in private social media conversations exposed rape culture. One month following the verdict, in the trial of a twenty-seven-year-old man accused of raping a seventeen-year-old girl, the defense told the jury to consider the girl's lace thong as evidence of consent. He was acquitted. Women all over Ireland protested again, some held signs with red lace thongs, and many demanded education about consent. The hope for consent education is not only about offering young people a vocabulary for understanding intimacy and boundaries, but also about shifting a larger public conversation to confront the sexism that enables impunity.[21]

## CONSENT ON CAMPUS

In 1991 Antioch College adopted the first affirmative consent policy. In 2011 the frequency of sexual assault on campus and the lack of adequate response led the Obama administration to send a "Dear Colleague" letter instructing colleges and universities to use a trauma-informed approach to truth-seeking in Title IX proceedings.[22] In 2014 Governor Jerry Brown signed a law in California that defined consent as affirmative and verbal, clarifying that people who are asleep, intoxicated, or unconscious cannot give consent. Affirmative consent aims to replace the unheeded "no" with the eminently hearable "yes." Consent has achieved its centrality due to a sincere effort to promote a clear antidote to such cultural clichés as "your lips say no, but your eyes say yes," or the trope in heterosexual screen romances that asserts women cannot say or do not know what they desire until a man gives it to them, or the more explicitly dangerous "no means yes," a negation of women's autonomy. Joseph Fischel argues that while affirmative consent is the "least-bad standard available for sexual assault law," it is lousy for sex politics because it offers no path toward a "democratically hedonic sexual culture."[23] Consent announces what no one should violate rather than what all should aspire to. In this, Fischel is an optimist. He wants something better for college students than not to get raped and for residential life messaging and campus policy to adopt more flexible language than the barebones "consent" and its amplifiers, "affirmative" and "enthusiastic." Campus sexual policies and education are admirable for centering consent, but they also misleadingly suggest that rape results from a communication error.

Feminist writer Kate Harding analyzes the features of college rape culture, linking who is most likely to rape and where they look for victims to who is most likely to be targeted and when. New students as especially vulnerable during their first few months on campus.[24] During this time, they are preyed on by serial rapists often associated with fraternities or sports teams. These are the key elements of sexual assault on campus: (1) a time frame so identifiably linked to sexual assault it is called "the red zone"; (2) experienced sexual predators with access to younger students who are often inexperienced drinkers and, as new students, lack an established support system; and (3) cultures like frats and some sports teams that are responsible for more rape. As a theory of sexual violence, none of these elements identifies women as an intrinsically vulnerable group. Instead, in examining rape, it finds a pattern of abuse rather than a problem with consent. What can consent education do to reduce sexual assault without policies that address the vulnerable time frame when students start school, fraternities as a site of sexual assault, and the ease with which students evade expulsion even when they are found responsible in disciplinary proceedings?

In 2011, with no fanfare, the Obama administration sent a letter instructing school districts, colleges, and universities to make changes to their Title IX proceedings: namely, to consider sexual harassment, and sexual violence, as sex discrimination that negatively affects students and therefore falls under the purview of Title IX. Moreover, because Title IX is not a criminal action, schools should use the burden of proof in civil cases, preponderance of the evidence, rather than criminal law, beyond a reasonable doubt.[25] Using the civil burden of proof levels the scales in disciplinary hearings where female students accuse male students, and where students accuse faculty. As reasonable as this correction appears to be to rampant sexual violence on campuses, one wonders why the burden had been raised to the level of criminal law in campus disciplinary hearings in the first place? Men can already rely on the benefit of the doubt and the "credibility discount" applied to women's testimony.[26] Male students accused of sexual assault thus have a structural advantage over accusers due to the gendering of doubt in the law. When Betsy DeVos, Trump's secretary of education, suspended the Obama letter in September 2017, she expressed concern that men would be disadvantaged if women's credibility was no longer diminished. She and other defenders of this rollback used legal language to inflame concern about a change in fairness, opining that men were being denied due process. Student disciplinary hearings, however, represent a means by which colleges and universities can address violations of student codes of behavior. They can offer support to victims, change dorm room locations, or class schedules, but they have no legal powers. Instead, they are seen as a softer, gentler form of discipline than turning students over to police for sexual assault cases. What they are not is criminal court, and suggesting they are disadvantages women.

Yet DeVos's view that an equal scale of doubt represented a change that would harm men is precisely the basis of a lawsuit a student accused of sexual assault brought after he was suspended for a year from Purdue University. A district court dismissed his suit, but the Seventh Circuit Court reversed that decision and, in an opinion written by Amy Coney

Barrett, now a Supreme Court justice, allowed the case to proceed. Barrett sympathized with John Doe's claim that he had been discriminated against *as a man*. He claimed he had been hurt when the burden of proof was lowered in Title IX cases and he sought protected class status under Title IX. Barrett agreed.

Purdue suspended John Doe for violating Jane Doe's consent.[27] The two were involved in a dating relationship that included consensual sex. Once when they were sharing a bed, Jane woke up to discover John groping her over her clothes. She protested and reprimanded him. He told her he had digitally penetrated her while she was asleep on a previous night. This allegation is at the core of the sexual misconduct case against him, which he denied. Both the process by which John Doe was investigated and the details of the allegations themselves are less than transparent. There is the issue not only of sexual assault occurring within a relationship that has on other occasions included consensual sex, but of the alleged violation of a sleeping person. There is also an issue about the process. Jane Doe did not file a complaint, but the university considered the allegation serious enough to pursue. After his suspension, John Doe brought two claims against Purdue in federal court. The first is the standard claim suspended students make: that the university's procedures were unfair and violated his constitutional right to due process. The second asserts Purdue acted on anti-male bias when it disciplined him and violated Title IX of the Education Amendments of 1972. Then-judge Barrett found the second argument persuasive, writing that it was "plausible" Purdue's investigation panel "chose to believe Jane [Doe] because she is a woman and to disbelieve John [Doe] because he is a man." She pointed to the "Dear Colleague" letter's reminder to schools of their responsibilities to victims, saying it "gives [Doe] a story about why Purdue might have been motivated to discriminate against males accused of sexual assault."[28]

In her analysis of this ruling in Barrett's jurisprudence, Alexandra Brodsky concludes that one "of the most disturbing parts of *Purdue* is that it treats the Department of Education's efforts to enforce survivors' Title IX rights as evidence of anti-male bias."[29] Barrett decided to hear a case testing the rising credibility of sexual violence victims as something that would diminish the benefit of the doubt that men accused of sexual misconduct can typically rely on. The worry that the foundations of law will shake if women might be believed rather than doubted reveals how deeply invested the law is in that imbalance, and how much male impunity seems to be the "fair" and default setting, especially in determining consent.

## CONSENT: A MEMOIR

When she was thirteen years old, Vanessa Springora met author Gabriel Matzneff, then in his late forties, at a dinner party her mother took her to. Matzneff targeted and groomed Springora, persuading her they were embarked on a great romance, under the noses of and with the apparent approval of Matzneff's contemporaries and Springora's mother. Her memoir, *Consent* (2020), makes it clear that she did not consent because she had no power to.[30] Although consent is a meaningless term for a child's coerced participation in sex with an adult, a sector of a French establishment elite gave permission to Matzneff on Springora's behalf. She indicts a cultural view, mingled with the law, that the trope of seduction indemnifies men for sexual abuse. Because she sees consent as a test of a society's views about the worth of girls and the women they become, Springora asks if how we talk about consent can prevent sexual violence. Her memoir is an act of narrative justice, and the answer it provoked is "yes." Following its publication, Matzneff was investigated for rape in connection with his admitted trips to the Philippines, where he had sex with children as young as eight years old, and is currently on trial for his public statements celebrating pedophilia in connection with Springora. *Consent* also propelled an effectively suppressed #MeToo breakthrough in France, prompting the passage of its first age-of-consent law, making sex with someone under fifteen punishable by a twenty-year sentence.[31]

The conditions of emergence were present in France before the 2017 #MeToo breakthrough. In 2012 Nafissatou Diallo, who was working as a hotel maid in Manhattan, claimed that Dominique Strauss-Kahn sexually assaulted her.[32] At the time of the assault, Strauss-Kahn was the head of the International Monetary Fund and a presumptive presidential candidate. The case resounded in France, spotlighting a permissiveness toward sexual harassment, assault, and even rape as sexual freedom. Author Tristane Banon, too, accused Strauss-Kahn of trying to rape her in 2002. Banon's allegations exposed the problem statutes of limitations pose to victims. Investigators concluded that there was prima facie evidence of sexual assault, a victory in itself, but were unable to prosecute because the clock had run out, granting Strauss-Kahn legal impunity. As Diallo's allegations were investigated, Strauss-Kahn and his legal team financed a smear campaign against her. Cyrus Vance, Jr., the Manhattan district attorney whose role in sexual assault cases involving powerful men I have previously discussed, decided not to charge Strauss-Kahn, but his political ambitions were tanked. Moreover, in a prefiguring of #MeToo, women, many of them immigrants like Diallo, protested in support of her and raised an outcry against the routine sexual harassment hotel maids experience on the job. The elements of saturation (so much sexual violence), visibility (international reporting, a powerful man, street protest by survivors showing up for each other), and participation (more women coming forward, some soul searching in France) were present and they produced the signature #MeToo form as women told their stories. But they were let down when Vance's office dropped its case, declaring they had lost confidence in Diallo.

In 2017 the Weinstein allegations resonated in France. The hashtag #BalanceTonPorc urged victims to name names. But #MeToo faced resistance as established figures of Strauss-Kahn's, Weinstein's, and Matzneff's generation decried American-style puritanical attacks against France's putatively liberal sexual culture. Famous actress Catherine Deneuve and Catherine Millet, author of the memoir *The Sexual Life of Catherine M* (2002), published an op-ed in *Le Monde* with one hundred signatories defending men's "right to bother" women and asserting that women weren't upset by and even enjoyed sexual harassment. Springora's memoir in 2020 helped to propel a reckoning in France with the sexual abuse of minors, highlighting in particular the open secret of pedophilia, including incest, as practiced by powerful men, especially intellectuals and authors whose defenses and deflections about these practices put victims on notice about who would have more credibility. Springora exposes the mismatch between the understanding of consent as volitional, a meaning that applies to all kinds of aspects of life in which one exercises agency, and the meaning of consent in laws about sexual violence. In every aspect of law except for laws about rape, consent represents a two-way street, a necessary willingness for civic and commercial engagement alike. Only with regard to sex is consent relegated to a gray area. This is especially true for age of consent.

Age-of-consent laws differ by locality. In some countries and in some states in the United States, the age has dipped into single digits, making it legal for girls to be married.[33] In the United States, age of consent is not standardized but is pegged, variously, at ages sixteen, seventeen, and eighteen, distinguishing it from the younger ages of twelve, thirteen, or fourteen, considered too young for anyone to have credibly consented. Most states supplement the minimum age at which an individual can consent to sexual intercourse with age differential statutes, so-called Romeo and Juliet laws. In the state of Washington, for example, sexual intercourse with someone who is at least fourteen and less than sixteen is illegal if the defendant is four or more years older than the victim. This allows courts leeway not to prosecute statutory rape against teenagers, while also recognizing that age compounds power differentials and provides evidence of coercion in sexual relationships. At the time Matzneff targeted Springora, and until as recently as 2020, France was an outlier with respect to age-of-consent and rape law. It had no age of consent. If a complaint for sexual assault or rape was brought, the victim had to prove they did not consent, a negative burden few met.

Springora's abuser was an esteemed writer whose literary reputation lent his pedophilia an aestheticized sheen. His abuse of dozens of children and adolescent girls and boys was not hidden. Matzneff wrote about it in novels, gave interviews in which he celebrated sex with children, and was enabled in his abuse by French literary culture. In 1974 he published "Les Moins de Seize Ans" (Under 16 Years Old), a sour bit of self-indulgence with such declarations as: "To sleep with a child, it's a holy experience, a baptismal event, a sacred adventure," and "When you have held in your arms, and kissed, caressed, possessed a thirteen-year-old boy, a fifteen-year-old-girl, everything else seems dull, heavy, insipid." Expounding on that text in a 1990 television interview, Matzneff congratulated himself again on having sex with boys and girls: "I think that adolescents, young children, say between age 10 and 16, are perhaps at the age where their emotional and sexual impulses are strongest, because they are new. And I think there is nothing more beautiful and fecund that can happen to an adolescent than to have a love affair, either with someone their age, but also perhaps with an adult who helps them to discover themselves."[34] While the rest of the guests tittered in agreement, only Denise Bombardier, a feminist journalist from Quebec, challenged him, speaking up for victims, asserting they were damaged by Matzneff, denying they could consent, and saying if he were in the United States, he would "already be in jail."[35] Bombardier was applauded by some, but she was excoriated by the French literary elite, told by her publisher that her reputation and current book sales in France would be negatively affected as ranks closed around Matzneff. She was summoned by President Mitterrand, a patron of Matzneff, who tried to brush off the defense of Matzneff as a bit of clumsy overstatement by French writers eager to appear liberal. The writer and publisher Philippe Sollers, husband of feminist theorist Julia Kristeva, called Bombardier a "stupid bitch."[36]

Springora introduces how the psychic residue of sexual trauma combines with gendering by opening *Consent* with a meditation on the warnings directed at girls in fairy tales: leave the party on time, be wary of the sweet-talking wolf, don't bite the apple, don't touch the spindle, and watch out for hunters. So many gendered warnings "that every child would be wise to follow to the letter" (vii). In her childhood, books are talismanic objects in themselves. In adulthood, after Matzneff has used her letters and diaries to present sexual abuse as romance in his books and to create a public cover for pedophilia, books are "poison" to Springora. That is, until she decides to channel what she calls her yearslong dreams of "murder and revenge" into memoir: "Why not ensnare the hunter in his own trap, ambush him within the pages of the book?" (viii). *New York Times* book critic Parul Sehgal calls *Consent* "a Molotov cocktail, flung at the face of the French establishment, a work of dazzling, highly controlled fury."[37] Buoyed by the #MeToo effect circling the globe, Springora's memoir delves into the traumatic impact of sexual abuse and led to the first age-of-consent laws in France.

In *Consent*, Springora primarily wants to tell her story and reclaim her image, her reputation, and her life. She wants to expose how the law enabled Matzneff to groom and rape her, to isolate her from friends her own age, and to make her drop out of school so he could have sex with her. He was investigated occasionally by protective services, but Springora believes he orchestrated and enjoyed his ability to court and elude punishment. Springora, like his other victims, appeared in his novels in barely disguised form. He elicited written declarations of affection from his victims, which he included in his books as evidence of consent. When Matzneff used a photograph of Springora without her permission for the cover of one of his books, she had no legal recourse. In the absence of justice through the courts, narrative justice through memoir became her goal.

The memoir is divided into six sections following the prologue: The Child, The Prey, The Stranglehold, Release, The Imprint, and Writing. In terse and direct prose, Springora the adult returns to the time of the two-year abuse to recount Matzneff's entrapment of her and the imprisonment she suffered as a girl with no means to escape. That his hold on her is sexual seals her within the isolation and shame of being a fourteen-year-old whose homework is controlled by the fifty-year-old who is penetrating her. As a lonely child, Springora initially welcomes the intense attention Matzneff directs at her, which he escalates through a relentless love-bombing campaign of letters and meetings. Matzneff is highly practiced at exploiting the desire for attention and affection of minors, but, as Springora shows, no one can consent to acts she does not understand and has not even pictured, let alone desired. If, as I am arguing, consent requires that the people involved have an equivalent understanding of the consequences of sex, then, with Springora, we must remove "consent" from the sexual predator's arsenal. Young people can be coerced into sex, but they cannot consent, no matter what they are persuaded to say or write. Springora takes aim at consent precisely because Matzneff attributes it to his victims as a means to protect himself from censure. As a form of epistemic violence, consent enables an abuser to put words in his victim's mouth that hearers are accustomed to thinking of as expressions of agency.

Springora's memoir shares with other retrospective accounts of sexual abuse the power to highlight the falseness of consent. It exposes how Matzneff manipulated Springora's lack of knowledge about what he initiated and the consequences it would have for her: "The role G. liked to give himself in his books was that of benefactor, responsible for the initiation of young people into the joys of sex; a professional, a veteran; in other words—if one might dare to be so bold—an expert" (144). In contrast to the image Matzneff creates, and which is acceded to by those who saw his victims as consenting, Springora writes that Matzneff accomplished none of these goals. His only "talent" was that he could penetrate young people without physical force, leaving them with a shameful confusion about their own desire: "Physical violence leaves a memory for a person to react against. It's appalling, but tangible. Sexual abuse, on the other hand, is insidious and perverse, and the victim might be barely aware of what is happening. . . . For many years I struggled with the very idea of the victim, and was incapable of seeing myself as one." She concludes that "an adult's desire can only ever be a trap for an adolescent" (145). Abusers like Matzneff offer things a young person might agree to, like affection or "the sum of money their family needs," but they will do so without regard to the long-term sentence they impose, a sentence young people cannot anticipate or consent to.

In his essay collection *How to Write an Autobiographical Novel* (2018), Alexander Chee writes with painful precision about the difficulty of extricating the abuser's image of the victim from his emerging sense of identity and desire. Sexual abuse entangles desire and damage. It imposes an uncertain path toward self-knowledge on survivors, in part, by attacking the resource of memory on which they must draw for healing and which abuse forces them to distrust. "We are not what we think we are" (226), Chee writes, as he describes the layers of harm he must navigate as he struggles to remember sexual abuse, a process so alienating that it feels as if a "copy of me had replaced me" (226–27). Chee describes watching the premiere of the 1993 independent documentary film *Sex Is . . .* , to which he had been invited as an interviewee: "I went and watched in horror as I described the sexual abuse I'd experienced in the boys' choir I'd once been in, declaring it an education, even a liberation, and that it hadn't harmed me at all." (227). He watched the abuser's language tumble out of "my huge, lying mouth" (227) through the aftershocks of PTSD. The deep mistrust of self, a form of testimonial quieting, is legible in the awful legacy of trauma that intertwines telling with annihilation: "Even now, though, as I try to write this essay, it dissolves in my hands. There is a part of me that insists what I'll tell you cannot be told. That insists if the truth were known I would be destroyed" (231).[38]

In a *New York Times* op-ed and her memoir from which it is adapted, *Girlhood*, Melissa Febos offers the term *empty consent* to name the ways in which unwanted touch teaches girls that their bodies do not belong to them.[39] The unsought gaze and unreciprocated touch of boys and men are directed at girls as they approach middle school and teach them how to be in the world. To be a girl is to be a body for others. Febos names the trained deference to, fear of, and inability to prevent or halt unwanted sexual touch "empty consent" because it is a "no" that men refuse to hear and girls and women grow unable to utter. Empty consent is the opposite of desire. There is a willfulness to sexual abuse like Matzneff's: it asserts that the enactment of his desire on Springora be read as her consent. It is the right to name her experience for her, to take away her self-knowledge, and to restrict her relationship with the world. Empty consent names the phenomenology of being gendered, a training in the lived and felt experience of being embodied *for* others that makes the experience of refusing, resisting, and speaking out difficult to manifest.

In feminist phenomenology, the body is understood as a habitation that is at once personal and cultural, a product of forces that mold it and, once molded, the expression of those forces. We can observe bodies so influenced by norms of gender, that weakness, submissiveness, and femininity appear to be external and natural manifestations of internal and essential qualities. In "Throwing Like a Girl," Iris Marion Young extended to gender the concepts and vocabulary of phenomenology developed by Maurice Merleau-Ponty.[40] She observed that girls are trained not to extend their bodies into space like boys are, but to restrict their movements to comport with norms of femininity. This lifelong practice of holding back is expressed in tentativeness about the body's capacity to reach out into the world. It also reinforces the sense that the world will meet your efforts with hostility or indifference. Young's example of a woman crossing a stream when she hikes captures the sense of inward withholding and lack of confidence in the body developed over time such that she no longer trusts whether her body will carry her from bank to bank. She is tentative. Her social sense of her body, which says, "you can't," overrides her assessment of whether she can make the jump. A lifetime of such discipline severs the reliable feedback loop of trust in one's own body. In female gendering, both the world and the body are an unreliable, even hostile, reflection of a diminished personhood. The message is: if you fall, it will be your fault. For Young, gender can be understood as a form of oppression that women internalize through an imposed and enforced system of limitations. It is structural rather than individual, cultural rather than natural, and, to a large extent, masked in its operations by routine practices. The messages are everywhere, and women, as bell hooks poignantly observes of her own mother, can be patriarchy's most enthusiastic enforcers.[41] If we think of consent as part of gender, then we better understand how it is instrumentalized by abusers against victims; that is, how abusers exploit a gendered power imbalance to impose unwanted touch and claim their victims consented.

Attorney and feminist writer Jill Filipovic argues that "yes means yes," or affirmative consent, is a better baseline than "no means no." An unambiguous, even enthusiastic "yes" as the standard for consent removes it from the gray area and makes "it harder for men to get away with rape."[42] Kate Harding, whose book *Asking for It* exposes rape culture and proposes solutions to change it, advocates for a real-world understanding of the renegotiations that unfold during sex and recommends a "check in with your partner" approach (218). Filipovic and Harding speak to a contemporary moment of consent education within a cultural

conversation enlarged by the #MeToo effect. Rebecca Traister defines
the enlarged conversations propelled by the rising credibility of women
as connecting sexual harassment, verbal abuse, sexual innuendo,
street harassment, and dating violence to workplace discrimination
and systemic inequalities.[43] Agreeing with Traister that #MeToo is
"really about work," Joseph Fischel insists that it is also "really about
sex." #MeToo exposes "gendered dominance" and "sexual one-sidedness"
across all the areas of life in which men with power set the terms.[44]
These definitions of consent connect individual agency and institutional critique. They recognize that desire arises within the power
imbalances that shape other areas of life, and in this, they argue for the
nonexceptional quality of #MeToo; namely, that sexual harassment is
routine and, as such, will require solutions that suit the harm and support survivors.

# CONCLUSION

## Promising Young Women—What We Owe Survivors

The prevalence and diversity of #MeToo stories underscores the reality of sexual violence in every phase and location of women's lives. As a paradigm-shifting frame of reference for hearing those stories, the #MeToo effect positions survivors in relation to each other, overcoming the power imbalance that defines he said / she said and generating collective credibility. Here, a range of separate activities and forms as diverse as protest marches, labor strikes, serial television, life writing, and fiction can be understood as testimony, not only as separate examples emerging after the 2017 breakthrough, but as part of a lineage of intersectional feminism and narrative activism countering longstanding norms of gendered violence and impunity. And, not only in the restricted sense of sworn statements in courts of law, but as truthtelling. Understood as testimony, these examples indict the routine silencing of survivors as evidence of a deep-seated problem rather than disconnected individual cases. When the #MeToo effect identified specific men in power, and the institutions that protect them, it raised the question of accountability: What do we owe survivors? Survivor testimony offers an archive of authoritative responses to this question. As a first principle, I have argued we must pay attention to these accounts. Not because speaking out magically changes things. The point is that it doesn't. But because witnessing stories of harassment and abuse tasks hearers with acting. Reading like a survivor and holding open the possibility that accounts of sexual violence are truthful joins tellers and hearers in a mutual relation of ethical responsibility.

The claim that survivors themselves are best positioned to propose solutions to sexual violence is often substantiated by reference to their narratives and how they generate visibility, which is necessary for political participation, social change, and healing. Tarana Burke placed identification and empathy at the center of the movement, and her memoir *Unbound* consistently uses the term "my story" as the shared referent of "me too," the basis on which survivors connect. She locates the germ of her movement in her initial refusal to listen to what she knew was a story of sexual abuse (a story she wanted to avoid because it was triggering) and her hard-earned recognition that the key to healing consisted in reframing the narrative scene as empowering.[1] In her memoir *Know My Name*, Chanel Miller connects the experience of sexual violence to the recognition that results from hearing another survivor's story. Life writing enables Burke and Miller to offer authoritative and nuanced accounts unavailable at trial (Miller) or in the swirling media coverage of #MeToo (Burke). With reference to Sylvia Plath and Anne Sexton, confessional poets who drew on personal experiences of sexual violence, Jacqueline Rose argues that such work offers the world "a voice that brilliantly orchestrates its own sorrow and rage." Rose argues that survivors tell us the worst: not under the constraints of a disciplinary hearing, distorted through cross-examination on the stand, or managed into the classic formula of false equivalence "he said/she said," but in voices that conjure grief and fury in their own terms. Rose identifies the survivor's voice as "one of women's best weapons against cruelty and injustice."[2]

As narrative activism, #MeToo storytelling has multiple benefits. It is (potentially) therapeutic for individuals because it enables agency over a story that has been taken away. It is foundational to reparative work within communities. It changes how publics understand sexual violence and whose voices they trust. Yet, as salutary as it is to tell one's story, the hurdles to gaining a hearing for it are high. Tanya Serisier cautions that there is much to be lost for survivors when they speak out in conditions of willful unhearing. Sara Ahmed observes how survivor speech can be limited when formal procedures drain the time and energy of those who seek to hold institutions accountable, waiting them out until they give up. I conclude by examining the use of collective witness to force accountability in three examples that take place within the temporal, epistemic, and hermeneutic framing of #MeToo: the film *Promising Young Woman*, the campaign to hold Andrew Cuomo responsible for sexual harassment while he was governor of New York, and a lawsuit brought by three graduate students against Harvard University. All three show how survivor trauma is compounded by obstructive processes, minimization of harm, and refusal to act on findings. They show how the protection of abusers and willingness to sacrifice survivors forms a social adhesive, binding beneficiaries together through bad faith, secrecy, and permissible abuse. They also help us to navigate toward future resolutions of #MeToo cases.

## PROMISING YOUNG WOMAN

The film *Promising Young Women* (2020) follows Cassie, played by Carey Mulligan, as she struggles in the aftermath of her best friend and fellow medical student's rape and suicide. It is written, coproduced, and directed by Emerald Fennell in her feature film directorial debut. The film won an Oscar, as well as Critic's Choice, Writer's Guild, and British Academy Film awards for best original screenplay, with nominations for Best Picture, Best Director, Best Film Editing, and Best Actress, and grossed $17 million worldwide. It was promoted as a "black comedy thriller" focused on revenge. The film opens with a series of scenes in which Cassie dresses in elaborate costumes, goes out to bars alone, and pretends to drink to incapacitation. Invariably, when she performs extreme vulnerability—slipping in and out of consciousness, slurred speech—she is targeted by men who offer to take her home under the pretext of care. It is critical to the film that each man's offer to help her and his plan to rape her are indistinguishable. After each "nice guy" carts her back to his place, dumps her on a bed, and prepares to penetrate her, she confronts him. Alert and sober, she asks, "What are you doing?" He is startled by a suddenly conscious victim, whom he insists consented, and blames her for playing a trick. That is, he does anything other than take responsibility for what he has planned and is on the verge of doing: raping her.

Her repetition of this ritual illustrates that Cassie is in the grip of trauma, endlessly reentering a scene she cannot figure out how to exit. The predictable performance by a series of individual and unrelated men confirms that the circumstances leading to trauma persist. As the necklace Cassie wears makes clear—one-half of a heart with best friend Nina's name on it—she and Nina are a sororal pair. During Nina's assault by a member of their medical school cohort at a party, no one intervened. Afterward, when Nina reports the crime, she is harassed into dropping charges by the rapist's lawyer, whom the medical school refuses to discipline, and dies by suicide. In the wake of this loss, Cassie is devastated and feels guilty that she was not able to protect her friend. She drops out of medical school and cuts ties with those who so casually countenanced her friend's undoing. All she is left with is her obligation to Nina.

Emerald Fennell started working on the script in 2017, the year in which #MeToo reached a global audience. The film originally ended with Cassie's murder, but financial backers urged a less negative conclusion. Although Fennell considered an alternative ending in which Cassie kills all the men at the bachelor party, the final version of the film ends with a twist: Cassie has a backup revenge plan to send evidence of the rape to the police, who swoop in to arrest Nina's rapist/now Cassie's killer. The question of genre preoccupied reviewers, baffling some, but the tension between narrativizing rape in film and the genres of revenge and melodrama in which it is typically depicted is one of *Promising Young Woman*'s central preoccupations: not only because of audience expectations, but because the film asks whether the trauma of sexual violence can end or must be endlessly replayed in the lives of those sentenced to bear its burden when justice fails. Fennell is working knowingly within and referencing film history as she poses this question: "I certainly don't think of the film as a vigilante film. It's angry, it's about grief and it's also about how we forgive, how we as a society are able to move forward."[3] Her question is whether telling the story differently changes it.

The promising young woman is a figure who bears the brunt of broken promises: to reward her efforts, keep her safe. When the promising young woman is injured, what is she owed? Nina is faulted for drinking, is hounded into dropping the charges, and dies by suicide. She fails to generate compassion, fails to put the rapist and the medical school on the hook. She takes the blame. Cassie shoulders the effort to hold the rapist accountable, but, as becomes clear through the film, she is drained by the endlessness of her task. She takes on the obligation others refuse. She strives to compel those she holds directly responsible to feel and know differently: through compassion for Nina rather than reflexive protection of men and the institutions that will never be held unaccountable. The promising young woman has a male foil: the nice guy. Cassie's ritual performance is a form of pedagogy directed at men who imagine themselves as nice guys. She insists they see themselves from her perspective, as rapists, a self-description they would strenuously deny. But the labor of staging serial confrontations with individual men is endless. Later in the film, as the violence of the denouement nears, Cassie warns a man that there are many women like her, so he should watch out. This is the first reference the film makes to any group affiliation for Cassie, and the implication is that each avenger, like her, is on a solo mission. They are not joined as activists, a form of political organization the film cannot imagine, or even friends. The #MeToo effect is thwarted as all testimony is halted on the threshold of shared speech and action. So many promising young women . . . to whom no one will be accountable. They are on their own.

After Cassie returns from the first of the nightly vigils depicted in the film, she takes out a ledger and makes a mark. She's keeping score using tally marks: four vertical lines and a fifth one struck through the group diagonally to make five. There are pages of these marks as well as a list of names. It becomes clear that the film, too, is organized by tallying. "I," in bubblegum pink, titles the scene with Madison McPhee, fellow classmate played by Alison Brie, who was at the party where Nina was raped and refuses to acknowledge any responsibility, blaming Nina for drinking. These carefully crafted confrontations identify an actual accessory to Nina's demise, but they have none of the rape-revenge genre's actual violence. By design, however, emotional violence is the desired effect in elaborately plotted encounters aimed at compelling the bystanders to Nina's assault and enablers of the rapist to feel worry, care, and a profound urge to act on behalf of victims. Cassie gets Madison drunk at lunch and hires a man to take her to a hotel room, leaving Madison with the impression that he sexually assaulted her while she was passed out.

Act "II" is the confrontation with Dean Walker, played by Connie Britton, who initially pretends not to remember Nina, but also blames her for making a "bad choice." She asks Cassie, "What would you have me do? Risk a man's life every time there's an accusation like this? You have to give him the benefit of the doubt. Innocent until proven guilty." When Dean Walker refuses any accountability, Cassie tells her that she dropped the dean's daughter off at a hotel room with members of a band. The dean's terror is palpable. The mask of indifference drops because she knows exactly what can happen to her daughter. Cassie reveals, as she will later with Madison, that she has created illustrative rather than actual scenarios of threat and tells the dean, "You just have to *think* about it the right way. I guess it *feels* different when it's someone you love." The impetus of this pedagogy is to wring right feeling as the prompt for right action from those who failed Nina. If affect prompts new knowledge, then the pedagogy works because it generates obligation, the feeling that one is on the hook and must act. "III" is aimed at Nina's rapist's lawyer, but he is already wracked with guilt following an attack of conscience and is eager to confess. In a moment of loosening, Cassie forgives him.

The film mixes the cat-and-mouse thriller genre implied in these elaborate set-ups with the rape-revenge exploitation plot and, surprisingly, the rom-com, as Cassie dates and falls in love with Ryan, one of the medical students who, unbeknownst to Cassie, was at the party where Nina was raped. There's even a musical montage splicing together cute scenes of their unfolding romance as they lip sync to a Paris Hilton song in the aisles of a drug store. Ryan is appealing, funny, self-deprecating, and patient. He is played by Bo Burnham, another of Fennell's canny casting choice of the "nice guys" whose previous roles and public personae induce audiences to sympathize with them. As Cassie begins to trust Ryan and they fall in love, she imagines another path for herself. She halts the weekly ritual of confronting men and even deletes the social media account she has used to discover that Nina's rapist Al Monroe is getting married. This healing trajectory is halted when Madison McPhee, who is frantic that "something happened" in the hotel room after lunch, gives Cassie an old phone that has the video of Nina's rape that the classmates shared widely. Ryan is shown witnessing the attack, laughing, and doing nothing to intervene. The rom-com is discarded as a way to end the story of sexual violence. The conclusion is unavoidable: there are no nice guys.

As the bubblegum pink "IIII" appears on screen, Cassie confronts Al Monroe at his bachelor party. She returns to the solo mission costumed as a stripper/nurse, gets the attendees drunk with sedative-laced alcohol, and takes Al upstairs. She wants Al to understand, as usual, but in this confrontation, it is not clear if she will cross the line from emotional to physical violence. She threatens to carve Nina's name on Al's body, but he breaks free and smothers her with a pillow. It would appear that the final and failed effort to end traumatic obligation with a transfer of shame and embodied accountability ends with Cassie's sacrificial death. There will be no settling of debts, no final tally mark. Cassie's confrontation with Ryan, however, reshuffled the ledger. Cassie sent the video of Nina's rape and the address of the party to the repentant attorney with instructions that it be shared with police "in the event of my disappearance." Between the bachelor party where Cassie is killed and the wedding, a missing persons investigation is opened for her. The detective initially focuses on whether "she hurt herself," a hypothesis Ryan readily endorses when questioned. As the consequences of Cassie's backup plan drop in the closing minutes of the film, police swarm the wedding, arresting Al as Ryan receives a series of programmed texts that read:

You didn't think it was the end did you?
It is now.

Enjoy the wedding.

Love, Cassie and Nina.

A final diagonal mark strikes the end of the tally. Is this justice? No disciplinary process, police, or court helped Nina, no chorus of survivors rose to amplify her credibility, and Cassie is dead at the end of the film. So many stories end this way. Cassie is disempowered from the beginning and resembles the minor characters I discussed earlier. Like Ismene, she is one of a sisterly pair. Like Philomela, she visually represents a spectacle of a woman-in-crisis who nonetheless struggles to find an adequate witness. Overarchingly, Cassie's plotting suggests the metaphor of a theater of participation to think through how various subjects are placed in relation to sexual violence, what each position compels them to do or permits them to get away with. There are victims and abusers, but also enablers, bystanders who would never imagine themselves taking part in sexual misconduct, and beneficiaries whose distance from harm enables them to shrug off responsibility. Going far beyond the perpetrator-victim dyad, sexual abuse draws a range of subjects into a theater of participation. The film asks how to make them accountable. The title underscores that promising young woman is both a trope and a trap: her promise can be blunted by abuse and the impunity of abusers. The #MeToo effect of collective witness offers an alternative to the solo mission and the traumatic obligation that cannot be discharged in *Promising Young Woman*.

In 2020, the #MeToo effect propelled accountability when Lindsey Boylan accused New York governor Andrew Cuomo of sexual harassment, and two more women who also worked for the state of New York came forward.[4] Their allegations were reported in the *New York Times* in February 2021, and Cuomo made a tepid stab at excusing his behavior as old-school, if handsy. As allegations accumulated and were verified by journalists, some called for Cuomo's impeachment or resignation. Instead, the New York attorney general's office undertook a full investigation, which found the allegations credible and also discovered the sexual harassment of a state trooper Cuomo had asked to be assigned to his security detail. At the end of the investigation, his behavior looked worse than it did at the beginning. The attorney general documented a pattern of sexual harassment and a culture of intimidation in Cuomo's office that permitted it. As the inquiry shifted away from he said / she said and the testimony of several women initiated the #MeToo effect, the scope of the investigation focused on the active enablement, patronage, and passivity through which abuse came to define the culture. Ultimately, the governor resigned.

This is what many survivors have been asking for: a full and fair investigation, a transparent reporting of the findings, and proportional consequences. Prior to Cuomo's resignation, a story broke implicating the leadership of TimesUp in vetting the governor's statement denying sexual harassment. The organization was founded in the wake of #MeToo to support women in making sexual discrimination claims.[5] As a result of this revelation, the leadership resigned. Both investigations and their outcomes met the demands of survivors to be heard. They represent a new benchmark for #MeToo cases that do not originate in court but travel instead from workplace complaints to fact-checking and reporting in reputable journalism and generate an investigation that, in turn, delivers findings that reverberate further. The full transit of this testimony demonstrates the necessary mobility of survivor narratives as they seek justice.

Based on the pattern I have analyzed in this book, the support survivors need is unlikely to come from the criminal-legal system. Police do not reliably investigate crimes of sexual violence, nor do prosecutors bring charges. Juries rarely convict, and when they do, probation officers recommend light sentences, which judges may whittle down. The burden of proof is high in criminal cases, beyond reasonable doubt, which is as it should be when the full force of the system bears down on the accused. However, it is a standard women are disadvantaged in meeting independent of the facts. Civil court, with its lower burden of proof, is better suited to women's claims in general, including sexual harassment claims. And not all forms of sexual misconduct are crimes. Many are best handled as disciplinary issues better resolved in workplaces and schools where the accommodations and support are about whom to reassign, whose class schedule to change, and whose office space or dorm assignment to move. Better, then, are appropriate venues outside the criminal system for handling many sexual harassment claims. Notably, there needs to be a third-party entity to which those who cannot access workplace protections may safely appeal. Sex workers, immigrants, domestic workers—all need a way to access support. Yet the law should not be abandoned as a tool in forcing accountability and may even offer a forum for narrative activism and redress, as in a lawsuit brought in 2022 by three women graduate students against Harvard after they sought an adequate resolution through Title IX.

## MARGARET G. CZERWIENSKI, LILIA M. KILBURN, AND AMULYA MANDAVA V. HARVARD UNIVERSITY

*Promising Young Woman* represents a fictional medical school deeply intertwined with rape culture (parties, constant accusations of rape, "2–3 a week" in the words of the dean, no due process for victims despite their efforts to report) and the criminal-legal system (attorneys are paid bonuses for settlements, victims are hounded, social media posts are cherry picked to influence juries). The parties, sexual assault, and silencing of victims are part of the school's common knowledge, as are the routine disclaimers about sexual violence that strangle testimony. In the film, everyone blames women, including a fellow female medical student and a female dean. Those who play along benefit: they receive medical education, degrees, and jobs; they are showered with praise and honors; their friendship networks remain intact. Both the transmission of expertise and sexual abuse that brutally culls promising young women from the ranks create a system of patronage. The lawsuit brought against Harvard asks what it will take to intervene in this system, to disrupt its repetition, and to end its reenactment of trauma in actual universities.

In 2022, three anthropology PhD students—Margaret G. Czerwienski, Lilia M. Kilburn and Amulya Mandava—filed a lawsuit against Harvard. In it, they allege that John Comaroff, a renowned professor of anthropology, used his "power and his perch at Harvard to exploit aspiring scholars." Specifically, "he kissed and groped students without their consent, made unwelcome sexual advances and threatened to sabotage students' careers if they complained." The lawsuit represents a strategy of last resort because when the students reported Comaroff to the university and sought to warn their peers about him, "Harvard watched as he retaliated by foreclosing career paths and ensuring that those students would have 'trouble getting jobs.'" The lawsuit alleges that the investigatory process itself became a tool in Comaroff's "campaign of professional blacklisting," as Harvard enabled him and turned the students into collateral damage. Specifically, Harvard obtained Lilia Kilburn's private therapy notes without her consent, shared them with Comaroff, and apparently attached the notes to its final report on the case, so everyone who had the report could read them. Comaroff allegedly used the information in there—that Ms. Kilburn had PTSD as a result of his harassment—to discredit her testimony, saying she couldn't be trusted.

The letter of support, a #MeToo genre I previously discussed, featured in the days before the lawsuit became public. Thirty-eight of Harvard's bold-faced faculty names cited a concern for due process that motivated them to sign a letter of support for Comaroff.[6] Despite its putative concern about process, the letter is a warm and personal endorsement of Comaroff himself: "We the undersigned know John Comaroff to be an excellent colleague, advisor and committed university citizen who has for five decades trained and advised hundreds of Ph.D. students of diverse backgrounds, who have subsequently become leaders in universities across the world." After the lawsuit was made public, a public outcry about the letter followed. Thirty-five of the thirty-eight retracted their signatures and insisted they were merely voicing a concern about process.[7]

The suit identifies two tools—sexual harassment and retaliation—that abusers use to maintain their networks of influence and how institutions enable them when they do. Naming these tools in the lawsuit unites three individual complaints into a collective demand for accountability at the highest levels. It charges that a decade-long pattern persists through the institutional procedures designed to investigate and sanction it. It claims Comaroff threatened retaliation and brandished his gatekeeping power. The chronology in this suit intertwines three timelines:

Comaroff's sexual harassment of specific people, the ongoing and thwarted efforts to report his misconduct, and his retaliation for potential, suspected, and actual reporting. Margaret G. Czerwienski learned in 2017 about Comaroff's sexual harassment at Harvard and tried to inform her professors and protect students. Similarly, and independently, Amulya Mandava reported harassment to professors and sought to warn students in 2017. Both allege that Comaroff threatened them with career-ending retaliation, effectively silencing them. Lilia Kilburn, as a result of Harvard's failure to act, was the direct target of Comaroff's sexual harassment in 2019, as the suit explains. The three students were effectively isolated from one another other until 2019, when they brought their concerns forward through a Title IX complaint. All three came forward at different times and to different entities but were met with inaction. Their suit anatomizes how the interlocking elements of a prestige-driven academic culture, an investigative process that stalled the women in their efforts to warn students about Comaroff, and a complacent institution created a culture in which abuse of power and professional development go hand in hand.

Together the women demonstrate the inadequate protections offered to them as silence breakers and also point a way toward a potential paradigm shift through narrative activism: they refused to stop complaining and connected their knowledge of unfair reporting practices about sexual harassment to their union organizing work. They united silence breaking and whistle blowing. By linking sexual harassment to other abuses of power, exposing the absence of real recourse through an independent process for survivors, and naming an institution as the responsible party, this case distills a critical insight of the #MeToo movement: it leverages collective credibility to expose a systemic problem that requires a structural solution to ensure accountability. #MeToo vividly demonstrates that the problem with sexual violence is not limited to isolated examples. It does not exist apart from other forms of abuse and is deeply rooted in hierarchal cultures, like the academy. In the Harvard lawsuit, the women's interlocking stories of trying to stop a sexual predator—and being thwarted by Harvard's processes—demonstrate that sexual harassment and retaliation are ready tools to maintain abuse of power as an institutionally protected practice. Sexual harassment allows some to flourish—as gatekeepers, beneficiaries of patronage, and bystanders—as it weeds out others who interrupt the reproduction of privilege and inequality. Thus solutions must focus on all the ways in which abuse of power is protected, including the disingenuous defense of "due process" where real recourse does not exist for survivors and whistle blowers.

As a tallying of actionable harms, the fate of the lawsuit is not yet settled. As narrative activism, however, the lawsuit leverages collective storytelling to generate obligation. Specifically, it combines elements that would be disparate in the law into a compelling story about how sexual abuse seeps into every aspect of a culture and what must be done to change this: three students, three complaints, three timelines, and the identification of an educational institution as a workplace. The lawsuit has a collective subject. As a group, the plaintiffs bind together the timelines into a single story. Just as "alone, together" describes the subjectivity and temporality of trauma navigated by *Promising Young Woman*, alone, each of the women was thwarted in her solo mission to report on Comaroff. Together, they became a different storyteller, one whose testimony refuses to be managed into "he said/she said" through which each could be doubted one at a time. As the disruptive and collective subject of #MeToo and the framework of credibility it summons, they leverage life writing as testimony.

Together, they tell one story about multiple events with a focus on accountability. Hence the lawsuit is brought against Harvard rather than Comaroff or the Anthropology Department, both of which are subject to discipline by Harvard, which the suit asserts is responsible for knowing about Comaroff's past allegations of sexual harassment and abuse at the University of Chicago. Harvard is constructed as a knowing and responsible subject: aware of Comaroff's predatory behavior, hence charged with the responsibility not to hire him, or, failing that, to warn students about him in a transparent way, and, failing that, remove him from advising and teaching. The lawsuit clarifies the cascading consequences that followed from a failure to act on this foreknowledge. The whole complaint is an obligation-generating story about what Harvard did and did not do, what happened as a result, and why the lawsuit is the last resort to make it comply. There is a final scene feel to this complaint that resonates with *Promising Young Woman*. After Cassie has ticked off all the enablers, she arrives at her final confrontation, as the graduates students do when they face down Harvard. They absorb Comaroff into the university in order to identify Harvard, that liberal bastion of worldwide renown, as a clear and present danger. Harvard is the final nice guy.

A person or institution that cannot accept its obligation, an obligation it expressly assumes in the practice of education, refuses accountability, and allows survivors to be expended as collateral damage in networks of patronage is a hard enemy. Most narratives that pit women against implacable authority end badly for them. Harvard is accused of "deliberate indifference," personified as a subject whose inaction "allowed Prof. Comaroff to repeatedly and forcibly kiss Ms. Kilburn, grope her in public, imagine aloud her rape and murder, cut her off from other professors, and derail her academic trajectory." Harvard becomes the responsible party for a litany of harms not only because of what Comaroff did as a professor there but because *it knew better*. The fact that institutions possess ample evidence to punish predators and protect students is central to the film and the lawsuit. The dean in *Promising Young Woman* suggests rape is so endemic on campus that reports of it reach her office twice a week. Numerous medical students shared the video of Nina's rape on their phones. The lawyer readily acknowledges that he was tasked with getting rapists off the hook. In the lawsuit, Harvard is accused of knowing about Comaroff when multiple students informed their professors of his reputation before his hiring.

The issue is bigger than the three complainants. As with #MeToo, they are representative rather than exclusive witnesses. By asserting that "plaintiffs are far from alone," they call in a history of known complaints as well as the enabling behavior of Harvard in permitting a "pattern of sexism, misogyny, and a sexual and gender-based behavior misconduct" to go "unchecked by a predominantly white, male faculty." This is a reference to the historic case (among others) I wrote about in chapter 1, of Jorge Domínguez, professor of government at Harvard, that continued for four decades.[8] In 2020 the *Harvard Crimson*, the student newspaper, detailed how three professors in the Anthropology Department had received multiple complaints of sexual harassment during the same decades of sexual misconduct engaged in by professors in the Government Department. Harvard had problems with ongoing sexual harassment reaching back decades. As complaints by the graduate students in anthropology about incidents as recent as 2017 show, impunity is institutionally entrenched. Writing about *itself*, a Harvard anthropology committee concluded that the university has condoned "a culture in which the abuse of power is normalized and accommodated."

Narrative activism takes us ethically where the law fails. Where the law builds in bias against women and survivors of all genders through doubt, and when rules of evidence separate race-based from gender-based harms, minimizing accountability for both, narrative connects the dots. Emerald Fennell uses narrative filmmaking to show how a larger system of abuse isolates Cassie and consigns her to death. Lindsey Boylan and the other silence breakers in Cuomo's office joined their voices to demand an independent inquiry and accountability. The anthropology students use legal narrative to establish the institutional context of abuse, Harvard's longstanding pattern of tolerating abuse of power and sexual abuse, and the impact of a specific person's predatory behavior on students within that history and place. In the choral voice of the collective witness, the afterlives of so many #MeToo narratives resound. Unheard in previous disciplinary decisions, silenced and muffled by processes that amplify institutional interests, and falsely isolated into solo missions, they are better understood as part of a long history of feminist activism and complaint.

I have argued that narrative activism better describes the scope and power of #MeToo than its characterization as an example of carceral feminism for two related reasons: the criminal-legal system has little interest in victims of sexual violence, and survivors rarely express faith in it or seek to increase its power over them. The mutual antipathy is evident. Where survivors need transparent processes for reporting, they encounter the false appearance of evidence-gathering. Rape-kits said to be "backlogged," which suggests an actual queue where evidence is slowly but diligently being analyzed, are simply warehoused.[9] Where survivors need processes that acknowledge that trauma delays how and when someone reports, statutes of limitations impose timelines that victims, especially young ones, cannot meet. Where they need a way to tell the story in such a way that it will end the reproduction of violence, they confront a system that builds in secondary violence as a routine feature of reporting. It is intolerable that institutions have so little regard and offer such meager relief to those whose stories they demand at every testimonial checkpoint.

Narrative activism drove the #MeToo effect by creating new conditions in which a multitude of stories of sexual violence could avoid these checkpoints and be heard as testimony—as truth-telling and justice-seeking. These stories broke through the minimization of survivor accounts in court as mere "she said" ballast on a scale tipped toward doubting women. He said / she said insists that we act against our knowledge about sexual violence and doubt every survivor, not because of any deficiency in a particular case, but as reflexive bias dressed up as rational doubt. Women and doubt are linked through the underlying association of women with the fictitious threat they pose to men. They are seen not as targets but as dangerous weapons. Not as those who deserve access to justice but as vengeful, putting men and the law itself at risk because they are under threat, angry, and demand a reckoning.

In writing this book, I have confronted the unexceptional quality of sexual violence in everyday life. Sexual harassment, assault, and rape do not just happen once to the unlucky ones who were in the wrong place at the wrong time. Rather, like all traumatic experience, they echo throughout lifetimes. When this violence is suppressed, as it typically is, it leaves a mark on the communities and organizations in which it happens, and it keeps happening. Survivor testimony teaches us about the costs entailed. Studying the factors that converged in the #MeToo breakthrough suggests that while it is impossible to predict which cases will force the puzzle pieces of saturation, visibility, participation, and lineage to join up in a way that galvanizes a broad public to demand change, those are the key elements. They can be harnessed to push forward changes in culture, policy, and law that will reduce sexual violence by creating the context for survivors to be heard together. Overall, I am struck by what a basic request the right to be heard represents. I have proposed narrative activism as a means to be hearable and addressable as a credible witness to one's own experience. This is not an alternative to other forms of justice, but a necessary complement to all of them. Any model of justice requires the right be heard and the means to compel accountability. Justice refers not only to what we aspire to, but to the institutional conditions through which individuals can seek it, and the forms of collective communication on which they can rely. Although we are ill equipped for this work, we can apply the knowledge gained from the #MeToo effect toward a sustained transformation of the status of survivors and those who abuse them and create a new norm of credibility and accountability where doubt and impunity previously ruled. *The #MeToo Effect* argues that the person who is sexually violated *is* a witness and their testimony *is* evidence, a claim that is established in every aspect of law except the law of sexual violence. Despite attacks on their credibility, survivors have produced a record of testimony that breaks through this framing, creating new pathways for witness through their narratives and the critical practice of survivor reading.

What do we owe survivors? Because survivors deserve to be heard as credible, I have offered literary criticism and feminist analysis to highlight the alternative lineage—testimonial and intersectional—that survivors have produced because courts and other formal processes halt them. Thus the question of whether #MeToo has "done anything" ought not only to be assessed in terms of law or policy, where it is often found lacking. Oppositional social movements do not simply obliterate the systems they arise to challenge, nor do we require them to in order to consider them meaningful. It is too much to ask #MeToo to end patriarchy for it be deemed worthy, harnessed for future work, and acknowledged for enfolding survivors within larger solidarities. The #MeToo effect offers a frame of reference for survivor testimony. It replaces he said / she said with a better standard for telling and acting on the truth about sexual violence.

# ACKNOWLEDGMENTS

I have many people to thank. First, thank you to survivors, advocates, activists, and everyone who shared their stories with me and answered my questions. Several people read full drafts of the manuscript, sometimes more than once, and always when I needed fresh eyes on the project. Thank you to Beth Marshall, Sharon Marcus, Craig Howes, Jim Phelan, Gillian Whitlock, Rosanne Kennedy, and Carol Dougherty. Thank you to those who invited me to present this work, in person or in print, and for helping me to improve it: Caroline Bicks and the University of Maine; Wallace Best, Anne McClintock, and Gayle Salamon at Princeton; Jennifer Cooke; Cloe Axelson and Franny Toth at *Cognoscenti*; Joy Castro and the University of Nebraska; Marilee Lindemann, Martha Nell Smith, and the University of Maryland; Kimberley Lamm, Priscilla Wald, and Ara Wilson at Duke; Helena Michie and Rice University; Theresa Kulbaga and Miami University; Vicki Madden and Maria Elena Torres-Quevedo; Laura Castor and Cassandra Falke at the Arctic University of Norway; Hülya Adak and Sabanaci University; Suzanna Walters and Northeastern University; Faculty of Law at Lund University, Sweden; Marlene Kenney and Riverside Trauma Center; and Cynthia Franklin, John Zuern, Ebony Coletu, Carol Stabile, Rebecca Wanzo, and the members of *Biography's* "Afterlives of #MeToo" workshop. Thank you to Jennifer Crewe, Nancy K. Miller, and Victoria

Rosner at Columbia University Press. Thank you to Ohio State University and my Project Narrative colleagues, Wellesley College, and Suzanne Stewart-Steinberg and Peter Szendy at the Pembroke Center, Brown University, for welcoming me to the "Narratives of Debt" seminar. Thank you to the Battered Women's Justice Project and Stop Domestic Violence in DC for invitations to share my work and learn from yours. Thank you to those who talked with me about this project before and during the pandemic. Thank you for sharing this heavy material and reminding me to celebrate: Hillary Chute, Marlene Kenney, Brette Lennon, William and Helen Pounds, Maggie Roberts, Allie Collins-Anderson, Christopher Castiglia, Susan Brison, Tahneer Oksman, Anne Van Cleve, Ellen Wilson, and Eden Osucha. A special thanks to Margaret Czerwienski, Lilia Kilburn, and Amulya Mandava for their courage and camaraderie. Whenever I thought I might leave sexual violence off the syllabus, or omit a visit from a rape crisis center staffer or Title IX officer to class, a student shared a story of sexual assault that underscored how necessary such resources are. This didn't happen once or twice, but every year over thirty years of teaching. I especially want to underscore that student survivors deserve narrative justice and more. They deserve all the support necessary to move on from abuse.

I turn to my family for particular appreciation. My siblings Sudee, Don, and David shared silly pet photos to offset the isolation of Covid and we pulled together to weather our mother's death in February 2022 and support our father. The faithfulness of those bonds—siblings and parents—is tied into the making of this book. Special thanks to my husband Tom Pounds and our beloved sons Finn and William for their support. The power of friendship and feminist support lies at the heart of this book. I dedicate it to Beth Marshall for being there every step of the way.

# NOTES

## PREFACE

1.  As I write this preface, the cover-up of rampant sexual within the Southern Baptist church has been exposed. Survivors have begged for years that the church leadership address sexual abuse, including the request to keep a list and share the names of credibly accused abusers with the congregations that employ them. The church hierarchy kept such a list in secret, but there is no evidence that they removed any of the accused from positions of power and influence. The three-hundred-page report was compiled by a third-party investigator and documents that national leaders "suppressed claims of sexual abuse and stymied proposals for reform for over two decades." See Ruth Graham, "Southern Baptists Release List of Alleged Sex Abusers," *New York Times*, May 26, 2022.

2.  Leigh Gilmore, *Tainted Witness: Why We Doubt What Women Say About Their Lives* (New York: Columbia University Press, 2017).

3.  This overvaluation of men applies especially to white cisgender heterosexual men. Men who are not white cannot rely on this unearned extra credit even when they benefit from patriarchy.

4.  My use of the term is grounded in a theory of gender that holds, simultaneously, that gender is not immutably grounded in biology, even as people are exploited and oppressed as if gender were real in precisely this way; that masculinity and femininity are produced in relation to social forms of power; and that anyone's experience of gender is real to them, but claiming to be a woman or a man has a different status from asserting that the gender binary is universally true.

5.  Lest literary culture seem too rarefied a context for survivor activism, antirape activists in the 1970s and 1980s used literary criticism to explore and explain sexual violence. Kate Millett's groundbreaking first book, *Sexual Politics* (1970), began as her

Ph.D. thesis and is a work of literary criticism that interrogates the sexism and het-erosexism of the novelists D. H. Lawrence, Henry Miller, and Norman Mailer and interprets Jean Genet as offering a critique of patriarchy and the family. Better known for partnering with feminist legal theorist Catherine MacKinnon to devise antipor-nography legislation, Andrea Dworkin used her earliest works, *Woman Hating* (1976) and *Pornography: Men Possessing Women* (1981), to develop a theory of male domi-nance grounded in close readings of literary texts. Millett and Dworkin brought skills to the analysis of sexual violence honed through academic training in the humani-ties, including close reading; a fluency of historical, aesthetic, and political reference; and an understanding of the significance of language in these realms. Audre Lorde's influential statement, "My silences had not protected me. Your silence will not pro-tect you," was delivered at the annual convention of the Modern Language Associa-tion in 1977 on a panel that included poet Adrienne Rich, and was later published in the essay "The Transformation of Silence Into Language and Action," in *Sister Out-sider: Essays and Speeches* (Trumansburg, N.Y.: Crossing, 1984).

# INTRODUCTION

1. James Phelan, *Somebody Telling Somebody Else: A Rhetorical Poetics of Narrative* (Columbus: Ohio State University Press, 2017), ix.

2. Tarana Burke launched the organization Just Be in 2006 to serve girls and women of color in Baltimore, which is the source of the Me Too movement.

3. Harriet Jacobs, *Incidents in the Life of a Slave Woman*, ed. Jean Fagan Yellin (Cam-bridge, Mass.: Harvard University Press, 2000).

4. Tarana Burke, *Unbound: My Story of Liberation and the Birth of the Me Too Move-ment* (New York: Flatiron, 2021), 152.

5. Burke, 157.

6. See Sarah J. Jackson, Moya Bailey, and Brooke Foucault Welles, *#Hashtag Activism: Networks of Race and Gender Justice* (Cambridge, Mass.: MIT Press, 2020).

7. For data analysis of survivor testimony on Twitter that is not typically classed as #MeToo, see Kim Albrecht, "The #MeToo Anti-Network," November 2020–November 2021, https://metoo.kimalbrecht.com, on the hashtag #WhyIDidn'tReport. Typically, these tweets were posted in response to #MeToo, described an experience of unre-ported sexual violence, and did not cite #MeToo. So many stories lie outside the frames still being developed to hear them as testimony.

8. For a full account of the women who went on the record about Weinstein and how Jodi Kantor and Megan Twohey reported the story in the *New York Times*, see their *She Said: Breaking the Sexual Harassment Story* (New York: Penguin, 2019).

9. Andrea Constand filed civil charges against Cosby in 2005. See "Andrea Constand's Victim Impact Statement," *New York Times*, September 25, 2018, https://www.nytimes.com/2018/09/25/arts/andrea-constand-statement-cosby.html. She was awarded a financial settlement in 2006. When other women brought additional allegations,

criminal charges were filed in 2016. Cosby was convicted on three counts in 2018 and sentenced to three to ten years in state prison. In 2021 his conviction was vacated by the Supreme Court of Pennsylvania because the district attorney who brought the civil charges in 2005 said he would not try Cosby on criminal charges. There is no official documentation of this agreement, just the asserted recollection of a deal made via press release. See my analysis in "Bill Cosby's Release Forces Us to Ask: How Far Can #MeToo Go?," *WBUR Cognoscenti*, July 7, 2021, https://www.wbur.org/cognoscenti/2021/07/07/bill-crosby-conviction-vacated-rape-andrea-constand-leigh-gilmore.

10. See Ronan Farrow's reporting, which highlights how NBC enabled Lauer, in Daniel Arkin, "Brooke Nevils Clearly Described Rape or Sexual Assault by Matt Lauer in NBC Meeting, Says Ronan Farrow," *NBC News*, October 11, 2019, https://www.nbcnews.com/news/us-news/brooke-nevils-unambiguously-described-rape-matt-lauer-nbc-meeting-ronan-n1064986.

11. Many young athletes accused Nassar before 2018. Reporting by the *Indy Star*, to which Denhollander submitted her allegations, was crucial to the investigation of Nassar's crimes and the multiple failures and outright refusals by authorities to stop him. See, for example, Justin L. Mack, "A List of the Gymnasts Who Have Publicly Accused Dr. Larry Nassar of Sexual Abuse," *Indy Star*, December 7, 2017, https://www.indystar.com/story/news/2017/12/07/list-gymnasts-who-have-publicly-accused-dr-larry-nassar-sexual-assault/930136001/.

12. I draw on my theorization of memoir as an alternative jurisdiction in *The Limits of Autobiography: Trauma and Testimony* (Ithaca, N.Y.: Cornell University Press, 2001).

13. Caitlin Flanagan and Daphne Merkin wrote in response to an account by "Grace," the pseudonym given a woman whose story was told on *Babe.net* magazine about what she described as sex she felt went too far with comedian Aziz Ansari. The story provoked backlash against #MeToo, but also conversation about dating norms. See Katie Way, "I Went on a Date with Aziz Ansari. It Turned Into the Worst Night of My Life," *Babe.net*, January 13, 2018, https://babe.net/2018/01/13/aziz-ansari-28355; Caitlin Flanagan, "The Humiliation of Aziz Ansari," *Atlantic*, January 14, 2018, https://www.theatlantic.com/entertainment/archive/2018/01/the-humiliation-of-aziz-ansari/550541/; and Daphne Merkin, "Publicly, We Say #MeToo. Privately, We Have Misgivings," *New York Times*, January 5, 2018, https://www.nytimes.com/2018/01/05/opinion/golden-globes-metoo.html.

14. Masha Gessen, "When Does a Watershed Become a Sex Panic," *New Yorker*, November 14, 2017; Catherine Deneuve, "Open Letter: Nous défendons une liberté d'importuner, indispensable à la liberté sexuelle." *Le Monde*, January 10, 2018, https://www.cnn.com/2018/01/10/europe/catherine-deneuve-france-letter-metoo-intl/index.html.

15. The metaphor of the pendulum in claims of #MeToo overreach is ubiquitous. See, for example, "We seem to be on a pendulum in this country where we've gone from believing no women to believing all women," quoted in Nicholas Fandos and Dana Rubinstein, "Why These Women Are Determined to Clear Cuomo's Name," *New York*

*Times,* February 2, 2022, https://www.nytimes.com/2022/02/02/nyregion/cuomo -supporters.html. Bari Weiss concocted the standard "believe all women" and attributed it to #MeToo. See Rebecca Traister's apt response in "'You Believe He's Lying'? The Latest Debate Captured Americans' Exhausting Tendency to Mistrust Women," *Cut,* February 26, 2020. See also Monica Hesse, "'Believe Women' Was a Slogan. 'Believe All Women' Is a Strawman," *Washington Post,* May 12, 2020.

16. Jessica A. Clarke, "The Rules of #MeToo," *University of Chicago Legal Forum* 2019 (November 31, 2019): 37–84.

17. Deborah Turkheimer, "Beyond #MeToo," *New York University Law Review* 94, no. 5 (November 2019): 1146–1208.

18. Sara Ahmed, *Complaint!* (Durham, N.C.: Duke University Press, 2021), 28.

19. Clarke, "The Rules of #MeToo," 37.

20. Lorna Bracewell, *Why We Lost the Sex Wars: Sexual Freedom in the #MeToo Era* (Minneapolis: University of Minnesota Press, 2021), 4, 5.

21. Dorothy Allison, *Bastard Out of Carolina* (New York: Dutton, 1992).

22. Combahee River Collective, "A Black Feminist Statement" (1977), in *The Second Wave: A Reader in Feminist Theory,* ed. Linda Nicholson (New York: Routledge, 1997): 63–70. See also Keeanga-Yamahtta Taylor, *How We Get Free: Black Feminism and the Combahee River Collective* (London: Haymarket, 2017).

23. CRC's articulation of intersectionality is anticapitalist. Although there are elements within the critique of patriarchy central to antirape politics from the 1970s onward that also reference Marxist-feminism, including by Catherine MacKinnon, as well as the anti-imperialism of Andrea Dworkin, CRC stands out for its deep engagement.

24. Tanya Serisier cautions that women who speak out are vulnerable to censure. See her *Speaking Out: Feminism, Rape, and Narrative Politics* (London: Palgrave Macmillan, 2018).

25. This operates mostly for white cisgender men. Men of color cannot rely on it routinely, but white women can sometimes harm men of color by accessing the power they possess within patriarchy. The most hierarchical structures combine sexism, homophobia, and racism. Queer, trans, and nonbinary people of color are least likely to be deemed more credible when they accuse cisgender white men.

26. Parul Sehgal, "The Case Against the Trauma Plot," *New Yorker,* December 27, 2021.

27. Cherríe Moraga and Gloria Anzaldúa, eds., *This Bridge Called My Back: Writings by Radical Women of Color* (Watertown, Mass.: Persephone, 1981).

28. For analysis of political resistance and formal experimentation in autobiography, see my *Autobiographics: A Feminist Theory of Women's Self-Representation* (Ithaca, N.Y.: Cornell 1994), especially chapter 3 on medieval women writers and chapter 6 on Gloria Anzaldúa, Cherríe Moraga, and *This Bridge Called My Back.*

29. In making this claim, I draw on my theorization of life writing as an alternative jurisdiction in "Jurisdictions: *I, Rigoberta Menchú, The Kiss,* and Scandalous Self-Representation in the Age of Memoir and Trauma," *Signs: Journal of Women in Culture and Society* 28, no. 2 (2002): 695–718; and *The Limits of Autobiography: Trauma and Testimony* (Ithaca, N.Y.: Cornell University Press, 2001).

30. In *Limits*, I theorize "limit cases" as texts that reside on the border of genre. Invok-
ing the conventions of more than one genre is a strategy writers use to evade highly
legalistic forms of judgment, including what Erin A. Spampinato calls "adjudicative
reading," or a tendency to read novels depicting sexual violence as if legal rules of
evidence applied. See her "Rereading Rape in the Critical Canon: Adjudicative Criticism and the Capacious Conception of Rape," *differences* 32, no. 2 (2021): 122–60.

31. Michèle LeDoeuff, *Hipparchia's Choice* (1991; New York: Columbia University Press,
2007). Quoted in Manon Garcia, *We Are Not Born Submissive: How Patriarchy Shapes
Women's Lives* (Princeton, N.J.: Princeton University Press, 2021), xiii.

32. Judith Lewis Herman, *Trauma and Recovery* (New York: Basic Books, 1997), 1.

33. There is a debate about how #MeToo has or has not changed the investigation and
prosecution of sex crimes. See Troy Closson, "R. Kelly's Last Criminal Trial Was in
2008. The World Has Changed Since," *New York Times*, August 17, 2021, https://www
.nytimes.com/2021/08/17/nyregion/r-kelly-trial-allegations.html.

## 1. THE #METOO EFFECT

1. Alison Leotta traces the legal origins of "he said / she said" to their source in English
law. See her article "I Was a Sex-Crimes Prosecutor. Here's Why 'He Said / She Said' Is
a Myth," *Time*, October 3, 2018, https://time.com/5413814/he-said-she-said-kavanaugh
-ford-mitchell/. The corroboration requirement blocked the prosecution of most rapes.
For example, a study in 1969 showed that New York City's corroboration requirement
resulted in 18 rape convictions out of 1,085 arrests. William M. Freeman, "Ex-magistrate
Ploscowe Dies; Criminal-Law Expert Was 71," *New York Times*, September 11, 1975,
https://www.nytimes.com/1975/09/22/archives/exmagistrate-ploscowe-dies-criminal
law-expert-was-71.html.

2. See my *Tainted Witness: Why We Doubt What Women Say About Their Lives* (New
York: Columbia University Press, 2017).

3. This overvaluation of men applies especially to white cisgender heterosexual men and
is inextricably related to white supremacy. Men who are not white cannot rely on this
unearned extra credit even when they benefit from patriarchy.

4. Jill Smolowe, "Sex, Lies and Politics: He Said, She Said," *Time*, October 21, 1991, http://
content.time.com/time/magazine/article/0,9171,974096,00.html.

5. In *Tainted Witness*, I drew on Jane Mayer and Jill Abramson's exhaustive research
into Hill's allegations. See their *Strange Justice: The Selling of Clarence Thomas* Boston: Houghton Mifflin, 1994). They begin their research assuming there are two versions of the events, a classic "he said / she said," but conclude there is no evidence to
suggest Hill fabricated anything or that Thomas's denials were rooted in fact.

6. See Angela Wright's interview, "Thomas Accuser Angela Wright Sticks to Claims,"
NPR, October 9, 2007, https://www.npr.org/templates/story/story.php?storyId
=15113601.

7.  See Michael Martin's interview with Sukari Hardnett, NPR, September 23, 2018, https://www.npr.org/2018/09/23/650956623/anita-hill-testimony-the-witness-not-called.

8.  United States Congress, Senate, Select Committee on Ethics, "Resolution for Disciplinary Action," 104th Congress, First Session, September 8, 1995, https://www.congress.gov/104/crpt/srpt137/CRPT-104srpt137.pdf.

9.  Patricia Holt, "Under Scrutiny: Anita Hill Describes Finding a New Life After the Devastating Clarence Thomas Hearings," *SFGate*, September 28, 1997, https://www.sfgate.com/books/article/Under-Scrutiny-Anita-Hill-describes-finding-a-2804765.php.

10. Excerpted in Barbara Boxer, *The Art of Tough* (New York: Hachette, 2016).

11. "Senator Packwood engaged in a pattern of abuse of his position of power and authority as a United States Senator by repeatedly committing sexual misconduct, making at least 18 separate unwanted and unwelcome sexual advances between 1969 and 1990. . . . In most of these instances, the victims were members of Senator Packwood's staff or individuals whose livelihoods were dependent upon or connected to the power and authority held by Senator Packwood. These improper acts bring discredit and dishonor upon the Senate and constitute conduct unbecoming a United States Senator." Select Committee on Ethics, "Resolution for Disciplinary Action."

12. External Review Committee to Review Sexual Harassment at Harvard University, "Report," January 2021, https://provost.harvard.edu/files/provost/files/report_of_committee_to_president_bacow_january_2021.pdf. It is important to note that in 2014 Harvard, along with fifty-five other institutions, was under investigation by the Department of Education for its failure to address campus sexual assault. See Jennifer Steinhauer and David S. Joachim, "55 Colleges Named in Federal Inquiry Into Handling of Sexual Assault Cases," *New York Times*, May 1, 2014, https://www.nytimes.com/2014/05/02/us/politics/us-lists-colleges-under-inquiry-over-sex-assault-cases.html. In 2016 a student filed a lawsuit against Harvard for compelling her to remain in the same dorm as her alleged rapist. See Christine Hauser, "Former Students Sue Harvard Over Handling of Sexual Crimes Complaints," *New York Times*, February 19, 2016, https://www.nytimes.com/2016/02/20/us/harvard-sexual-crimes-complaints-alyssa-leader.html. I want to highlight the cultural attitudes and structures through which institutions enable sexual violence to continue, even as they are compelled (and even attempt) to address it.

13. David L. Chandler, "3Q: Sheila Widnall on Sexual Harassment in STEM," *MIT News*, September 17, 2018, https://news.mit.edu/2018/sheila-widnall-sexual-harassment-STEM-0917.

14. James S. Bikales, "Protected by Decades-Old Power Structures, Three Renowned Harvard Anthropologist Face Allegations of Sexual Harassment," *Harvard Crimson*, May 29, 2020, "https://www.thecrimson.com/article/2020/5/29/harvard-anthropology-gender-issues/.

15. United States District Court for the District of Massachusetts, case 1:22-cv-10202, document 1, filed February 8, 2022, https://www.sanfordheisler.com/documents/Czerwienski-et-al.-v.-Harvard-University-File-Stamped.pdf.

16.  T. Christian Miller and Ken Armstrong reported "An Unbelievable Story of Rape," in *ProPublica*, December 16, 2015, https://www.propublica.org/article/false-rape -accusations-an-unbelievable-story.

17.  T. Christian Miller and Ken Armstrong, *A False Report: A True Story of Rape in Amer- ica* (New York: Crown 2018), 38. The book became the basis for the eight-episode Netflix series *Unbelievable* (2019).

18.  "Believe women" is a perfectly understandable standard for several reasons: (1) it is clearly intended to correct the overwhelming presence of doubt; (2) rape is under- reported and there are so many obstacles to being heard that when a woman does make a claim, it is more likely than not that she is telling the truth; (3) there is noth- ing exceptional about false claims of rape except that people tend to make such claims a little less frequently than about other things; and (4) there is no benefit to claiming to be a victim of rape. For the power of the "believe women" stance, see Jessica Val- enti and Jaclyn Friedman, eds., *Believe Me: How Trusting Women Can Change the World* (New York: Seal, 2020).

## 2. BUILDUP

1.  Tim Baysinger, "This Is How Many People Watched the Oscars this Year," *Time*, Feb- ruary 27, 2017, https://time.com/4684709/oscars-2017-nielsen-ratings/.

2.  Andrew Flanagan, "Taylor Swift Wins Sexual Assault Lawsuit Against Former Radio Host," NPR, August 14, 2017, https://www.npr.org/sections/therecord/2017/08/14 /543473684/taylor-swift-wins-sexual-assault-lawsuit-against-former-radio-host.

3.  See Sharon Marcus, *The Drama of Celebrity* (Princeton, N.J.: Princeton University Press, 2019), for analysis of how "celebrity defiance powerfully symbolizes social dynamics" (25) and can sometimes change them. Lady Gaga and Taylor Swift invited audiences to relish the power they wield in situations that are otherwise disempow- ering. Their solidarity with victims rather than their difference from them contrib- uted to the growing awareness that sexual violence crosses all lines.

4.  Chanel Miller, *Know My Name: A Memoir* (New York: Viking, 2019).

5.  Anna Silman, "'Emily Doe' from the Brock Turner Case Is Ready for You to Know Her Name," *Cut*, September 4, 2019, https://www.thecut.com/2019/09/chanel-miller -from-brock-turner-case-wants-us-to-know-her-name.html.

6.  Miller's statement appears in Katie J. M. Baker, "Here's the Powerful Letter the Stan- ford Victim Read to Her Attacker," *Buzzfeed*, June 3, 2016, https://www.buzzfeednews .com/article/katiejmbaker/heres-the-powerful-letter-the-stanford-victim-read-to -her-ra.

7.  Miller, *Know My Name*, 2.

8.  Miller, 6.

9.  I am grateful to Elizabeth Marshall for conversations about the cultural logics of mas- culinity in this case. See Bill Scher, "After Kavanaugh, #MeToo Should Launch a New Temperance Movement," *Politico Magazine*, October 9, 2018, https://www

.politico.com/magazine/story/2018/10/09/kavanaugh-metoo-temperance-suffragettes
-221141/.

10.  I have previously presented "the rape defense" in my article "Stanford Sexual Assault: What Changed with the Survivor's Testimony," *Conversation*, June 16, 2016, https:// theconversation.com/stanford-sexual-assault-what-changed-with-the-survivors -testimony-60913.

11.  Legal teams often give clients a visual makeover, but Brock Turner and convicted St. Paul's rapist Owen Labrie appeared strikingly differently in court than in their mug shots.

12.  Rebecca Wanzo, *The Suffering Will Not Be Televised: African American Women and Sentimental Political Storytelling* (Albany: SUNY Press, 2009).

13.  See Heyes's chapter "Dead to the World: Rape, Unconsciousness, Social Media," in *Anaesthetics of Existence: Essays on Experience at the Edge* (Durham, N.C.: Duke University Press, 2020), 53.

14.  Joanna Bourke, *Rape: Sex, Violence, History* (Berkeley: Counterpoint, 2007), 54.

15.  "The Incriminating Statement by Cosby Referred to by Judge," Associated Press, September 25, 2018, https://apnews.com/article/bill-cosby-pa-state-wire-entertainment -us-news-celebrities-bb64abed0ae04c62900fe99e805e90e4.

16.  Emanuella Grinberg and Catherine E. Shoichet, "Brock Turner Released from Jail After Serving Three Months for Sexual Assault," *CNN*, September 2, 2016, https:// www.cnn.com/2016/09/02/us/brock-turner-release-jail/index.html.

17.  Michele Dauber, Twitter, June 4, 2016, https://twitter.com/mldauber/status/739320 585222660096/photo/1.

18.  Wanzo, *The Suffering Will Not Be Televised*, 8. Wanzo's anatomization of the scene of sympathy presciently describes how Turner's testimony affected Aaron Persky. She continues: "Perhaps most importantly, detractors understand sentimentality as marked by an excessive or simplistic expression of angst or happiness in response to traumatic or other transformative events that are allegedly difficult to represent through tear-inducing texts. In other words, sentimentality supposedly represents something other than 'real' emotion."

19.  "'20 Minutes of Action': Father Defends Stanford Student Son Convicted of Sexual Assault," *Guardian*, June 6, 2016, https://www.theguardian.com/us-news/2016/jun/06 /father-stanford-university-student-brock-turner-sexual-assault-statement.

20.  Deborah Epstein, "Discounting Credibility: Doubting the Stories of Women Survivors of Sexual Harassment," *Seton Hall Law Review* 51, no. 2 (2020): 289–329.

21.  The term *predator*, like perpetrator and victim, is complicated. It obscures the complexity of abusive relationships, layering over and obscuring more intimate terms like boyfriend, classmate, colleague, or mentor. FBI director J. Edgar Hoover used the term *sexual predator* to criminalize a type of person rather than to address how some abusers groom and harm multiple victims. The term has been used in the discourse of criminology to demonize and caricature queer sexuality rather than describe actual harm. For analysis of the limitations and homophobia of this discourse, see Gillian Harkins, *Virtual Pedophilia: Sexual Offender Profiling and U.S. Security Culture*

(Durham, N.C.: Duke University Press, 2020), 48–49. The term is warranted here as a description of Trump, who, like Weinstein, has a lengthy history of preying on vulnerable girls and women.

22. Ariella Azoulay, "The Natural History of Rape" *Journal of Visual Culture* 17, no. 2 (August 2018): 166–76.

23. Susanna Capelouto, "Nancy O'Dell: The Woman Who Rebuffed Trump," *CNN*, October 8, 2016, https://www.cnn.com/2016/10/08/us/nancy-odell-bio/.

24. No Stupid Questions, Reddit, https://www.reddit.com/r/NoStupidQuestions/com ments/5p9vih/what_does_i_moved_on_her_like_a_bitch_even_mean1./

25. Michael Rothberg, *The Implicated Subject: Beyond Victim and Perpetrator* (Stanford: Stanford University Press, 2019); Bruce Robbins, *The Beneficiary* (Durham, N.C.: Duke University Press, 2017).

26. In her brilliant book *The Life and Death of Latisha King: A Critical Phenomenology of Transphobia* (New York: New York University Press, 2018), Gayle Salamon fuses feminist phenomenology and close reading in an analysis of transphobia, homophobia, sexism, and racism in a murder trial. Salamon shows the importance of attending to the words and gestures that attorneys and witnesses employ to cocreate the scenes they describe. These seemingly neutral descriptions carry judgment, including sympathy for the white teen murderer and homophobia directed at the victim, a trans girl of color. Stereotypes are smuggled via description and violent ideas are cloaked as common sense. Salamon's work informs my attention to how bystanders are beckoned and implicated as participants, and how forms of white male bonding are built on shared heterosexism and racism.

27. The widely shared story of the march's origin focuses on how a single Facebook post went viral in the aftermath of Hillary Clinton's defeat, an idea that spread not only as millions in the United States had the same impulse, but also through Clinton's H4A campaign staff and other activist networks and organizations, including Planned Parenthood.

28. Kaveh Waddell, "The Exhausting Work of Tallying America's Largest Protest," *Atlantic*, January 23, 2017.

29. On how illustrators, comics creators, and other visual artists drew on social justice movements and the iconography of protest to picture MeToo, see my "Graphic Witness: Visual and Verbal Testimony in the #MeToo Movement," in *The New Feminist Literary Studies*, ed. Jennifer Cooke (Cambridge: Cambridge University Press, 2020), 25–40.

30. The importance of speech acts to signal lineage can be seen in the rhetorical use of citation. For example, the authors of the Declaration of Sentiments asserted when they assembled at Seneca Falls in 1848 "that all men and women are created equal," to echo and revise the Declaration of Independence. "Women's rights are human rights," asserted by then first lady Hillary Rodham Clinton at the Fourth International Women's Conference in Beijing in 1995, is a speech act that declares an alliance of women with the rights granted in international law and custom as human rights. #BlackLivesMatter is a speech act authored by the founding members Patrisse Cullors, Alicia Garza, and Opal Tometi.

31.   J. L. Austin's speech act theory is useful here in charting the performative power of #MeToo. #MeToo is both locutionary and illocutionary, to use Austin's terminology. As a locutionary act, #MeToo is an actual utterance that draws its power from its shared social meaning and its performance on social media. As an illocutionary act, it had the power to create additional effects through its repetition and the meanings that accrued. Thanks to Jim Phelan for comments on this section.

32.   Lacy M. Johnson, *The Reckonings: Essays on Justice for the Twenty-First Century* (New York: Scribner, 2018), 20.

33.   Brittney Cooper, *Eloquent Rage: A Black Feminist Discovers Her Superpower* (New York: St. Martin's, 2018), 152.

34.   Soraya Chemaly, *Rage Becomes Her: The Power of Women's Anger* (New York: Atria, 2019).

35.   Rebecca Traister, *Good and Mad: The Revolutionary Power of Women's Anger* (New York: Simon and Schuster, 2019), 2.

36.   The "angry black woman" stereotype has been used to signal to white audiences that Black women are a threat. Michelle Obama spoke about being caricatured through the application of this trope, as has tennis champion Serena Williams, who has been criticized for being angry, hence out of control and even dangerous, when she challenges her treatment within her sport as an expression of racism. The racial past of the stereotype does not disappear as white women embrace anger because anger has a history. That history influences who can access it and with what consequences.

37.   Audre Lorde, "The Transformation of Silence Into Language and Action," in *Sister Outsider: Essays and Speeches* (Trumansburg, N.Y.: Crossing, 1984).

38.   White women tend to vote as their white husbands do, and 47 percent voted for Trump in 2016 (https://time.com/5422644/trump-white-women-2016/). The term *women* can be wielded transphobically as a term of exclusion.

## 3. BREAKTHROUGH

1.   Deborah Turkheimer, "Incredible Women: Sexual Violence and the Credibility Discount," *University of Pennsylvania Law Review* 166, no. 1 (2017), https://scholarship.law.upenn.edu/penn_law_review/vol166/iss1/1/.

2.   Patriarchal retrenchment, as was on display during Anita Hill's testimony in 1991, generated feminist activism, as anger over Hill's treatment propelled a record number of women into elected office the following year. This breakthrough was followed by a backlash, evidence of a historical pattern analyzed by Susan Faludi in her *Backlash: The Undeclared War Against American Women* (New York: Crown, 1991).

3.   See Judith Butler, *Giving an Account of Oneself* (New York: Fordham University Press, 2005), in which, drawing on Theodor Adorno, Butler theorizes the "conditions of emergence" required for a self to bring a narrative into existence. Many factors contribute to this possibility, and the self cannot control many of them (7, 19). The prevailing ethos shapes the account one can give, but Butler reads Michel

Foucault as offering a way to assert agency and ethical deliberation even when the subject is ungrounded (i.e., not able to determine the conditions in which an account is given).

4. In February 2018 the *New York Times* reported on three studies: a new national online survey conducted in January, a *Washington Post*/ABC News poll, and new findings from the largest continuing study by the National Intimate Partner and Sexual Violence Survey by the Centers for Disease Control and Prevention. The *Post* poll reported that one in two women said they had experienced "unwanted sexual behavior," but the use of this catchall term and the absence of any examples of specific behavior mean that the one in two number is likely too low as a result of confusion about the category, according to an analysis of the survey data conducted by Anita Raj, director of UC San Diego's Center on Gender Equity and Health. Other surveys, in contrast, sought to gather specific data about workplace harassment or assault. One which asked a thousand women and a thousand men "about verbal harassment, sexual touching, cyber sexual harassment, being followed on the street, genital flashing and sexual assault": 77 percent of women and 34 percent of men said they had encountered verbal sexual harassment; 51 percent of women and 17 percent of men experienced unwanted sexual touching; 41 percent of women and 22 percent of men said they were sexually harassed online; 34 percent of women and 10 percent of men were physically followed; 30 percent of women and 12 percent of men were flashed; and 27 percent of women and 7 percent of men reported sexual assaults. See Susan Chira, "Numbers Hint at Why #MeToo Took Off: The Sheer Number Who Can Say 'Me, Too,'" *New York Times*, February 21, 2018, https://www.nytimes.com/2018/02/21/upshot/pervasive-sexual-harassment-why-me-too-took-off-poll.html.

5. Centers for Disease Control and Prevention, "Sexual Violence Is Preventable," April 19, 2021, https://www.cdc.gov/injury/features/sexual-violence/index.html.

6. See Marci A. Hamilton, *Justice Denied: What America Must Do to Protect Its Children* (Cambridge: Cambridge University Press, 2012), for the critical importance of abolishing statutes of limitation for child victims of clergy sexual abuse.

7. Laura Santhanam, "1 in 6 U.S. Women Say Their First Sexual Intercourse Was Rape," *PBS News Hour*, September 16, 2019, https://www.pbs.org/newshour/health/1-in-16-u-s-women-say-their-first-sexual-intercourse-was-rape.

8. The WHO did not release data on abusers other than to highlight the prevalence of intimate partner violence. Most men who sexually harass and abuse women know and live with them. They are spouses, boyfriends, and family members. The data shows that no space is free of sexual violence. World Health Organization, "Devastatingly Pervasive: 1 in 3 Women Globally Experience Violence," March 9, 2021, https://www.who.int/news/item/09-03-2021-devastatingly-pervasive-1-in-3-women-globally-experience-violence.

9. See Alyson Cole, "(Re)Made in America: Survivorship After the Shoah," *European Journal of Cultural Studies* 24, no. 1 (2021): 28–44. Cole traces the rise of the term *survivor* to replace *victim* and the shifting meanings of these terms. Following the example of many organizations aimed at ending sexual abuse, I prioritize

self-identification and self-naming, understanding that there are many reasons to choose either term (http://www.generationfive.org). *Victim*, in this context, often refers to someone still in the situation or relationship where they are being hurt. *Survivor* marks a decision to identify with having survived. These definitions are dynamic and reflect the range of decisions people make as they process abuse, including how to identify. There is also a temporal aspect to self-naming, and some identify as survivors to clarify a then/now context for healing.

10.  Jelani Cobb, "An American Spring of Reckoning," *New Yorker*, June 22, 2020, https://www.newyorker.com/magazine/2020/06/22/an-american-spring-of-reckoning.

11.  As I discuss in chapter 4, in the nineteenth century white feminists sought to shift the burden onto men for what they considered assaults on autonomy and dignity granted by legal marriage. Victoria Woodhull, a free-love advocate and controversial figure in the women's rights movement, argued that marriage entrapped women economically and coerced them sexually. She asserted that marriage was as flawed and anachronistic as slavery, and therefore its end was inevitable. In public remarks and private correspondence, Elizabeth Cady Stanton and Susan B. Anthony compared legal marriage to slavery to highlight that marriage entailed rape and forced childbearing and childrearing for white women. This analogy underscored how marriage tied white women to white husbands in relations of sexual bondage and was aimed at white audiences. For previously enslaved women like Harriet Jacobs, writing in the 1850s, a critique of white marriage targeted the complicity of white women and men in the rape of Black girls and women. When white feminists borrowed from the experience of Black women to make knowable something about their suffering through analogy, they obscured the actual bondage of enslaved women.

12.  Cobb, "American Spring."

13.  A profusion of important work makes this point, including Walter Jones, *The Broken Heart of America St. Louis and the Violent History of the United States* (New York: Basic Books, 2020); Elizabeth S. Hinton, *America on Fire: The Untold History of Police Violence and Black Rebellion Since the 1960s* (New York: Liveright, 2021); Angela Davis, *Are Prisons Obsolete?* (New York: Seven Stories, 2003), Keeanga-Yamahtta Taylor, *Race for Profit: How Banks and the Real Estate Industry Undermined Black Homeownership* (Chapel Hill: University of North Carolina Press, 2019), and *From #BlackLives Matter to Black Liberation* (Chicago: Haymarket, 2016); and the 1619 Project. Also, there has been a surge in popular culture, with *Black Panther*, novels by Colson Whitehead rooted in historical events like *The Nickel Boys* (New York: Penguin, 2019) and *The Underground Railroad* (New York: Penguin, 2016); nonfiction like Saidiya Hartman's *Wayward Lives, Beautiful Experiments* (New York: Norton, 2019); and the success of the television series about queer and trans people, *Pose*. These all revealed the vivid presences of the past to mainstream white audiences and official cultural commentators accustomed to ignoring Black, Latinx, Indigenous, and queer culture. The centering by Black Lives Matter and Say Her Name of Black and brown people killed by the police has been amply historicized. Within the annals of suffering inflicted by slavery and its afterlives is a legacy of Black joy, desire, and faith.

14. See Sarah J. Jackson, Moya Bailey, and Brooke Foucault Welles, *#Hashtag Activism: Networks of Race and Gender Justice* (Cambridge, Mass.: MIT Press, 2020), 20–22, for analysis of #MeToo within "a discernible genealogy that has important cultural resonances."

15. Of its founding, Tarana Burke notes, "We call 'me too.' a *movement* because our goal is to educate and activate millions of women and girls across the country who are survivors of Sexual Abuse, Assault and Exploitation (S.A.A.E.). Our philosophy of 'empowerment through empathy' is the tool we use to connect millions of women and girls who have spent, for some, years in a dark place feeling isolated and alone. We want all survivors to move beyond survival into a thriving life and the 'me too.' movement is our vehicle to do just that." Tarana Burke, *JustBEInc.*, https://justbeinc .wixsite.com/justbeinc/donate.

16. Morning talk shows, news programs, and entertainment programming all regularly included reference to Tarana Burke. Burke and Milano gave several interviews together.

17. Personal email correspondence with Charlotte Clymer and Kaci Beeler, June 11, 2020.

18. It is interesting in this context to think of the legacy of anonymous attribution in women's writing. Harriet Jacobs, to whom I turn later in the chapter, wrote under a pseudonym to protect her family members who were still enslaved and others who were free but could be violently harassed to disclose where Jacobs was living. Virginia Woolf references the history of preventing women from publishing their work in their own names when she writes, "I would venture to guess that Anon, who wrote so many poems without signing them, was a woman" (*A Room of One's Own*, 1929 [London: Harcourt, 2005]).

19. Jodi Kantor and Megan Twohey, "Harvey Weinstein Paid Off Sexual Harassment Accusers for Decades," *New York Times*, October 5, 2017, https://www.nytimes.com /2017/10/05/us/harvey-weinstein-harassment-allegations.html.

20. Jodi Kantor and Megan Twohey, *She Said: Breaking the Sexual Harassment Story* (New York: Penguin, 2019).

21. "Weinstein," transcript, *PBS Frontline*, https://www.pbs.org/wgbh/frontline/film /weinstein/transcript/.

22. "Weinstein," transcript.

23. Ronan Farrow's *Catch and Kill: Lies, Spies, and a Conspiracy to Protect Predators* (New York: Little, Brown, 2019) fills in the investigative picture by exposing how victims are silenced through threats of retaliation and nondisclosure agreements.

24. *Catch and Kill* describes how NBC killed Farrow's investigation into allegations about Weinstein. Farrow took his reporting to David Remnick at the *New Yorker*, where it appeared in print. Farrow believes NBC suppressed the Weinstein story because it would point to NBC and a similar story about Matt Lauer.

25. For example, when settlements with the victims of Roger Ailes and Bill O'Reilly at FOX, whose serial predatory sexual harassment and assault cost the company millions, were exposed, responsibility for the longstanding practice of shielding abusers landed squarely with boards of directors who had authorized coercive settlements.

26.  "Weinstein," transcript.

27.  Kantor and Twohey present lawyer David Boies, for example, as a diehard Weinstein defender bent on destroying the women who accuse his client. Famous feminist mother-daughter legal icons Lisa Bloom and Gloria Allred are exposed as exploiting their knowledge of sexual assault victims' vulnerabilities to pressure them into signing NDAs. Bloom netted for herself a hefty percentage of the money generated by NDAs struck with Weinstein's victims. Kantor and Twohey include in the book Bloom's letter to Weinstein outlining how she would help him destroy Rose McGowan, who accused him of rape, and rehabilitate his image. She argued that his alliance with her as a feminist would rescue his reputation.

28.  Cyrus Vance, Jr., "Manhattan D.A. Cyrus Vance on Weinstein Verdict and Why His Office Didn't Prosecute in 2015," interview by Amna Nawaz, *PBS News Hour*, February 25, 2020, https://www.pbs.org/newshour/show/manhattan-da-cyrus-vance-on -weinstein-verdict-and-why-his-office-didnt-prosecute-in-2015.

29.  James C. McKinley, Jr., "Cy Vance Defends Decision Not to Pursue Case Against Harvey Weinstein," *New York Times*, October 11, 2017, https://www.nytimes.com/2017/10 /11/nyregion/cy-vance-defends-weinstein-decision.html.

30.  Irin Camon, "The Woman Who Taped Harvey Weinstein," *Cut*, February 18, 2020, https://www.thecut.com/2020/02/ambra-battilana-gutierrez-on-the-harvey -weinstein-trial.html.

31.  Strauss-Kahn was apprehended after he had boarded a flight to France. Following his arrest, he orchestrated a smear campaign against Diallo, and although further incriminating information came out about Strauss-Kahn, Vance declined to charge him because his office had lost faith in Diallo. Several features of this case are important to #MeToo. The crime occurred in a jurisdiction in which powerful men like Weinstein and Jeffrey Epstein evaded charges. Women who worked as maids throughout New York City showed up to protest the character assassination of Diallo, highlighting the routine sexual abuse that women in the hotel industry face. The case shares the conditions of emergence of the #MeToo breakthrough. See my *Tainted Witness: Why We Doubt What Women Say About Their Lives* (New York: Columbia University Press, 2017), 133–55, for analysis of this case.

32.  Nishita Jha, "The Judge in the Harvey Weinstein Trial Told Potential Jurors the 'Case Is Not a Referendum on #MeToo,'" *BuzzFeed News*, January 16, 2020, https://www .buzzfeednews.com/article/nishitajha/harvey-weinstein-judge-referendum-metoo.

33.  Eric Levenson, Lauren del Valle, and Sonia Moghe, "Harvey Weinstein Sentenced to 23 Years in Prison After Addressing His Accusers in Court," *CNN*, March 11, 2020, https://www.cnn.com/2020/03/11/us/harvey-weinstein-sentence/index.html.

34.  McKinley, "Cy Vance Defends Decision."

35.  Madison Pauly, "She Was a Rising Star at a Major University. Then a Lecherous Professor Made Her Life Hell," *Mother Jones*, September 8, 2017, https://www.motherjones .com/politics/2017/09/she-was-a-rising-star-at-a-major-university-then-a-lecherous -professor-made-her-life-hell/.

36. Susan Lekach, "Team Behind Time's Person of the Year Issue Was All Women," *Mashable.com*, December 6, 2017, https://mashable.com/2017/12/06/time-person-of-the-year-women-behind-issue/.

37. Paula A. Johnson, Sheila Widnall, and Frazier F. Benya, eds., *Sexual Harassment of Women: Climate, Culture, and Consequences in Academic Sciences, Engineering, and Medicine* (Washington, D.C.: National Academies, 2018).

38. Jerhonda Pace accused R. Kelly of molesting her months before #MeToo. On the difficulty in breaking the R. Kelly case, see Jim DeRogatis, "The Woman Who Said R. Kelly Abused Her Refuses to Be Silenced," *BuzzFeed News*, March 13, 2018, https://www.buzzfeednews.com/article/jimderogatis/jerhonda-pace-r-kelly-me-too-tarana-burke#.qcqlOXaZz.

39. David Folkenflik and Colin Dwyer, "Matt Lauer Accused of Rape in New Book: Former NBC Star Denies 'False Stories,'" NPR, October 9, 2019, https://www.npr.org/2019/10/09/768527936/matt-lauer-accused-of-rape-in-new-book-former-nbc-star-denies-false-stories.

40. Whisper networks are an example of informal reporting. They provide information about sexual abusers with the aim of keeping women safe. Examples abound; two with specific connections to #MeToo show the role of social media. In 1990 students at Brown University wrote the names of alleged rapists inside the doors of bathroom stalls in women's restrooms. In an echo of past activism, students resumed this practice in 2017, and in 2021 the Instagram account @voicesofbrown invited students to share stories of sexual assault. Moira Donegan created *Shitty Media Men List* as an anonymous, crowd-sourced Google spreadsheet. The document was intended as a resource for people in media to protect themselves from sexual predators. See Moira Donegan, "I Started the Media Men List," *Cut*, January 10, 2018, https://www.thecut.com/2018/01/moira-donegan-i-started-the-media-men-list.html. On informal reporting, see Deborah Turkheimer, "Unofficial Reporting in the #MeToo Era," *University of Chicago Legal Forum* 2019, article 10 (2019); Jordan A. Thomas, "How to Make It Easier for Women to Report Sexual Harassment," *Quartz at Work*, January 3, 2018, https://qz.com/work/1170489/how-to-make-it-easier-for-women-to-report-sexual-harassment-according-to-a-lawyer-who-represents-whistleblowers/.

41. When whistleblowers expose classified information, whether these are military or state secrets, they cannot expect protection, as the cases of Chelsea Manning and Edward Snowden demonstrate.

42. I discuss the case of the public letter that Harvard faculty signed in support of Professor John Comaroff in the conclusion of this book.

43. See "Letters: Open Letter Against Media Treatment of Junot Díaz," *Chronicle of Higher Education*, May 14, 2018, https://www.chronicle.com/blogs/letters/open-letter-against-media-treatment-of-junot-diaz/?cid2=gen_login_refresh&cid=gen_sign_in.

44. Shreerekha, "In the Wake of His Damage," *Rumpus*, May 12, 2018, https://therumpus.net/2018/05/12/in-the-wake-of-his-damage/; Marianella Belliard, "Junot Díaz's Mask:

This Is How He Lost It," *Latino Rebels*, May 10, 2018, https://www.latinorebels.com /2018/05/10/junotdiazsmask/.

45.  Claire Valentine, "Author Junot Díaz Responds to Allegations of Sexual Misconduct and Verbal Abuse," *Paper*, May 4, 2018, https://www.papermag.com/junot-diaz-me -too--2565930804.html.

46.  Mark Shanahan and Stephanie Ebbert, "Junot Díaz Case May Be a #MeToo Turning Point," *Boston Globe*, June 30, 2018, https://www.bostonglobe.com/metro/2018/06/30 /junot-diaz-case-may-metoo-turning-point/3TMFseenE4Go1eVsqbFSxM/story .html.

47.  Louis CK and Kevin Spacey, for example, both denied allegations of sexual harassment that circulated for years. After admitting wrongdoing, both stirred discussion about accountability when they sought to resume their professional careers.

48.  Michel Foucault, *The History of Sexuality*, vol. 1 (New York: Vintage, 1978), 61.

49.  John Frow, "Discursive Justice," *SAQ* 100, no. 2 (2001): 334.

50.  See Michel Foucault, *Fearless Speech*, ed. Joseph Pearson (Los Angeles: Semiotexte, 2001).

51.  Sara Ahmed, *Living a Feminist Life* (Durham, N.C.: Duke University Press, 2017), 82.

## 4. BACKDROP

1.  Hortense Spillers, "Mama's Baby, Papa's Maybe: An American Grammar Book," in *Black, White, and in Color: Essays on American Literature and Culture* (Chicago: University of Chicago Press, 2003), 203–29.

2.  See Rosanne Kennedy and Hannah McCann, "Splitting from Halley: Doing Justice to Race, Unwantedness, and Campus Sexual Assault," *Signs: Journal of Women in Culture and Society* 46, no. 1 (2020): 79–102.

3.  Darlene Clark Hine, "Rape and the Inner Lives of Black Women in the Middle West: Preliminary Thoughts on the Culture of Dissemblance," *Signs: Journal of Women in Culture and Society* 14, no. 4 (1989): 912–20.

4.  Hazel V. Carby, *Reconstructing Womanhood: The Emergence of the Afro-American Woman Novelist* (New York: Oxford University Press, 1987). 39.

5.  Hine, "Rape and the Inner Lives of Black Women," 912.

6.  See Leigh Gilmore and Elizabeth Marshall, *Witnessing Girlhood: Toward an Intersectional Tradition of Life Writing* (New York: Fordham University Press, 2019).

7.  Frederick Douglass and Harriet A. Jacobs, *Narrative of the Life of Frederick Douglass, an American Slave* and *Incidents in the Life of a Slave Girl*, intro. Anthony K. Appiah (New York: Modern Library, 2000), xi; Henry Louis Gates, ed., *The Classic Slave Narratives* (New York: New American Library, 1987), xiii; Hortense Spillers, *Black, White, and in Color: Essays on American Literature and Culture* (Chicago: University of Chicago Press, 2003), 35.

8.  See Jean Fagan Yellin, ed., *The Harriet Jacobs Family Papers*, vol. 1 (Chapel Hill: University of North Carolina Press, 2008), for letters exchanged between Jacobs and Amy Post from the late 1840s through the publication of *Incidents*.

9.  Jean Fagan Yellin documented the process of reauthenticating Jacobs's authorship in *Harriet Jacobs: A Life* (New York: Basic Books, 2004).

10. Spillers, *Black, White, and in Color*, 470.

11. Catherine Jacquet, *The Injustices of Rape: How Activists Responded to Sexual Violence, 1950–1980* (Chapel Hill: University of North Carolina Press, 2019), 8.

12. Susan Brownmiller, *Against Our Will: Men, Women, and Rape* (New York: Simon and Schuster, 1975), 397.

13. Moya Bailey and Trudy, "On Misogynoir: Citation, Erasure, and Plagiarism," *Feminist Media Studies* 18, no. 4 (2018): 762–68.

14. Kimberlé Crenshaw's work in 1989 examined three Title VII cases to demonstrate the obstacles to litigation Black women faced: *DeGraffenreid v. General Motors*, *Moore v. Hughes Helicopter*, and *Payne v. Travenol*. See her "Demarginalizing the Intersection of Race and Sex: A Black Feminist Critique of Antidiscrimination Doctrine, Feminist Theory and Antiracist Politics," *University of Chicago Legal Forum* 1989, no. 1, art. 8: 139–67.

15. Vrushali Patil and Jyoti Puri, "Colorblind Feminisms: Ansari-Grace and the Limits of #MeToo Counterpublics." *Signs: Journal of Women in Culture and Society* 46, no. 3 (Spring 2020): 690–91. See also Heather Berg, "Left of #MeToo," *Feminist Studies* 46, no. 2 (2020): 259–86.

16. Shoniqua Roach, "(Re)turning to 'Rape and the Inner Lives of Black Women': A Black Feminist Forum on the Culture of Dissemblance," *Signs: Journal of Women in Culture and Society* 45, no. 3 (Spring 2020): 515–19.

## 5. #METOO STRESS TEST

1.  Anita Hill, *Believing: Our Thirty-Year Journey to End Gender Violence* (New York: Viking, 2021), 5; see also Jane Mayer and Jill Abramson, *Strange Justice: The Selling of Clarence Thomas* (Boston: Houghton Mifflin, 1994).

2.  This phrase was used variously by every Democrat on the committee beginning with chair Dianne Feinstein's opening remarks.

3.  The nomination hearings represent a forum that has been transforming into an increasingly trial-like setting since the failed nomination of Robert Bork in 1987, not only pitting members of the Senate Judiciary Committee against one another in an adversarial relationship along party lines but also subjecting those who testify to hostile questioning.

4.  I discuss the use of life narrative as politics-by-narrative means in the Hill-Thomas hearings in *Tainted Witness: Why We Doubt What Women Say About Their Lives* (New York: Columbia University Press, 2017).

5.  See Mayer and Abramson, *Strange Justice.*

6.  Testimony is a fraught racial construct. Legacies of slavery produce the scene of witness for girls and women of color as a location of injustice and misrecognition, which philosopher Kristie Dotson theorizes as epistemic violence in "Tracking Epistemic

Violence, Tracking Practices of Silencing," *Hypatia* 26, no. 2 (Spring 2011): 236–57. With reference to the juridical roots of Kimberlé Crenshaw's definition of intersectionality (1989), the Senate Judiciary Committee's hearings imposed the burden of arguing their way into legitimacy on the witnesses. To track the ways in which multiple oppressions can intersect with the site of witness and turn the subject who is bearing witness into a figure without standing resonates especially with Crenshaw's analysis. See her "Demarginalizing the Intersection of Race and Sex: A Black Feminist Critique of Antidiscrimination Doctrine, Feminist Theory and Antiracist Politics," *University of Chicago Legal Forum* 1989, no. 1, art. 8: 139–67

7.  This draws on James Phelan's claim that narrative is rhetorical in precisely this way, in *Somebody Telling Somebody Else: A Rhetorical Poetics of Narrative* (Columbus: Ohio State University Press, 2017).

8.  Li Zhou, "Susan Collins Thinks Lawyers Should Be Able to Cross-examine Kavanaugh and Ford on Sexual Assault Allegations," *Vox*, September 18, 2018, https://www.vox.com/2018/9/18/17874938/supreme-court-brett-kavanaugh-susan-collins.

9.  Renae Reints, "Trump Calls Christine Blasey Ford a 'Very Credible Witness,'" *Fortune*, September 28, 2018, http://fortune.com/2018/09/28/trump-ford-credible-witness/.

10.  Gilmore, *Tainted Witness*.

11.  Gilmore, 5.

12.  Caitlin Flanagan, "The Abandoned World of 1982," *Atlantic*, September 25, 2019, https://www.theatlantic.com/ideas/archive/2018/09/kavanaugh-ford/571066/.

13.  Carol Gilligan, *In a Different Voice: Psychological Theory and Women's Development* (Cambridge, Mass.: Harvard University Press, 1982).

14.  "Full Transcript: Christine Blasey Ford's Opening Statement to the Senate Judiciary Committee," *Politico*, September 26, 2018, https://www.politico.com/story/2018/09/26/christine-blasey-ford-opening-statement-senate-845080.

15.  Amanda Holpuch, "Anita Hill: Kavanaugh Confirmation Hearing 'Disservice to the American Public,'" *Guardian*, October 10, 2018.

16.  "Protestors Confront Flake in Elevator," transcript, *Rachel Maddow Show*, MSNBC, September 28, 2018, http://www.msnbc.com/transcripts/rachel-maddow-show/2018-09-28.

17.  "Read Lead Prosecutor Rachel Mitchell's Memo About the Kavanaugh-Ford Hearing," *Axios*, October 1, 2018, https://www.axios.com/brett-kavanaugh-rachel-mitchell-prosecutor-memo-2c3233cc-1d42-416b-af04-02700aa9a711.html.

## 6. READING LIKE A SURVIVOR

1.  My thanks to friends and colleagues who have shared the importance of this point based on their work in specific communities, especially Marlene Kenney and Meg Jensen.

2. Anti–sexual violence organization Rape, Abuse & Incest National Network (RAINN), for example, advocates for changes in statutes of limitations and addressing the rape kit backlog. It provides information about sexual violence by state and offers a sexual assault hotline. Rape crisis centers and intimate partner violence organizations offer legal advocacy as well as education and community outreach programs.

3. Roxane Gay, ed., *Not That Bad: Dispatches from Rape Culture* (New York: Harper, 2018).

4. Jill Christman, "Slaughterhouse Island," in Gay, *Not That Bad*, 28.

5. Vanessa Mártir, "What I Told Myself," in Gay, *Not That Bad*, 104.

6. Gayatri Spivak, "Can the Subaltern Speak?," in *Marxism and the Interpretation of Culture*, ed. Cary Nelson and Lawrence Grossberg (London: Macmillan, 1988), 280.

7. Miranda Fricker, *Epistemic Injustice: Power and the Ethics of Knowing* (Oxford: Oxford University Press, 2007).

8. Kristie Dotson, "Tracking Epistemic Violence, Tracking Practices of Silencing," *Hypatia* 26, no. 2 (Spring 2011): 236–57.

9. After use of undue force, the second highest complaint against police is sexual assault. See Cato Institute, National Police Misconduct Reporting Project, 2010 Annual Report, https://www.leg.state.nv.us/Session/77th2013/Exhibits/Assembly/JUD/AJUD 338L.pdf.

10. Joel Fischel, "In the Fight for Policing Reform, LGBT Is a Threadbare Alliance," *Boston Review*, June 17, 2020, https://bostonreview.net/gender-sexuality/joseph-j-fischel -fight-policing-reform-lgbt-threadbare-alliance.

11. Alliance for a Safe and Diverse DC, *Move Along: Policing Sex Work in Washington, D.C.* (Washington, D.C.: Different Avenues, 2008), https://dctranscoalition.files .wordpress.com/2010/05/movealongreport.pdf.

12. Daniel Holtzclaw et al. are examples of police who rape women they detain. It is legal in thirty-five states as of 2018 for police to have sex with women in custody. One hundred percent of the time, police claim these coerced acts are consensual. Albert Samaha, "An 18-Year-Old Said She Was Raped While in Police Custory. The Officers Say She Consented," *BuzzFeed News*, February 7, 2018, https://www.buzzfeednews .com/article/albertsamaha/this-teenager-accused-two-on-duty-cops-of-rape-she -had-no. #MeToo emerges at a convergence of a "rising credibility of survivors and the falling credibility of police." Anne Gray Fischer, "Police Sexual Violence Is Hidden in Plain Sight," *Boston Review*, July 30, 2020, https://bostonreview.net/law-justice /anne-gray-fischer-reform-wont-end-police-violence.

13. Katharine Bodde and Erika Lorshbough, "There's No Such Thing as 'Consensual Sex' When a Person Is in Police Custody," ACLU, February 23, 2018, https://www.aclu.org /blog/criminal-law-reform/reforming-police/theres-no-such-thing-consensual-sex -when-person-police.

14. Natasha Lennard, "In Secretive Court Hearing, NYPD Cops Who Raped Brooklyn Teen in Custody Get No Jail Time," *Intercept*, August 30, 2019, https://theintercept .com/2019/08/30/nypd-anna-chambers-rape-probation/. The list is too long to convey here, but the role of authorities in police unions to norm this violence is

demonstrable. In August 2020, for example, the former president of the Boston Police Patrolmen's Association was charged with multiple counts related to the alleged sexual assault of a family member in a series of incidents from the time the girl was seven through twelve years old. Patrick M. Rose, Sr., served for twenty years in the department before heading the union.

15.   Gilmore, *Tainted Witness.*

16.   Emily Martin, "The Egg and the Sperm: How Science Has Constructed a Romance Based on Stereotypical Male-Female Roles," *Signs: Journal of Women in Culture and Society* 16, no. 3 (1991): 485–501.

17.   Scholars including Marianne Hirsch, Michael Rothberg, Bruce Robbins, and Gillian Whitlock have sought to contribute critical language to awaken the complexities of witness. Hirsch's "postmemory" and Whitlock's "testimony of things" express how legacies of trauma are transmitted generationally, reflected in what people save and make, and how pain travels beyond its official commemoration. There is always more to tell and more to hear. Rothberg offers the "implicated subject" to expand the study of violence beyond a focus on victims and perpetrators. His notion of "implication" refers to the responsibilities of bystanders, not only to urge new thinking about intervention, but also to explore moral and political responsibility beyond the most obvious position of complicity. In this, he draws on Bruce Robbins's discussion of how some become *beneficiaries* of violence, especially those who would never do harm, and often imagine themselves as sympathetic to sufferers rather than as accomplices to harm. Beneficiaries, like those who possess white privilege and male privilege, receive a portion of their status through their relation to a violence they assent to.

18.   Sarah J. Jackson, Moya Bailey, and Brooke Foucault Welles, *#Hashtag Activism: Networks of Race and Gender Justice* (Cambridge, Mass.: MIT Press, 2020).

19.   See my *The Limits of Autobiography: Trauma and Testimony* (Ithaca, N.Y.: Cornell University Press, 2001).

20.   Susan Brison, *Aftermath: Violence and the Remaking of a Self* (Princeton, N.J.: Princeton University Press, 2001), 7. Brison's memoir carved a new path in nonfiction by fusing scholarship about trauma with a vivid personal account. *Aftermath* focuses on the extraordinary burden placed on rape survivors by the legal system in the "best-case" scenario in which a rapist is tried and convicted. Brison broke new ground in philosophy by insisting that her experience augmented her scholarly authority. *Aftermath* demonstrated the diversity of expertise that writers in the memoir boom brought to the self-representation of trauma and offers a context for how Christine Blasey Ford's research on trauma informed her testimony about sex assault during the Kavanaugh hearings.

21.   Tanya Serisier, "Speaking Out, Public Judgements and Narrative Politics," in *MeToo, Feminist Theory, and Surviving Sexual Violence in the Academy*, ed. Laura A. Gray-Rosendale (Lanham, Md.: Lexington, 2020), 179.

22.   *Allen v. Farrow*, HBO, season 1, episode 3, https://tvshowtranscripts.ourboard.org/viewtopic.php?f=943&t=43001.

23.   Brison, *Aftermath*, 71.

24.  Lacy Crawford, *Notes on a Silencing* (New York: Little, Brown 2020).

25.  There are two memoirs of rape at St. Paul's boarding school, both of which offer harrowing accounts of predatory sexual behavior by students and cover-ups by the school administration. In addition to Crawford's memoir, written as an adult, Chessy Prout has written a memoir about being sexually assaulted by senior Owen Labrie. When Prout was a fifteen-year-old freshman, Labrie lured her and then sexually assaulted her as part of the "senior salute" tradition in which male seniors rack up points for sexual conquests. Prout went public when St. Paul's tried to ensure her silence by threatening to expose her name. See Kristi Palma, "Chessy Prout Went Public with Her Name to 'Take Back the Internet,'" *Boston.com*, September 12, 2016, https://www .boston.com/news/crime/2016/09/12/chessy-prout-went-public-with-her-name-to -take-back-the-internet.

26.  Julie K. Brown of the *Miami Herald* has pursued the Epstein story and describes how Epstein evaded responsibility. See Julie K. Brown, "Perversion of Justice: Jeffrey Epstein," *Miami Herald*, December 19, 2019, https://www.miamiherald.com/news/local /article220097825.html. See also the Netflix docuseries, *Jeffrey Epstein: Filthy Rich*.

27.  Postcritique strategies following Eve Kosofsky Sedgwick's reparative reading include Sharon Marcus and Stephen Best (surface reading), Christopher Castiglia (practices of hope), Gayle Salamon (critical phenomenology), Leigh Gilmore and Elizabeth Marshall (accompaniment), and Saidiya Hartman (resignification).

28.  Sophocles, *Antigonick*, trans. Anne Carson (New York: New Directions, 2012).

29.  Virginia Woolf, *A Room of One's Own*, 1929 (London: Harcourt, 2005).

30.  Michel Foucault, *Wrong-Doing and Truth-Telling: The Function of Avowal in Justice*, ed. Fabienne Brion and Bernard E. Harcourt, trans. Stephen W. Sawyer (Chicago: University of Chicago Press, 2014), 60.

31.  Bonnie Honig, *Antigone, Interrupted* (Cambridge: Cambridge University Press, 2013).

32.  In her short book about a long history of silencing women, *Women and Power* (London: Liveright 2017), classicist Mary Beard draws a line from Penelope in *The Odyssey* to Hillary Clinton and Elizabeth Warren.

33.  Richard David, "Drains of Eale," *Shakespeare Survey* 10 (1957): 1.

34.  J. C. Trewin, *Shakespeare on the English Stage, 1900–1964* (London: Barrie and Rockliff, 1964), 235–37. For a discussion of how Brooks's production inspired subsequent productions at the Oregon Shakespeare Festival and the Papp Theater, see G. Harold Metz, "Stage History of *Titus Andronicus*," *Shakespeare Quarterly* 28, no. 2 (Spring 1977): 154–69. Metz suggests that the staging of *Titus* by these storied companies helps show the development of Shakespearean tragedy.

35.  Juliet Macur and Nate Schweber, "Rape Case Unfolds on Web and Splits City," *New York Times*, December 16, 2012, https://www.nytimes.com/2012/12/17/sports /high-school-football-rape-case-unfolds-online-and-divides-steubenville-ohio .html.

36.  Sophocles, *Antigonick*, trans. Carson, 32, 45.

37.  Emily Ogden, *On Not Knowing: How to Love and Other Essays* (Chicago: University of Chicago Press, 2022), 41.

38.   Ben Montgomery, *Grandma Gatewood's Walk: The Inspiring Story of the Woman Who Saved the Appalachian Trail* (Chicago: Chicago Review, 2014).

39.   On the consolation of literary language, see David James, *Discrepant Solitude: Contemporary Literature and the Work of Consolation* (Oxford: Oxford University Press, 2019).

# 7. #METOO STORYTELLING

1.    See, for example, Richard Brody, "'The Last Duel,' Reviewed," *New Yorker*, October 15, 2021, https://www.newyorker.com/culture/the-front-row/the-last-duel-reviewed -ridley-scotts-wannabe-metoo-movie.

2.    There are more docuseries, including "Room 2806: The Accusation," about Dominique Strauss-Kahn. In her discussion of the brilliant *I May Destroy You*, Rebecca Wanzo identifies Coel's achievement, in part, as resetting expectations for representation by figuring sexual violence as "both commonplace and disruptive of the everyday. But Coel is defiant in her refusal to let *I May Destroy You* be entirely about despair." Wanzo, "Rethinking Rape and Laughter: Michaela Coel's *I May Destroy You*," *Los Angeles Review of Books*, September 22, 2020.

3.    Maya Angelou, *I Know Why the Caged Bird Sings* (New York: Random House, 1970); Maxine Hong Kingston, *The Woman Warrior: A Memoir of a Girlhood Among Ghosts* (New York: Knopf, 1976).

4.    See Katharine Chamberlain, "Spotlight on Censorship: I Know Why the Caged Bird Sings," *Intellectual Freedom* (blog), September 26, 2010, https://www.oif.ala.org/oif /spotlight-on-censorship-i-know-why-the-caged-bird-sings/.

5.    In "Limit Cases," I coin the term *memoir boom* to describe the rise in self-representational texts that take up trauma as representative rather than marginal subject matter for autobiography and transforms whose lives and experience could be seen as significant. See Leigh Gilmore, "Limit-Cases: Trauma, Self-Representation, and the Jurisdictions of Identity," *Biography* 24, no. 1 (December 2001): 128–39.

6.    Elizabeth Wurtzel, *Prozac Nation: Young and Depressed in America* (Boston: Houghton Mifflin, 1994); Mary Karr, *Liar's Club: A Memoir* (New York: Viking Penguin, 1995).

7.    I have written about the critical reception of *The Kiss* (New York: Random House, 1997) in "Jurisdictions: *I, Rigoberta Menchú, The Kiss*, and Scandalous Self-Representation in the Age of Memoir and Trauma," *Signs: Journal of Women in Culture and Society* 28, no. 2 (Winter 2003): 695–718.

8.    Roxane Gay, *Hunger: A Memoir of (My) Body* (New York: Harper, 2017), 14.

9.    Ellen Bass and Laura Davis, *The Courage to Heal: A Guide for Women Survivors of Child Sexual Abuse* (New York: Collins Living, 1988).

10.   Terese Marie Mailhot, *Heart Berries: A Memoir* (Berkeley: Counterpoint, 2018), 1, 6. I draw on my essay in *Biography* for my analysis of *Heart Berries*.

11.   Shelly Oria, ed., *Indelible in the Hippocampus: Writings from the MeToo Movement* (San Francisco: McSweeney's 2019).

12. See Gilmore, *Tainted Witness.*

13. Paisley Rekdal, "Nightingale: A Gloss: A Special APR Supplement," *American Poetry Review* 46, no. 5 (September/October 2017): 21–24.

14. Lacy M. Johnson, *The Reckonings: Essays on Justice for the Twenty-First Century* (New York: Scribner, 2018), 68.

15. Kristen Roupenian, "Cat Person," *New Yorker*, December 11, 2017, https://www .newyorker.com/magazine/2017/12/11/cat-person.

16. "Why didn't' she leave?" is the question some raised about the pseudonymous Grace and her story about Aziz Ansari published in *Babe.net.* Grace described a date in which she felt initially flattered and starstruck by Ansari's attention and then violated by his approach to sex with her at his apartment. They met at an Emmy Awards after-party in 2017. She was a photographer and approached Ansari when she saw him taking photos with a film camera. They exchanged contact info and flirted over text for a week before he asked her out on a date she described as "the worst night of my life." Caitlin Flanagan called the story a hit piece: the assassination of a brown man by a white woman who should have known enough to leave his apartment. See Flanagan, "The Humiliation of Aziz Ansari," *Atlantic*, January 14, 2018, https:// www.theatlantic.com/entertainment/archive/2018/01/the-humiliation-of-aziz -ansari/550541/.

17. Mary Gordon, *Payback* (New York: Pantheon, 2020), 95.

## 8. CONSENT BEFORE AND AFTER #METOO

1. Joel Fischel, *Screw Consent: A Better Politics of Sexual Justice* (Berkeley: University of California Press, 2019).

2. Katherine Angel, *Sex Will Be Good Again Tomorrow: Women and Desire in the Age of Consent* (London: Verso, 2021), 114.

3. Michelle J. Anderson, "All-American Rape," *St. John's Law Review* 79, no. 3 (Summer 2005): 625–44, https://scholarship.law.stjohns.edu/lawreview/vol79/iss3/2/.

4. Harriet Jacobs, *Incidents in the Life of a Slave Girl*, ed. Jean Fagan Yellin (Cambridge, Mass.: Harvard University Press, 2000).

5. Catharine A. MacKinnon, *Feminism Unmodified* (Cambridge, Mass.: Harvard University Press, 1987), argues that the customary distinction between sex and rape is a legal artifact that does not apply in real life. See also MacKinnon, *Toward a Feminist Theory of the State* (Cambridge, Mass.: Harvard University Press, 1989), for the claim that coercion defines women's relation to sex under patriarchy.

6. It is important to recognize children and youth as unable to consent under my definition. In cases of economic constraint and sex work, for example, children, in my definition of consent, can be compelled to seek sex but cannot consent to it. Those who have sex with children often rewrite the trauma they inflict as seduction. A survivor-centered and trauma-informed understanding of sexual violence does not allow the abuser to define consent.

7.    Sung Hoon Song and John R. Fernandes, "Comparison of Injury Patterns in Consensual and Nonconsensual Sex," *Academy of Forensic Pathology* 7, no. 4 (December 2017): 619–31, https://www.ncbi.nlm.nih.gov/pmc/articles/PMC6474446/.

8.    Sharon Marcus argues that rape is structured like a language and that there are ways to rewrite rape scripts in real time. Her "Fighting Bodies, Fighting Words" brings an astute use of feminist literary criticism to the analysis of sexual violence and rape prevention. Marcus focuses on the temporality of assault with the aim of locating pressure points where it could be deflected and turned away from assault to survival. See "Fighting Bodies, Fighting Words: A Theory and Politics of Rape Prevention" in *Feminists Theorize the Political*, ed. Judith Butler and Joan W. Scott (London: Routledge, 1992), 385–403.

9.    See Olatz G. Abrisketa and Marian G. Abrisketa, "It's Okay, Sister, Your Wolf-Pack Is Here: Sisterhood as Public Feminism in Spain." *Signs: Journal of Women in Culture and Society* 45, no. 4 (June 2020): 931–53.

10.   Christina Morales, "Court Overturns Sex Crime Conviction Because Victim Was 'Voluntarily Intoxicated,'" *New York Times*, March 31, 2021, https://www.nytimes.com/2021/03/31/us/minnesota-supreme-court-rape-ruling.html.

11.   See Jessica Valenti's analysis of the incoherence of consent and rape law, "American Rape Laws Make No Sense," In *All in Her Head by Jessica Valenti*, blog, April 7, 2021, https://jessica.substack.com/p/american-rape-laws-make-no-sense. Her essay brought this research to my attention: Scott A. Johnson, "Intoxicated Perpetrators of Sexual Assault and Rape Know What They Are Doing Despite Intoxication," *Journal of Forensic Sciences and Criminal Investigation* 1, no. 4 (January 2017): https://juniperpublishers.com/jfsci/pdf/JFSCI.MS.ID.555570.pdf.

12.   On the incest case against Olivier Duhamel, see "French Intellectual Duhamel Won't Face Incest Charges, Prosecutor Says," *France24*, June 14, 2021, https://www.france24.com/en/europe/20210614-french-intellectual-duhamel-won-t-face-incest-charges-paris-prosecutor-says; and Constant Méheut, "France Drops Rape Investigation of Prominent Intellectual," *New York Times*, June 4, 2021, https://www.nytimes.com/2021/06/14/world/europe/olivier-duhamel-france.html. Although Duhamel confessed, French officials refused to charge him because the statute of limitations had expired.

13.   See Carole Pateman, *The Sexual Contract* (London: Polity, 1988).

14.   Estelle Freedman, *Redefining Rape: Sexual Violence in the Era of Suffrage and Segregation* (Cambridge, Mass.: Harvard University Press, 2013).

15.   For analysis of degrees of rape and how absence of force and absence of consent lead to a lesser charge, see Kit Kinports, "Rape and Force: The Forgotten *Mens Rea*," *Buffalo Criminal Law Review* 4, no. 2 (2001): 755–99.

16.   The country's law does not name rape victims. Her identity is permanently shielded. During the trial, however, her name was printed in the British press. I will not circulate her name because she has not chosen to identify herself publicly.

17.   Conor Gallagher, "Belfast Trial: Doctor Criticises Medical Examination of Alleged Rape Victim," *Irish Times*, February 21, 2018, https://www.irishtimes.com/news/crime

-and-law/belfast-trial-doctor-criticises-medical-examination-of-alleged-rape -victim-1.3400137.

18.  Gallagher, "Belfast Trial."

19.  Conor Gallagher, "Inside the Court 12: The Complete Story of the Belfast Rape Trial," *Irish Times*, March 28, 2018, https://www.irishtimes.com/news/crime-and-law/inside -court-12-the-complete-story-of-the-belfast-rape-trial-1.3443620.

20.  Gallagher, "Belfast Trial."

21.  In 2015 British police uploaded a consent education video, "Tea and Consent," that was widely shared following Brock Turner's lenient sentence. The video uses stick figures to act out scenarios in which initiating sex should be thought of as asking someone if they'd like a cup of tea. It explicitly states that people may withdraw consent, that unconscious people cannot consent to sex, and that no one is obligated to have sex. It concludes: "consent is everything." See "Tea and Consent," *Washington Post*, June 10, 2016, https://www.washingtonpost.com/video/national/tea-and-consent/2016 /06/10/38e3e220-2f15-11e6-b9d5-3c3063f8332c_video.html. In a spectacular failure of consent education, Australia's government commissioned a video that also used the food/drink analogy for sex. It cost $3.8million, featured milkshakes and tacos, and was so confusing, it was immediately removed from circulation. See Naaman Zhou and Matilda Boseley, "Milkshake Consent Video Earlier Script Referred to 'Modern Progressive' 1950s," *Guardian*, April 22, 2021, https://www.theguardian.com /australia-news/2021/apr/23/milkshake-consent-video-earlier-script-referred-to -modern-progressive-1950s. Thank you to Gillian Whitlock for the example from Australia.

22.  United States Department of Education, Office for Civil Rights, "Dear Colleague," April 4, 2011, https://www2.ed.gov/about/offices/list/ocr/letters/colleague-201104.pdf.

23.  Fischel, *Screw Consent*, 3.

24.  Kate Harding, *Asking for It: The Alarming Rise of Rape Culture—and What We Can Do About It* (Boston: Da Capo, 2015).

25.  U.S. Department of Education, "Dear Colleague."

26.  Deborah Epstein and Lisa Goodman, "Discounting Women: Doubting Domestic Violence Survivors' Credibility and Dismissing Their Experiences," *University of Pennsylvania Law Review* 167 (2019): 399–461.

27.  *Doe v. Purdue University*, No. 17-3565 (Cir. 2019), *Justia*, https://law.justia.com/cases /federal/appellate-courts/ca7/17-3565/17-3565-2019-06-28.html.

28.  See Alexandra Brodsky's analysis of what this case reveals about Amy Coney Barrett's anti–civil rights jurisprudence, in "Understanding Judge Barrett's Opinion in Doe v. Purdue," *Public Justice*, September 24, 2020, https://www.publicjustice.net /understanding-judge-barretts-opinion-in-doe-v-purdue/.

29.  Brodsky, "Understanding Judge Barrett's Opinion."

30.  Vanessa Springora, *Consent: A Memoir*, trans. Natasha Lehrer (New York: Harper-Collins, 2021).

31.  "France Toughens Law on Sex with Minors Under 15," *DW.com*, April 15, 2021, https://p .dw.com/p/3s5ap.

32. See my *Tainted Witness: Why We Doubt What Women Say About Their Lives* (New York: Columbia University Press, 2017), for analysis of the Diallo case.

33. For information about age-of-consent laws in the United States, see Asaph Glosser, Karen Gardiner, and Mick Fishman, *Statutory Rape: A Guide to State Laws and Reporting Requirements*, Department of Health and Human Services, December 15, 2004, https://aspe.hhs.gov/sites/default/files/migrated_legacy_files//42881/report.pdf.

34. Lise Ravery, "Denise Bombardier Deserves Credit for Unmasking French Author," *Montreal Gazette*, December 30, 2019, https://montrealgazette.com/opinion/columnists /lise-ravery-denise-bombardier-deserves-credit-for-unmasking-french-author.

35. Clément Thiery, "Denise Bombardier: 'In America, Mr. Matzneff Would Already Be in Jail,'" *France-Amérique*, January 23, 2020, https://france-amerique.com/en/denise -bombardier-in-america-mr-matzneff-would-already-be-in-jail/.

36. Lara Marlowe, "Paris Letter: Most Shocking Thing About Matzneff Affair Is Everybody Knew," *Irish Times*, January 27, 2020, https://www.irishtimes.com/news/world /europe/paris-letter-most-shocking-thing-about-matzneff-affair-is-everybody -knew-1.4153065.

37. Alexander Chee, *How to Write an Autobiographical Novel* (New York: Mariner, 2018). 226–27, 231.

38. Parul Sehgal, " 'Consent,' a Memoir That Shook France, Recalls Living a 'Perverse Nightmare,'" *New York Times*, February 16, 2021, https://www.nytimes.com/2021/02 /16/books/review-consent-memoir-vanessa-springora.html.

39. Melissa Febos, "I Spent My Life Consenting to Touch I Didn't Want," *New York Times Magazine*, March 31, 2021, https://www.nytimes.com/2021/03/31/magazine/consent .html; Febos, *Girlhood* (New York: Bloomsbury, 2021).

40. Iris Marion Young, On *Female Body Experience: "Throwing Like a Girl" and Other Essays* (Oxford: Oxford University Press, 2005).

41. bell hooks, *Feminism Is for Everybody* (London: Pluto, 2000).

42. Jill Filipovic, "Offensive Feminism: The Conservative Gender Norms That Perpetuate Rape Culture, and How Feminists Can Fight Back," in *Yes Means Yes: Visions of Female Sexual Power and a World Without Rape*, ed. Jaclyn Friedman and Jessica Valenti (Berkeley: Seal, 2008), 13–28.

43. Rebecca Traister, *Good and Mad: The Revolutionary Power of Women's Anger* (New York: Simon and Schuster, 2018).

44. Fischel, *Screw Consent*, 182.

## CONCLUSION

1. Tarana Burke, *Unbound: My Story of Liberation and the Birth of the Me Too Movement* (New York: Flatiron, 2021), 157.

2. Jacqueline Rose, "Feminism and the Abomination of Violence," *Cultural Critique* 94 (2016): 4–25. See also *On Violence and On Violence Against Women* (New York: Farrar, Straus and Giroux, 2021), 23.

3. Amy Fleming, "'It's wild!' Carey Mulligan and Emerald Fennell on Making Oscars History," *Guardian*, March 19, 2021, https://www.theguardian.com/film/2021/mar/19/its-wild-carey-mulligan-and-emerald-fennell-on-making-oscars-history.

4. Luis Ferré-Sadurní and Mihir Zaveri, "Sexual Harassment Claims Against Cuomo: What We Know So Far," *New York Times*, November 11, 2021, https://www.nytimes.com/article/cuomo-sexual-harassment-nursing-homes-covid-19.html.

5. Ultimately, head of the organization Tina Tchen resigned, as did attorney Roberta Kaplan.

6. Isabella B. Cho and Ariel H. Kim, "38 Harvard Faculty Sign Open Letter Questioning Results of Misconduct Investigations Into Prof. John Comaroff," *Harvard Crimson*, February 4, 2022, https://www.thecrimson.com/article/2022/2/4/comaroff-sanctions-open-letter/.

7. Ariel H. Kim and Meimei Xu, "35 Harvard Professors Retract Support for Letter Questioning Results of Comaroff Investigations," *Harvard Crimson*, February 11, 2022.

8. "Report of the External Review Committee to Review Sexual Harassment at Harvard University," Harvard University, January 2021, https://provost.harvard.edu/files/provost/files/report_of_committee_to_president_bacow_january_2021.pdf. It is important to note that in 2014 Harvard, along with fifty-five other institutions, was under investigation by the Department of Education for its failure to address campus sexual assault.

9. See Michele Bowdler, *Is Rape a Crime? A Memoir, an Investigation, and a Manifesto* (New York: Macmillan, 2020).

# BIBLIOGRAPHY

Abrisketa, Olatz G., and Marian G. Abrisketa. "It's Okay, Sister, Your Wolf-Pack Is Here: Sisterhood as Public Feminism in Spain." *Signs: Journal of Women in Culture and Society* 45, no. 4 (June 2020): 931–53.

Ahmed, Sara. *Complaint!* Durham, N.C.: Duke University Press, 2021.

——. *Living a Feminist Life.* Durham, N.C.: Duke University Press, 2017.

Albrecht, Kim. "The #MeToo Anti-Network." November 2020–November 2021. https://metoo .kimalbrecht.com.

Alliance for a Safe and Diverse DC. *Move Along: Policing Sex Work in Washington, D.C.* Washington, D.C.: Different Avenues, 2008. https://dctranscoalition.files.wordpress.com /2010/05/movealongreport.pdf.

Allison, Dorothy. *Bastard Out of Carolina.* New York: Dutton, 1992.

Anderson, Michelle J. "All-American Rape." *St. John's Law Review* 79, no. 3 (Summer 2005): 625–44. https://scholarship.law.stjohns.edu/lawreview/vol79/iss3/2.

Angel, Katherine. *Sex Will Be Good Again Tomorrow: Women and Desire in the Age of Consent.* London: Verso, 2021.

Angelou, Maya. *I Know Why the Caged Bird Sings.* New York: Random House, 1970.

Anzaldúa, Gloria, and Cherríe Moraga, eds. *This Bridge Called My Back: Writings by Radical Women of Color.* Watertown, Mass.: Persephone, 1981.

Arkin, Daniel. "Brooke Nevils Clearly Described Rape or Sexual Assault by Matt Lauer in NBC Meeting, Says Ronan Farrow." *NBC News*, October 11, 2019. https://www.nbcnews .com/news/us-news/brooke-nevils-unambiguously-described-rape-matt-lauer-nbc -meeting-ronan-n1064986.

Associated Press. "The Incriminating Statement by Cosby Referred to by Judge," September 25, 2018. https://apnews.com/article/bill-cosby-pa-state-wire-entertainment-us-news -celebrities-bb64abed0ae04c62900fe99e805e90e4.

Axios. "Read Lead Prosecutor Rachel Mitchell's Memo About the Kavanaugh-Ford Hearing." October 1, 2018. https://www.axios.com/brett-kavanaugh-rachel-mitchell-prosecutor-memo-2c3233cc-1d42-416b-af04-02700aa9a711.html.

Azoulay, Ariella. "The Natural History of Rape." *Journal of Visual Culture* 17, no. 2 (August 2018): 166–76.

Bailey, Moya, and Trudy. "On Misogynoir: Citation, Erasure, and Plagiarism." *Feminist Media Studies* 18, no. 4 (2018): 762–68.

Baker, Katie J. M. "Here's the Powerful Letter the Stanford Victim Read to Her Attacker." *Buzzfeed*, June 3, 2016. https://www.buzzfeednews.com/article/katiejmbaker/heres-the-powerful-letter-the-stanford-victim-read-to-her-ra.

Bass, Ellen, and Laura Davis. *The Courage to Heal: A Guide for Women Survivors of Child Sexual Abuse*. New York: Collins Living, 1988).

Baysinger, Tim. "This Is How Many People Watched the Oscars this Year." *Time*, February 27, 2017. https://time.com/4684709/oscars-2017-nielsen-ratings/.

Beard, Mary. *Women and Power*. London: Liveright, 2017.

Belliard, Marianella. "Junot Díaz's Mask: This Is How He Lost It." *Latino Rebels*, May 10, 2018. https://www.latinorebels.com/2018/05/10/junotdiazsmask/.

Bikales, James S. "Protected by Decades-Old Power Structures, Three Renowned Harvard Anthropologist Face Allegations of Sexual Harassment." *Harvard Crimson*, May 29, 2020. "https://www.thecrimson.com/article/2020/5/29/harvard-anthropology-gender-issues/.

Bodde, Katharine, and Erika Lorshbough. "There's No Such Thing as 'Consensual Sex' When a Person Is in Police Custody." ACLU, February 23, 2018. https://www.aclu.org/blog/criminal-law-reform/reforming-police/theres-no-such-thing-consensual-sex-when-person-police.

Bourke, Joanna. *Rape: Sex, Violence, History*. Berkeley: Counterpoint, 2007.

Bowdler, Michele. *Is Rape a Crime? A Memoir, an Investigation, and a Manifesto*. New York: Macmillan, 2020.

Boxer, Barbara. *The Art of Tough*. New York: Hachette, 2016.

Bracewell, Lorna. *Why We Lost the Sex Wars: Sexual Freedom in the #MeToo Era*. Minneapolis: University of Minnesota Press, 2021.

Brison, Susan. *Aftermath: Violence and the Remaking of a Self*. Princeton, N.J.: Princeton University Press, 2002.

Brodsky, Alexandra. "Understanding Judge Barrett's Opinion in Doe v. Purdue." *Public Justice*. September 24, 2020. https://www.publicjustice.net/understanding-judge-barretts-opinion-in-doe-v-purdue/.

Brody, Richard. "'The Last Duel,' Reviewed." *New Yorker*, October 15, 2021. https://www.newyorker.com/culture/the-front-row/the-last-duel-reviewed-ridley-scotts-wannabe-metoo-movie.

Brown, Julie K. "Perversion of Justice: Jeffrey Epstein." *Miami Herald*, December 19, 2019. https://www.miamiherald.com/news/local/article220097825.html.

Brownmiller, Susan. *Against Our Will: Men, Women, and Rape*. New York: Simon and Schuster, 1975.

Burke, Tarana. *Unbound: My Story of Liberation and the Birth of the Me Too Movement*. New York: Flatiron, 2021.

Butler, Judith. *Giving an Account of Oneself*. New York: Fordham University Press, 2005.

Capelouto, Susanna. "Nancy O'Dell: The Woman Who Rebuffed Trump." *CNN*, October 8, 2016. https://www.cnn.com/2016/10/08/us/nancy-odell-bio/.

Camon, Irin. "The Woman Who Taped Harvey Weinstein." *Cut*, February 18, 2020. https://www.thecut.com/2020/02/ambra-battilana-gutierrez-on-the-harvey-weinstein-trial.html

Carby, Hazel V. *Reconstructing Womanhood: The Emergence of the Afro-American Woman Novelist*. New York: Oxford University Press.

Centers for Disease Control and Prevention. "Sexual Violence Is Preventable." April 19, 2021. https://www.cdc.gov/injury/features/sexual-violence/index.html.

Chamberlain, Katharine. "Spotlight on Censorship: I Know Why the Caged Bird Sings." *Intellectual Freedom* (blog), September 26, 2010. https://www.oif.ala.org/oif/spotlight-on-censorship-i-know-why-the-caged-bird-sings/.

Chandler, David L. "3Q: Sheila Widnall on Sexual Harassment in STEM." *MIT News*, September 17, 2018. https://news.mit.edu/2018/sheila-widnall-sexual-harassment-STEM-0917.

Chee, Alexander. *How to Write an Autobiographical Novel*. New York: Mariner, 2018.

Chemaly, Soraya. *Rage Becomes Her: The Power of Women's Anger*. New York: Atria, 2019.

Chira, Susan. "Numbers Hint at Why #MeToo Took Off: The Sheer Number Who Can Say 'Me, Too.'" *New York Times*, February 21, 2018. https://www.nytimes.com/2018/02/21/upshot/pervasive-sexual-harassment-why-me-too-took-off-poll.html.

Cho, Isabella B., and Ariel H. Kim. "38 Harvard Faculty Sign Open Letter Questioning Results of Misconduct Investigations Into Prof. John Comaroff." *Harvard Crimson*, February 4, 2022. https://www.thecrimson.com/article/2022/2/4/comaroff-sanctions-open-letter/.

Clarke, Jessica A. "The Rules of #MeToo." *University of Chicago Legal Forum* 2019 (November 31, 2019): 37–84.

Closson, Troy. "R. Kelly's Last Criminal Trial Was in 2008. The World Has Changed Since." *New York Times*, August 17, 2021. https://www.nytimes.com/2021/08/17/nyregion/r-kelly-trial-allegations.html.

Cobb, Jelani. "An American Spring of Reckoning." *New Yorker*, June 22, 2020. https://www.newyorker.com/magazine/2020/06/22/an-american-spring-of-reckoning.

Cole, Alyson. "(Re)Made in America: Survivorship After the Shoah." *European Journal of Cultural Studies* 24, no. 1 (2021): 28–44.

Combahee River Collective. "A Black Feminist Statement" (1977). In *The Second Wave: A Reader in Feminist Theory*, ed. Linda Nicholson, 63–70. New York: Routledge, 1997.

Constand, Andrea. "Andrea Constand's Victim Impact Statement." *New York Times*, September 25, 2018. https://www.nytimes.com/2018/09/25/arts/andrea-constand-statement-cosby.html.

Cooper, Brittney. *Eloquent Rage: A Black Feminist Discovers Her Superpower*. New York: St. Martin's, 2018.

Crawford, Lacy. *Notes on a Silencing*. New York: Little, Brown, 2020.

Crenshaw, Kimberlé. "Demarginalizing the Intersection of Race and Sex: A Black Feminist Critique of Antidiscrimination Doctrine, Feminist Theory and Antiracist Politics." *University of Chicago Legal Forum* 1989, no. 1, art. 8: 139–67.

David, Richard. "Drains of Eale." *Shakespeare Survey* 10 (1957).

Deneuve, Catherine. "Open Letter: Nous défendons une liberté d'importuner, indispensable à la liberté sexuelle." *Le Monde*, January 10, 2018. https://www.cnn.com/2018/01/10/europe /catherine-deneuve-france-letter-metoo-intl/index.html

DeRogatis, Jim. "The Woman Who Says R. Kelly Abused Her Refuses to Be Silenced." *Buzzfeed News*, March 13, 2018. https://www.buzzfeednews.com/article/jimderogatis /jerhonda-pace-r-kelly-me-too-tarana-burke#.qcqlOXaZz.

Donegan, Moira. "I Started the Media Men List." *Cut*, January 10, 2018. https://www.thecut .com/2018/01/moira-donegan-i-started-the-media-men-list.html.

Dotson, Kristie. "Tracking Epistemic Violence, Tracking Practices of Silencing." *Hypatia* 26, no. 2 (Spring 2011): 236–57.

Douglass, Frederick, and Harriet A. Jacobs. *Narrative of the Life of Frederick Douglass, an American Slave* and *Incidents in the Life of a Slave Girl*. Intro. Anthony K. Appiah. New York: Modern Library, 2000.

Dworkin, Andrea. *Pornography: Men Possessing Women*. New York: Putnam, 1981.

——. *Woman Hating*. New York: Dutton, 1974.

Epstein, Deborah. "Discounting Credibility: Doubting the Stories of Women Survivors of Sexual Harassment." *Seton Hall Law Review* 51, no. 2 (2020): 289–329.

Epstein, Deborah, and Lisa Goodman, "Discounting Women: Doubting Domestic Violence Survivors' Credibility and Dismissing Their Experiences," *University of Pennsylvania Law Review* 167 (2019): 399–461.

External Review Committee to Review Sexual Harassment at Harvard University. "Report." January 2021. https://provost.harvard.edu/files/provost/files/report_of_committee_to _president_bacow_january_2021.pdf.

Faludi, Susan. *Backlash: The Undeclared War Against American Women*. New York: Crown, 1991.

Fandos, Nicholas, and Dana Rubinstein. "Why These Women Are Determined to Clear Cuomo's Name." *New York Times*, February 2, 2022. https://www.nytimes.com/2022/02/02 /nyregion/cuomo-supporters.html.

Farrow, Ronan. *Catch and Kill: Lies, Spies, and a Conspiracy to Protect Predators*. New York: Little, Brown, 2019.

Febos, Melissa. *Girlhood*. New York: Bloomsbury, 2021.

——. "I Spent My Life Consenting to Touch I Didn't Want." *New York Times Magazine*, March 31, 2021. https://www.nytimes.com/2021/03/31/magazine/consent.html.

Ferré-Sadurní, Luis, and Mihir Zaveri. "Sexual Harassment Claims Against Cuomo: What We Know So Far." *New York Times*, November 11, 2021. https://www.nytimes.com/article /cuomo-sexual-harassment-nursing-homes-covid-19.html.

Filipovic, Jill. "Offensive Feminism: The Conservative Gender Norms That Perpetuate Rape Culture, and How Feminists Can Fight Back." In *Yes Means Yes: Visions of Female Sexual Power and a World Without Rape*, ed. Jaclyn Friedman and Jessica Valenti, 13–28. Berkeley: Seal, 2008.

Fischel, Joel. "In the Fight for Policing Reform, LGBT Is a Threadbare Alliance." *Boston Review*, June 17, 2020. https://bostonreview.net/gender-sexuality/joseph-j-fischel-fight -policing-reform-lgbt-threadbare-alliance.

———. *Screw Consent: A Better Politics of Sexual Justice*. Berkeley: University of California Press, 2019.

Fischer, Anne Gray. "Police Sexual Violence Is Hidden in Plain Sight." *Boston Review*, July 30, 2020. https://bostonreview.net/law-justice/anne-gray-fischer-reform-wont-end-police -violence.

Flanagan, Andrew. "Taylor Swift Wins Sexual Assault Lawsuit Against Former Radio Host." NPR, August 14, 2017. https://www.npr.org/sections/therecord/2017/08/14/543473684 /taylor-swift-wins-sexual-assault-lawsuit-against-former-radio-host.

Flanagan, Caitlin. "The Abandoned World of 1982." *Atlantic*, September 25, 2019. https://www .theatlantic.com/ideas/archive/2018/09/kavanaugh-ford/571066/.

———. "The Humiliation of Aziz Ansari." *Atlantic*, January 14, 2018. https://www.theatlantic .com/entertainment/archive/2018/01/the-humiliation-of-aziz-ansari/550541/.

Fleming, Amy. "'It's wild!' Carey Mulligan and Emerald Fennell on Making Oscars History." *Guardian*, March 19, 2021, https://www.theguardian.com/film/2021/mar/19/its-wild-carey -mulligan-and-emerald-fennell-on-making-oscars-history.

Folkenflik, David, and Colin Dwyer. "Matt Lauer Accused of Rape in New Book: Former NBC Star Denies 'False Stories.'" NPR, October 9, 2019. https://www.npr.org/2019/10/09 /768527936/matt-lauer-accused-of-rape-in-new-book-former-nbc-star-denies-false -stories.

Foucault, Michel. *Fearless Speech*, ed. Joseph Pearson. Los Angeles: Semiotexte, 2001.

———. *The History of Sexuality*. Vol. 1. New York: Vintage, 1978.

———. *Wrong-Doing and Truth-Telling: The Function of Avowal in Justice*, ed. Fabienne Brion and Bernard E. Harcourt, trans. Stephen W. Sawyer. Chicago: University of Chicago Press, 2014.

France24. "French Intellectual Duhamel Won't Face Incest Charges, Prosecutor Says," *France24*, June 14, 2021. https://www.france24.com/en/europe/20210614-french -intellectual-duhamel-won-t-face-incest-charges-paris-prosecutor-says.

Freedman, Estelle, *Redefining Rape: Sexual Violence in the Era of Suffrage and Segregation*. Cambridge, Mass.: Harvard University Press, 2013.

Fricker, Miranda. *Epistemic Injustice: Power and the Ethics of Knowing*. Oxford: Oxford University Press, 2007.

Frow, John. "Discursive Justice." *SAQ* 100, no. 2 (2001): 334.

Gallagher, Conor. "Belfast Trial: Doctor Criticises Medical Examination of Alleged Rape Victim." *Irish Times*, February 21, 2018. https://www.irishtimes.com/news/crime-and-law /belfast-trial-doctor-criticises-medical-examination-of-alleged-rape-victim-1.3400137.

———. "Inside the Court 12: The Complete Story of the Belfast Rape Trial." *Irish Times*, March 28, 2018. https://www.irishtimes.com/news/crime-and-law/inside-court-12-the -complete-story-of-the-belfast-rape-trial-1.3443620.

Gates, Henry Louis, ed. *The Classic Slave Narratives*. New York: New American Library, 1987.

Gay, Roxane. *Hunger: A Memoir of (My) Body*. New York: Harper, 2017.

——, ed. *Not That Bad: Dispatches from Rape Culture*. New York: Harper, 2018.

Gessen, Masha. "When Does a Watershed Become a Sex Panic." *New Yorker*, November 14, 2017.

Gilligan, Carol. *In a Different Voice: Psychological Theory and Women's Development*. Cambridge, Mass.: Harvard University Press, 1982.

Gilmore, Leigh. *Autobiographics: A Feminist Theory of Women's Self-Representation*. Ithaca, N.Y.: Cornell University Press, 1994.

——. "Bill Cosby's Release Forces Us to Ask: How Far Can #MeToo Go?" *WBUR Cognoscenti*, July 7, 2021. https://www.wbur.org/cognoscenti/2021/07/07/bill-crosby-conviction-vacated-rape-andrea-constand-leigh-gilmore.

——. "Graphic Witness: Visual and Verbal Testimony in the #MeToo Movement." In *The New Feminist Literary Studies*, ed. Jennifer Cooke, 25–40. Cambridge: Cambridge University Press, 2020.

——. "Jurisdictions: *I, Rigoberta Menchú*, *The Kiss*, and Scandalous Self-Representation in the Age of Memoir and Trauma." *Signs: Journal of Women in Culture and Society* 28, no. 2 (Winter 2003): 695–718.

——. "Limit-Cases: Trauma, Self-Representation, and the Jurisdictions of Identity." *Biography* 24, no. 1 (December 2001): 128–39.

——. *The Limits of Autobiography: Trauma and Testimony*. Ithaca, N.Y.: Cornell University Press, 2001.

——. "Stanford Sexual Assault: What Changed with the Survivor's Testimony." *Conversation*, June 16, 2016. https://theconversation.com/stanford-sexual-assault-what-changed-with-the-survivors-testimony-60913.

——. *Tainted Witness: Why We Doubt What Women Say About Their Lives*. New York: Columbia University Press, 2017.

Gilmore, Leigh, and Elizabeth Marshall. *Witnessing Girlhood: Toward an Intersectional Tradition of Life Writing*. New York: Fordham University Press, 2019.

Gordon, Mary. *Payback*. New York: Pantheon, 2020.

Graham, Ruth. "Southern Baptists Release List of Alleged Sex Abusers." *New York Times*, May 26, 2022.

Grinberg, Emanuella, and Catherine E. Shoichet. "Brock Turner Released from Jail After Serving Three Months for Sexual Assault." *CNN*, September 2, 2016. https://www.cnn.com/2016/09/02/us/brock-turner-release-jail/index.html.

Hamilton, Marci A. *Justice Denied: What America Must Do to Protect Its Children*. Cambridge: Cambridge University Press, 2012.

Harding, Kate. *Asking for It: The Alarming Rise of Rape Culture—and What We Can Do About It*. Boston: Da Capo, 2015.

Hardnett, Sukari. "Anita Hill Testimony: The Witness Not Called." Michael Martin, interviewer. *NPR*. September 23, 2018.

Harkins, Gillian. *Virtual Pedophilia: Sexual Offender Profiling and U.S. Security Culture*. Durham, N.C.: Duke University Press, 2020.

Harrison, Kathryn. *The Kiss*. New York: Random House, 1997.

Hauser, Christine. "Former Students Sue Harvard Over Handling of Sexual Crimes Complaints." *New York Times*, February 19, 2016. https://www.nytimes.com/2016/02/20/us/harvard-sexual-crimes-complaints-alyssa-leader.html.

Herman, Judith Lewis. *Trauma and Recovery*. New York, Basic Books, 1997.

Hesse, Monica. "'Believe Women' Was a Slogan. 'Believe All Women' Is a Strawman." *Washington Post*, May 12, 2020.

Heyes, Cressida. *Anaesthetics of Existence: Essays on Experience at the Edge*. Durham, N.C.: Duke University Press, 2020.

Hill, Anita. *Believing: Our Thirty-Year Journey to End Gender Violence*. New York: Viking, 2021.

——. "The Thomas Nomination: Prof. Anita Hill: 'I Felt That I Had to Tell the Truth.'" *New York Times*, October 12, 1991.

Hine, Darlene Clark. "Rape and the Inner Lives of Black Women in the Middle West: Preliminary Thoughts on the Culture of Dissemblance." *Signs: Journal of Women in Culture and Society* 14, no. 4 (1989): 912–20.

Holpuch, Amanda. "Anita Hill: Kavanaugh Confirmation Hearing 'Disservice to the American Public.'" *Guardian*, October 10, 2018.

Holt, Patricia. "Under Scrutiny: Anita Hill Describes Finding a New Life After the Devastating Clarence Thomas Hearings." *SFGate*, September 28, 1997. https://www.sfgate.com/books/article/Under-Scrutiny-Anita-Hill-describes-finding-a-2804765.php.

Honig, Bonnie. *Antigone, Interrupted*. Cambridge: Cambridge University Press, 2013.

hooks, bell. *Feminism Is for Everybody*. London: Pluto, 2000.

Hunt, Elle. "'20 Minutes of Action': Father Defends Stanford Student Son Convicted of Sexual Assault." *Guardian*. June 5, 2016.

Jackson, Sarah J., Moya Bailey, and Brooke Foucault Welles. *#Hashtag Activism: Networks of Race and Gender Justice*. Cambridge, Mass.: MIT Press, 2020.

Jacobs, Harriet. *Incidents in the Life of a Slave Girl*, ed. Jean Fagan Yellin. Cambridge, Mass.: Harvard University Press, 2000.

Jacquet, Catherine. *The Injustices of Rape: How Activists Responded to Sexual Violence, 1950–1980*. Chapel Hill: University of North Carolina Press, 2019.

James, David. *Discrepant Solitude: Contemporary Literature and the Work of Consolation*. Oxford: Oxford University Press, 2019.

Jha, Nishita. "The Judge in the Harvey Weinstein Trial Told Potential Jurors the 'Case Is Not a Referendum on #MeToo.'" *Buzzfeed News*, January 16, 2020. https://www.buzzfeednews.com/article/nishitajha/harvey-weinstein-judge-referendum-metoo.

Johnson, Lacy M. *The Reckonings: Essays on Justice for the Twenty-First Century*. New York: Scribner, 2018.

Johnson, Paula A., Sheila Widnall, and Frazier F. Benya, eds. *Sexual Harassment of Women: Climate, Culture, and Consequences in Academic Sciences, Engineering, and Medicine*. Washington, D.C.: National Academies, 2018.

Kahn, Mattie. "Cathy Park Hong and Chanel Miller on Making Art Out of Grief: A Conversation." *Glamour*. March 24, 2021.

Kantor, Jodi, and Megan Twohey. "Harvey Weinstein Paid Off Sexual Harassment Accusers for Decades." *New York Times*, October 5, 2017. https://www.nytimes.com/2017/10/05/us /harvey-weinstein-harassment-allegations.html.

——. *She Said: Breaking the Sexual Harassment Story*. New York: Penguin, 2019.

Karr, Mary. *Liar's Club: A Memoir*. New York: Viking Penguin, 1995.

Kennedy, Rosanne, and Hannah McCann. "Splitting from Halley: Doing Justice to Race, Unwantedness, and Campus Sexual Assault." *Signs: Journal of Women in Culture and Society* 46, no. 1 (September 2020): 79–102.

Kim, Ariel H., and Meimei Xu. "35 Harvard Professors Retract Support for Letter Questioning Results of Comaroff Investigations." *Harvard Crimson*, February 11, 2022.

Kingston, Maxine Hong. *The Woman Warrior: A Memoir of a Girlhood Among Ghosts*. New York: Knopf, 1976.

Kinports, Kit. "Rape and Force: The Forgotten *Mens Rea*." *Buffalo Criminal Law Review* 4, no. 2 (2001): 755–99.

LeDoeuff, Michèle. *Hipparchia's Choice*. 1991. New York: Columbia University Press, 2007.

Lekach, Susan. "Team Behind Time's Person of the Year Issue Was All Women." *Mashable .com*, December 6, 2017. https://mashable.com/2017/12/06/time-person-of-the-year -women-behind-issue/.

Lennard, Natasha. "In Secretive Court Hearing, NYPD Cops Who Raped Brooklyn Teen in Custody Get No Jail Time." *Intercept*, August 30, 2019. https://theintercept.com/2019/08 /30/nypd-anna-chambers-rape-probation.

Leotta, Allison. "I Was a Sex-Crimes Prosecutor. Here's Why 'He Said / She Said' Is a Myth." *Time*, October 3, 2018. https://time.com/5413814/he-said-she-said-kavanaugh-ford -mitchell/.

Levenson, Eric, Lauren del Valle, and Sonia Moghe. "Harvey Weinstein Sentenced to 23 Years in Prison After Addressing His Accusers in Court." CNN, March 11, 2020. https://www .cnn.com/2020/03/11/us/harvey-weinstein-sentence/index.html.

Lorde, Audre. "The Transformation of Silence Into Language and Action." In *Sister Outsider: Essays and Speeches*. Trumansburg, N.Y.: Crossing, 1984.

Mack, Justin L. "A List of the Gymnasts Who Have Publicly Accused Dr. Larry Nassar of Sexual Abuse." *Indy Star*, December 7, 2017. https://www.indystar.com/story/news/2017 /12/07/list-gymnasts-who-have-publicly-accused-dr-larry-nassar-sexual-assault /930136001/.

MacKinnon, Catharine A. *Feminism Unmodified*. Cambridge, Mass.: Harvard University Press, 1987.

——. *Toward a Feminist Theory of the State*. Cambridge, Mass.: Harvard University Press, 1989.

Macur, Juliet, and Nate Schweber. "Rape Case Unfolds on Web and Splits City." *New York Times*, December 16, 2012. https://www.nytimes.com/2012/12/17/sports/high-school -football-rape-case-unfolds-online-and-divides-steubenville-ohio.html.

Mailhot, Terese Marie. *Heart Berries: A Memoir*. Berkeley: Counterpoint, 2018.

Marcus, Sharon. *The Drama of Celebrity*. Princeton, N.J.: Princeton University Press, 2019.

——. "Fighting Bodies, Fighting Words: A Theory and Politics of Rape Prevention." In *Feminists Theorize the Political*, ed. Judith Butler and Joan W. Scott, 385–403. London: Routledge, 1992.

Lara Marlowe, "Paris Letter: Most Shocking Thing About Matzneff Affair Is Everybody Knew." *Irish Times*, January 27, 2020. https://www.irishtimes.com/news/world/europe/paris-letter-most-shocking-thing-about-matzneff-affair-is-everybody-knew-1.4153065.

Martin, Emily. "The Egg and the Sperm: How Science Has Constructed a Romance Based on Stereotypical Male-Female Roles." *Signs: Journal of Women in Culture and Society* 16, no. 3 (Spring 1991): 485–501.

Martin, Michael. Interview with Sukari Hardnett. NPR, September 23, 2018. https://www.npr.org/2018/09/23/650956623/anita-hill-testimony-the-witness-not-called.

Mayer, Jane, and Jill Abramson. *Strange Justice: The Selling of Clarence Thomas*. Boston: Houghton Mifflin, 1994.

McKinley, James C., Jr. "Cy Vance Defends Decision Not to Pursue Case Against Harvey Weinstein." *New York Times*, October 11, 2017. https://www.nytimes.com/2017/10/11/nyregion/cy-vance-defends-weinstein-decision.html.

Méheut, Constant. "France Drops Rape Investigation of Prominent Intellectual." *New York Times*, June 4, 2021. https://www.nytimes.com/2021/06/14/world/europe/olivier-duhamel-france.html.

Merkin, Daphne. "Publicly, We Say #MeToo. Privately, We Have Misgivings." *New York Times*, January 5, 2018. https://www.nytimes.com/2018/01/05/opinion/golden-globes-metoo.html.

Metz, G. Harold. "Stage History of *Titus Andronicus*." *Shakespeare Quarterly* 28, no. 2 (Spring 1977): 154–69.

Miller, Chanel. *Know My Name: A Memoir*. New York: Viking, 2019.

Miller, T. Christian, and Ken Armstrong. *A False Report: A True Story of Rape in America*. New York: Crown, 2018.

——. "An Unbelievable Story of Rape," *ProPublica*, December 16, 2015, https://www.propublica.org/article/false-rape-accusations-an-unbelievable-story.

Millett, Kate. *Sexual Politics*. New York: Doubleday, 1970.

Montgomery, Ben. *Grandma Gatewood's Walk: The Inspiring Story of the Woman Who Saved the Appalachian Trail*. Chicago: Chicago Review, 2014.

Morales, Christina. "Court Overturns Sex Crime Conviction Because Victim Was 'Voluntarily Intoxicated.'" *New York Times*, March 31, 2021, https://www.nytimes.com/2021/03/31/us/minnesota-supreme-court-rape-ruling.html.

Ogden, Emily. *On Not Knowing: How to Love and Other Essays*. Chicago: University of Chicago Press, 2022.

Oria, Shelley. *Indelible in the Hippocampus: Writings from the MeToo Movement*. San Francisco: McSweeney's, 2019.

Palma, Kristi. "Chessy Prout Went Public with Her Name to 'Take Back the Internet.'" *Boston.com*, September 12, 2016. https://www.boston.com/news/crime/2016/09/12/chessy-prout-went-public-with-her-name-to-take-back-the-internet.

Pateman, Carole. *The Sexual Contract*. London: Polity, 1988.

Patil, Vrushali, and Jyoti Puri. "Colorblind Feminisms: Ansari-Grace and the Limits of #MeToo Counterpublics." *Signs: Journal of Women in Culture and Society* 46, no. 3 (Spring 2020): 689–713.

Pauly, Madison. "She Was a Rising Star at a Major University. Then a Lecherous Professor Made Her Life Hell." *Mother Jones*, September 8, 2017. https://www.motherjones.com /politics/2017/09/she-was-a-rising-star-at-a-major-university-then-a-lecherous -professor-made-her-life-hell/.

Phelan, James. *Somebody Telling Somebody Else: A Rhetorical Poetics of Narrative.* Columbus: Ohio State University Press, 2017.

*Politico.* "Full Transcript: Christine Blaey Ford's Opening Statement to the Senate Judiciary Committee." *Politico*, September 26, 2018. https://www.politico.com/story/2018/09/26 /christine-blasey-ford-opening-statement-senate-845080.

Probation Officer. "Probation Report, People v. Brock Allen Turner." Superior Court, California, Santa Clara County. June 2, 2016.

"Protestors Confront Flake in Elevator." Transcript. *Rachel Maddow Show*, MSNBC, September 28, 2018. http://www.msnbc.com/transcripts/rachel-maddow-show/2018-09-28.

Ravery, Lise. "Denise Bombardier Deserves Credit for Unmasking French Author." *Montreal Gazette*, December 30, 2019. https://montrealgazette.com/opinion/columnists/lise-ravary -denise-bombardier-deserves-credit-for-unmasking-french-author.

Reints, Renae. "Trump Calls Christine Blasey Ford a 'Very Credible Witness.'" *Fortune*, September 28, 2018. http://fortune.com/2018/09/28/trump-ford-credible-witness/.

Rekdal, Paisley. "Nightingale: A Gloss: A Special APR Supplement." *American Poetry Review* 46, no. 5 (September/October 2017): 21–24.

"Report of the External Review Committee to Review Sexual Harassment at Harvard University." Harvard University. January 2021. https://provost.harvard.edu/files/provost/files /report_of_committee_to_president_bacow_january_2021.pdf.

Roach, Shoniqua. "(Re)turning to 'Rape and the Inner Lives of Black Women': A Black Feminist Forum on the Culture of Dissemblance." *Signs: Journal of Women in Culture and Society* 45, no. 3 (Spring 2020): 515–19.

Robbins, Bruce. *The Beneficiary.* Durham, N.C.: Duke University Press, 2017.

Rose, Jacqueline. "Feminism and the Abomination of Violence." *Cultural Critique* 94 (2016): 4–25.

——. *On Violence and on Violence Against Women.* New York: Farrar, Straus and Giroux, 2021.

Rothberg, Michael. *The Implicated Subject: Beyond Victim and Perpetrator.* Stanford: Stanford University Press, 2019.

Roupenian, Kristen. "Cat Person." *New Yorker*, December 11, 2017. https://www.newyorker .com/magazine/2017/12/11/cat-person.

Salamon, Gayle. *The Life and Death of Latisha King: A Critical Phenomenology of Transphobia.* New York: New York University Press, 2018.

Samaha, Albert. "An 18-Year-Old Said She Was Raped While in Police Custory. The Officers Say She Consented." *BuzzFeed News*, February 7, 2018. https://www.buzzfeednews.com /article/albertsamaha/this-teenager-accused-two-on-duty-cops-of-rape-she-had-no.

Santhanam, Laura. "1 in 6 U.S. Women Say Their First Sexual Intercourse Was Rape." *PBS News Hour*, September 16, 2019. https://www.pbs.org/newshour/health/1-in-16-u-s-women -say-their-first-sexual-intercourse-was-rape.

Scher, Bill. "After Kavanaugh, #MeToo Should Launch a New Temperance Movement." *Politico Magazine*, October 9, 2018. https://www.politico.com/magazine/story/2018/10/09 /kavanaugh-metoo-temperance-suffragettes-221141/.

Sehgal, Parul. "The Case Against the Trauma Plot." *New Yorker*, December 27, 2021.

——. " 'Consent,' a Memoir That Shook France, Recalls Living a 'Perverse Nightmare.' " *New York Times*, February 16, 2021. https://www.nytimes.com/2021/02/16/books/review -consent-memoir-vanessa-springora.html.

Serisier, Tanya. *Speaking Out: Feminism, Rape, and Narrative Politics*. London: Palgrave Macmillan, 2018.

——. "Speaking Out, Public Judgements and Narrative Politics." In *MeToo, Feminist Theory, and Surviving Sexual Violence in the Academy*, ed. Laura A. Gray-Rosendale, 167–80. Lanham, Md.: Lexington, 2020.

Shanahan, Mark, and Stephanie Ebert. "Junot Díaz Case May Be a #MeToo Turning Point." *Boston Globe*, June 30, 2018. https://www.bostonglobe.com/metro/2018/06/30/junot-diaz -case-may-metoo-turning-point/3TMFseenE4Go1eVsqbFSxM/story.html.

Shreerekha. "In the Wake of His Damage." *Rumpus*, May 12, 2018, https://therumpus.net /2018/05/12/in-the-wake-of-his-damage/.

Silman, Anna. " 'Emily Doe' from the Brock Turner Case Is Ready for You to Know Her Name." *Cut*, September 4, 2019. https://www.thecut.com/2019/09/chanel-miller-from -brock-turner-case-wants-us-to-know-her-name.html.

Smolowe, Jill. "Sex, Lies and Politics: He Said, She Said." *Time*, October 21, 1991. http://content .time.com/time/magazine/article/0,9171,974096,00.html.

Song, Sung Hoon, and John R. Fernandes. "Comparison of Injury Patterns in Consensual and Nonconsensual Sex." *Academy of Forensic Pathology* 7, no. 4 (December 2017): 619– 31. https://www.ncbi.nlm.nih.gov/pmc/articles/PMC6474446/.

Sophocles. *Antigonick*, trans. Anne Carson. New York: New Directions, 2012.

Spampinato, Erin A. "Rereading Rape in the Critical Canon: Adjudicative Criticism and the Capacious Conception of Rape." *differences* 32, no. 2 (September 2021): 122–60.

Spillers, Hortense. *Black, White, and in Color: Essays on American Literature and Culture*. Chicago: University of Chicago Press, 2003.

Spivak, Gayatri. "Can the Subaltern Speak?" In *Marxism and the Interpretation of Culture*, ed. Cary Nelson and Lawrence Grossberg, 271–313. London: Macmillan, 1988.

Springora, Vanessa. *Consent: A Memoir*, trans. Natasha Lehrer. Paris: Editions Grasset & Fasquelle, 2020; New York: HarperCollins, 2021.

Steinhauer, Jennifer, and David S. Joachim. "55 Colleges Named in Federal Inquiry Into Handling of Sexual Assault Cases." *New York Times*, May 1, 2014. https://www.nytimes .com/2014/05/02/us/politics/us-lists-colleges-under-inquiry-over-sex-assault-cases .html.

Taylor, Keeanga-Yamahtta. *How We Get Free: Black Feminism and the Combahee River Collective*. London: Haymarket, 2017.

Thiery, Clément. "Denise Bombardier: 'In America, Mr. Matzneff Would Already Be in Jail.'" *France-Amérique*, January 23, 2020. https://france-amerique.com/en/denise-bombardier -in-america-mr-matzneff-would-already-be-in-jail/.

Thomas, Jordan A. "How to Make It Easier for Women to Report Sexual Harassment." *Quartz at Work*, January 3, 2018. https://qz.com/work/1170489/how-to-make-it-easier-for-women -to-report-sexual-harassment-according-to-a-lawyer-who-represents-whistleblowers/.

Traister, Rebecca. *Good and Mad: The Revolutionary Power of Women's Anger.* New York: Simon and Schuster, 2018.

——. "'You Believe He's Lying'? The Latest Debate Captured Americans' Exhausting Tendency to Mistrust Women." *Cut.* February 26, 2020.

Trewin, J. C. *Shakespeare on the English Stage, 1900–1964.* London: Barrie and Rockliff, 1964.

Turkheimer, Deborah. "Beyond #MeToo." *New York University Law Review* 94, no. 5 (November 2019): 1146–1208.

——. "Incredible Women: Sexual Violence and the Credibility Discount." *University of Pennsylvania Law Review* 166, no. 1 (2017). https://scholarship.law.upenn.edu/penn_law _review/vol166/iss1/1/.

——. "Unofficial Reporting in the #MeToo Era." *University of Chicago Legal Forum* 2019, article 10 (2019).

United States Congress, Senate. Select Committee on Ethics. "Resolution for Disciplinary Action." 104th Congress, First Session, September 8, 1995. https://www.congress.gov/104 /crpt/srpt137/CRPT-104srpt137.pdf.

Valenti, Jessica. "American Rape Laws Make No Sense." In *All in Her Head by Jessica Valenti.* Blog, April 7, 2021. https://jessica.substack.com/p/american-rape-laws-make-no -sense.

Valenti, Jessica, and Jaclyn Friedman, eds. *Believe Me: How Trusting Women Can Change the World.* New York: Seal, 2020.

Valentine, Claire. "Author Junot Díaz Responds to Allegations of Sexual Misconduct and Verbal Abuse." *Paper,* May 4, 2018. https://www.papermag.com/junot-diaz-me-too- -2565930804.html.

Vance, Cyrus, Jr. "Manhattan D.A. Cyrus Vance on Weinstein Verdict and Why His Office Didn't Prosecute in 2015." Interview by Amna Nawaz. *PBS News Hour,* February 25, 2020. https://www.pbs.org/newshour/show/manhattan-da-cyrus-vance-on-weinstein-verdict -and-why-his-office-didnt-prosecute-in-2015.

Waddell, Kaveh. "The Exhausting Work of Tallying America's Largest Protest." *Atlantic,* January 23, 2017.

Wanzo, Rebecca. "Rethinking Rape and Laughter: Michaela Coel's *I May Destroy You.*" *Los Angeles Review of Books,* September 22, 2020.

——. *The Suffering Will Not Be Televised: African American Women and Sentimental Political Storytelling.* Albany: SUNY Press, 2009.

Way, Katie. "I Went on a Date with Aziz Ansari. It Turned Into the Worst Night of My Life." *Babe.net,* January 13, 2018. https://babe.net/2018/01/13/aziz-ansari-28355.

Woolf, Virginia. *A Room of One's Own.* 1929. London: Harcourt, 2005.

World Health Organization. "Devastatingly Pervasive: 1 in 3 Women Globally Experience Violence." March 9, 2021. https://www.who.int/news/item/09-03-2021-devastatingly -pervasive-1-in-3-women-globally-experience-violence.

Wright, Angela. "Thomas Accuser Angela Wright Sticks to Claims." NPR, October 9, 2007. https://www.npr.org/templates/story/story.php?storyId=15113601.

Wurtzel, Elizabeth, *Prozac Nation: Young and Depressed in America*. Boston: Houghton Mifflin, 1994.

Yellin, Jean Fagan, ed. *Harriet Jacobs: A Life*. New York: Basic Books, 2004.

——. *The Harriet Jacobs Family Papers*, vol. 1. Chapel Hill: University of North Carolina Press, 2008.

Young, Iris Marion. *On Female Body Experience: "Throwing Like a Girl" and Other Essays*. Oxford: Oxford University Press, 2005.

Zhou, Li. "Susan Collins Thinks Lawyers Should Be Able to Cross-examine Kavanaugh and Ford on Sexual Assault Allegations." *Vox*, September 18, 2018. https://www.vox.com/2018 /9/18/17874938/supreme-court-brett-kavanaugh-susan-collins.

# INDEX